"Read this excellent primer and read the Bible better as a result."
—Darrell Bock
Research Professor of New Testament Studies, Dallas Theological Seminary

"Well written and carefully researched, I believe *40 Questions About Interpreting the Bible* is an invaluable resource for anyone who has serious questions about the Holy Scriptures."
—Daniel Akin, President,
Southeastern Baptist Theological Seminary

"Aristotle once said that those who wished to succeed must ask the right preliminary questions. Plummer asks forty of them. Even better: he answers them, providing beginning students with all they need to know about biblical interpretation in general and the specific kinds of texts found in the Old and New Testaments in particular to begin interpreting the Bible profitably."
—Kevin J. Vanhoozer,
Blanchard Professor of Theology, Wheaton College

"How appropriate that Plummer's *40 Questions About Interpreting the Bible* is itself eminently understandable, crystal clear, and thoroughly engaging. The organization and breadth of coverage makes this book both a delight to read and highly instructive. Each chapter concludes with reflection questions and suggested resources for further study. I can't imagine a more helpful introduction to the subject of biblical interpretation than Plummer has produced."
—Bruce A. Ware, Professor of Christian Theology,
The Southern Baptist Theological Seminary

"Nuanced sufficiently for seminary courses and accessible enough for church groups, *40 Questions About Interpreting the Bible* helpfully acquaints students and church leaders alike to central principles of biblical interpretation and related matters like inspiration, canon, translation, and current discussions. This warm and engaging work would make a superb textbook for university and seminary courses on biblical interpretation."
—Christopher W. Morgan, Professor of Theology,
California Baptist University

"It is a wonderful thing to teach a person the Bible. It is even more wonderful to teach people how to study the Bible for themselves. Plummer has given us a helpful survey relative to how to understand the Bible. You will profit greatly from his insights."

—Jerry Vines,
Pastor-Emeritus, First Baptist Church, Jacksonville, FL

"*40 Questions About Interpreting the Bible* is a condensed discussion of a wide variety of important issues for the beginning student in the area of biblical studies. The question-answer format is a nice way to pique the students' interest and provide an answer to their questions at the same time."

—Paul D. Wegner
Professor of Old Testament, Phoenix Seminary

40 QUESTIONS SERIES

40 QUESTIONS ABOUT
Interpreting the Bible

Robert L. Plummer

Benjamin L. Merkle, Series Editor

40 Questions About Interpreting the Bible
© 2010 by Robert L. Plummer

Published by Kregel Publications, a division of Kregel, Inc., P.O. Box 2607, Grand Rapids, MI 49501.

This book is a title in the 40 Questions Series edited by Benjamin L. Merkle.

The Greek font SymbolU and the Hebrew font New JerusalemU are both available from www.linguistsoftware.com/lgku.htm, +1-425-775-1130.

Library of Congress Cataloging-in-Publication Data
Plummer, Robert L. (Robert Lewis), 1971-
   40 questions about interpreting the Bible / Robert L. Plummer.
      p. cm.
   Includes bibliographical references (p. 329) and index.
   1. Bible—Hermeneutics—Textbooks.   I. Title.   II. Title: Forty questions about interpreting the Bible.
   BS476.P58 2010
   220.6'1—dc22

2009035530

ISBN 978-0-8254-3498-3

Printed in the United States of America
10 11 12 13 14 / 5 4 3 2 1

To Mark Seifrid and Robert Stein
Scholars, Teachers, Friends

Contents

Part 3: Approaching Specific Texts

Section A: Shared Genres (Questions Apply Equally to Old and New Testaments)

Section B: Primarily Old Testament Genres

Section C: Primarily New Testament Genres

Part 4: Issues in Recent Discussion

Foreword

Who introduced the chapter and verse divisions regularly found in our current Bibles? What do we mean by "autographs"? What is the proper definition of "inerrancy"? How were the biblical manuscripts copied and transmitted over the centuries? What is the oldest extant fragment of the New Testament, and what is its date? Who determined what was included in the canon? What is the Apocrypha? Is the canon closed? What is the best available English Bible translation? What is the overarching message of the Bible? Why can't people agree on what the Bible means?

In this fascinating and well-crafted book, Robert Plummer takes up these and many other questions related to understanding the Bible. Informed by recent scholarship and presented in an accessible format that is both practical and relevant, this volume is a joy to read. The author has, in essence, provided us with a book on biblical interpretation broken up into digestible bits and pieces, using a format that makes it easier to stomach a subject that often gets stuck in beginning students' throats.

Plummer quotes one of his mentors, Robert Stein, who once told him, "I wrote my text on hermeneutics because I could not understand the other books on the subject." As one who is just now attempting to write a book on biblical interpretation myself (*Invitation to Biblical Interpretation*, forthcoming with Kregel), and as one who has taught biblical interpretation on the college, masters, and doctoral levels for more than fifteen years, I appreciate the challenges confronting those who would write a work on interpreting the Bible that readers can understand.

The present volume resoundingly succeeds in making the task and process of biblical interpretation transparent and in initiating the beginning student to a lifetime of study of God's Word. As Paul wrote to Timothy, "Do your best to present yourself to God as one approved, a workman who does not need to be ashamed and who correctly handles the word of truth" (2 Tim 2:15). For anyone who aspires to acquire the skills necessary to handle God's Word of truth correctly, this book will prove invaluable. I highly recommend it.

Andreas J. Köstenberger, Founder, Biblical Foundations™
Professor of New Testament and Biblical Theology, Director of Ph.D. Studies
Southeastern Baptist Theological Seminary, Wake Forest, NC

Introduction

This book is intended to help you understand the Bible. As a New Testament professor, I regularly teach an introductory course on biblical hermeneutics (interpretation) at The Southern Baptist Theological Seminary in Louisville, Kentucky. I have had difficulty finding a textbook that covers briefly and accurately all the issues that we survey in the course. (Topics covered in my course include: canon, manuscript transmission, English Bible translations, general interpretive questions, approaches to the major literary types in the Bible, and current hermeneutical debates.) I wrote this book in order to address these issues in one volume. Ideally, this book will serve as a textbook for an introductory Bible course at a college or seminary, but I endeavored to write so that the book will be beneficial to any curious Christian. My goal was to be accessible without being simplistic and scholarly without being pedantic, while always keeping an eye to practical questions and real-life application by the Christian reader.

Although you may choose to read through the entire book in order, it is organized so that particular topics may be accessed without knowledge of the prior contents. I encourage you to scan the forty questions in the table of contents before beginning to read. Is there a particular topic that catches your attention? Why not start there? Each chapter also closes with discussion questions and books recommended for further study.

There are many people whom I should thank for helping make this book a reality. Foremost, I would like to express my appreciation to the trustees and administration of Southern Seminary, who graciously granted me a sabbatical leave for 2008, during which this book was written. Thanks are in order to my dear friend, the series editor Ben Merkle, who provided constant encouragement. I also want to express thanks to my assistants, Andy Hassler, Ben Stubblefield, and Matt Smethurst for proofreading and research assistance. Others who offered helpful comments on the manuscript include Robert Stein, Danny Akin, Chuck Deglow, Laura Roberts, Wes Smith, Jonathan Pennington, and Robert Peterson. Special appreciation goes to Valerie Angel for checking the Scripture index. Thanks also to the helpful staff at the Southern Seminary library, not least Michael Strackeljahn.

My dear wife, Chandi, and three beautiful daughters (Sarah Beth, Chloe, and Anabelle) have kept me anchored in reality even as the mental demands of writing have tipped me more toward the eccentric band on the personality spectrum. Indeed, without them, I might have become a hermit or worse. As I wrote this book, I thought regularly of my young daughters, whom I hope will one day read it and benefit from their father's advice about how to approach the Bible. I continue to grow in my understanding of the Scriptures. If given a chance to revise this book in the future, I'm sure that there will be additions and changes.

This book is dedicated to two of my former professors, Robert Stein and Mark Seifrid. Both served on my doctoral dissertation committee. Dr. Stein infected me with his commonsense approach to interpretation and his exemplary clarity in communication. Mark Seifrid, my doctoral supervisor and now also a colleague, has become a dear friend over the last decade. His attention to the nuances of Scripture, as well as his understanding of several thorny interpretive issues, have helped me see much farther than I could have on my own. His genuine Christian friendship is a rare and treasured one.

Even as I thank these many persons who have helped create this book, I also take personal responsibility for the final product—flaws and all. I am encouraged that God uses all things—even our weaknesses and failures—to bring about ultimate good for us, conforming us to the image of his Son and lifting up Jesus as the greatest treasure (Rom. 8:28–30).

Abbreviations

AB	Anchor Bible
ABD	*The Anchor Bible Dictionary*. Edited by D. N. Freedman. New York: Doubleday, 1992.
ANF	*Ante-Nicene Fathers*, ed. A. Roberts and J. Donaldson. 10 vols. 1885. Peabody, MA: Hendrickson, reprint, 2004.
BDAG	W. Bauer, F. W. Danker, W. F. Arndt, and F. W. Gingrich. *Greek-English Lexicon of the New Testament and Other Early Christian Literature*. 3rd ed. Chicago: University of Chicago Press, 2000.
BECNT	Baker Exegetical Commentary on the New Testament
BT	*The Bible Translator*
CEV	Contemporary English Version
DJG	*Dictionary of Jesus and the Gospels*. Edited by Joel B. Green, Scot McKnight, and I. Howard Marshall. Downers Grove, IL: InterVarsity Press, 1992.
DNTB	*Dictionary of New Testament Background*. Edited by Craig A. Evans and Stanley E. Porter. Downers Grove, IL: InterVarsity Press, 2000.
DPL	*Dictionary of Paul and His Letters*. Edited by Gerald F. Hawthorne, Ralph P. Martin, and Daniel G. Reid. Downers Grove, IL: InterVarsity Press, 1993.
EBC	The Expositor's Bible Commentary. Edited by Frank E. Gaebelein.
EDNT	*Exegetical Dictionary of the New Testament*. Edited by H. Balz and G. Schneider. Grand Rapids: Eerdmans, 1990–1993.
HCSB	Holman Christian Standard Bible
ICBI	International Council on Biblical Inerrancy
JBR	*Journal of Bible and Religion*
JETS	*Journal of the Evangelical Theological Society*
JSNT	*Journal for the Study of the New Testament*
JSNTSup	Journal for the Study of the New Testament: Supplement Series
LB	Living Bible
MSG	The Message
NAC	New American Commentary

NCV	New Century Version
NICOT	New International Commentary on the Old Testament
NIDNTT	*New International Dictionary of New Testament Theology.* Edited by Colin Brown. 4 vols. Grand Rapids: Zondervan, 1975–1985.
NIGTC	New International Greek Testament Commentary
NPNF1	*Nicene and Post-Nicene Fathers*, 1st series. Edited by Philip Schaff. 14 vols. 1886–1889, reprint, Peabody: MA: Hendrickson, 2004.
NTS	*New Testament Studies*
OTP	*The Old Testament Pseudepigrapha.* Vol. 1. Edited by J. H. Charlesworth. New York: Doubleday, 1983.
REB	Revised English Bible
RSV	Revised Standard Version
SBJT	*The Southern Baptist Journal of Theology*
TDNT	*Theological Dictionary of the New Testament*
TEV	Today's English Version
TNIV	Today's New International Version
TNTC	Tyndale New Testament Commentaries
TrinJ	*Trinity Journal*
TS	*Theological Studies*
TynBul	*Tyndale Bulletin*
W.A.	*D. Martin Luthers Werke, kritische Gesammtausgabe.* Edited by J. K. F. Knaake et al. 57 vols. Weimar: Hermann Böhlau, 1883ff.
WTJ	*Westminster Theological Journal*

PART 1

Getting Started:
Text, Canon, and Translation

What Is the Bible?

M ost people who pick up this book will be familiar with the Bible. Yet, I am including this first, basic question for two reasons: (1) There will be some people who happen upon this book who have little to no knowledge of the Christian Scriptures. If that describes you, there is no better place to start than right here. (2) Even people who have spent many years reading the Bible can benefit from returning to the fundamentals. It is my hope that the answer below will be understandable to people ignorant of the Bible but not so simplistic as to be of no benefit to those already well versed in the Christian Scriptures.

Overview of the Bible

The Bible is a collection of writings that Christians consider uniquely inspired and authoritative. While it is one unified book, the Bible is also a compilation of sixty-six smaller books, or literary works. These works, produced by men of various historical time periods, backgrounds, personalities, and cultures, claim the Holy Spirit as the ultimate authority and safeguard behind their writing. As 2 Timothy 3:16 asserts, "All Scripture is God-breathed."

The Bible can be divided into two large sections—the Old Testament and the New Testament. The word *testament* comes from the Latin word *testamentum*, meaning "covenant" or "agreement." Thus, in its basic division, the Bible records two covenantal relationships between God and humanity. The first (old) covenant relationship was ratified at Mount Sinai between God and the Jewish nation (Exod. 19–31). This covenant was anticipatory and pointed to a new covenant, promised in Jeremiah 31:31, when God would draw a people to himself from all nations and write his words on their hearts (Isa. 49:6). In fact, this new covenant was in reality nothing other than a fulfillment of the many saving promises God had made throughout history—that Satan would be crushed by a human descendent of Eve (Gen. 3:15), that through Abraham's offspring all the nations of the world would be blessed (Gen. 22:18), etc.

Within the Old Testament are thirty-nine books of various genres (historical narratives, proverbs, poetry, psalms, etc.). The New Testament contains twenty-seven books, again made up of various literary types (historical narratives, letters, parables, etc.) See question 2 for more information on the organization of the Bible (that is, order of books, origin of chapter and verse divisions, etc.). Also, see the latter half of this book for interpretive approaches to specific biblical genres.

The Purpose of the Bible

The Bible itself is evidence of one of its main claims—that is, that the God who made the heavens, earth, and sea, and everything in them is a communicator who delights to reveal himself to wayward humans. We read in Hebrews 1:1–2, "In the past God spoke to our forefathers through the prophets at many times and in various ways, but in these last days he has spoken to us by his Son, whom he appointed heir of all things, and through whom he made the universe."

These verses in Hebrews point to the culmination of biblical revelation in the eternal Son of God. This Son became incarnate in Jesus of Nazareth, forever uniting God and man in one person—100 percent God and 100 percent man (John 1:14). The prophecies, promises, longings, and anticipations under the old covenant find their fulfillment, meaning, and culmination in the life, death, and resurrection of Jesus Christ. As the apostle Paul says in 2 Corinthians 1:20, "For no matter how many promises God has made, they are 'Yes' in Christ."

The purpose of the Bible, then, is "to make [a person] wise for salvation through faith in Christ Jesus" (2 Tim. 3:15). The Bible is not an end in itself. As Jesus said to the religious experts in his day, "You diligently study the Scriptures because you think that by them you possess eternal life. These are the Scriptures that testify about me" (John 5:39). So, under divine superintendence, the goal of the Bible is to bring its readers to receive the forgiveness of God in Christ and thus to possession of eternal life in relationship with the triune God (John 17:3).

Basic Story Line of the Bible

The Bible explains the origin of the universe (God made everything, Gen. 1–2). The Bible also reveals why there is sin, disease, and death (humans rebelled against God and brought sin and decay into the world, Gen. 3:1–24). And, the Bible promises that God will send a Messiah (Jesus) who will defeat death and Satan and ultimately renew all things (Gen. 3:15; Rev. 22:1–5).

God prepared for the coming of this Messiah by focusing his revelatory and saving work on the descendants of Abraham—that is, the Israelites or the Jews. Even as God gave his holy laws and sent his prophets to the one nation Israel, it was clear that he planned a worldwide blessing flowing forth from the Jews at a future time. God promised Abraham, "*All peoples on earth will be blessed through you*" (Gen. 12:3, my emphasis). Likewise, in the book of Isaiah, we read of God speaking prophetically to the coming Messiah: "It is too small a thing for you to be my servant to restore the tribes of Jacob and bring back those of Israel I have kept. *I will also make you a light for the Gentiles, that you may bring my salvation to the ends of the earth*" (Isa. 49:6, my emphasis). According to the Bible, Jesus has now inaugurated this worldwide salvation, which will be consummated at his return. While all persons are justly condemned under God's holy wrath, Jesus' death on the cross provides forgiveness for those who trust in him. A person becomes a part of God's people—a subject of King Jesus' domain— by turning away from his rebellion and trusting in the Savior's substitutionary death for his sin. As we read in John 3:36, "Whoever believes in the Son has eternal life, but whoever rejects the Son will not see life, for God's wrath remains on him."

The consummation of God's salvation is yet to be revealed. The Bible teaches that Jesus certainly will come again (1 Thess. 4:13–18). While scholars debate some of the specifics concerning Jesus' return, the Scriptures are clear that death and sin (now already defeated by the cross) then will be done away with forever (Rev. 20:14–21:4). All who have received God's forgiveness in Christ will dwell with God forever in endless joy (John 14:2–3; 17:24). Those who have remained in rebellion against God will not be given a postmortem, second chance at repentance; they will be punished through eternal separation from God (John 3:36; Matt. 25:46).

Functions of the Bible

Under the overarching purpose of revealing God and bringing people into a saving relationship with him through Jesus Christ, there are a number of related functions of the Bible, including the following.

- *Conviction of Sin.* The Holy Spirit applies God's Word to the human heart, convicting people of having failed to meet God's holy standard and convincing them of their just condemnation and need for a Savior (Rom. 3:20; Gal. 3:22–25; Heb. 4:12–13).

- *Correction and Instruction.* The Bible corrects and instructs God's people, teaching them who God is, who they are, and what God expects of them. Both through a believer's individual study and through the church's gifted teachers, God edifies and corrects his people (Josh. 1:8; Ps. 119:98–99; Matt. 7:24–27; 1 Cor. 10:11; Eph. 4:11–12; 2 Tim. 3:16; 4:1–4).

- *Spiritual Fruitfulness.* As the Word of God takes deep root in true believers, it produces a harvest of righteousness—a genuine manifestation of love for God and love for others (Mark 4:1–20; James 1:22–25).

- *Perseverance.* Empowered by the Holy Spirit, believers hold fast to the saving message of the Scriptures through the trials and temptations of life. Through this perseverance, they gain increasing confidence in God's promise to keep them until the end (John 10:28–29; 1 Cor. 15:2; 2 Cor. 13:5; Gal. 3:1–5; Phil. 1:6; Col. 1:23; 1 Tim. 3:13; 1 John 2:14).

- *Joy and Delight.* To those who know God, the Bible is a source of unending joy and delight. As Psalm 19:9–10 attests, "The ordinances of the LORD are sure and altogether righteous. They are more precious than gold, than much pure gold; they are sweeter than honey, than honey from the comb."

- *Ultimate Authority in Doctrine and Deed.* The Bible is the ultimate authority for the Christian in terms of behavior and belief (Luke 10:26; 24:44–45; John 10:35; 2 Tim. 3:16; 4:1–4; 2 Peter 3:16). The correctness of all preaching, creeds, doctrines, or opinions is decisively settled by this question: What does the Bible say? As John Stott notes, "Scripture is the royal scepter by which King Jesus governs his church."[1]

Chronology of the Bible's Composition

The first five books in the Old Testament, the books of Moses (Genesis, Exodus, Leviticus, Numbers, Deuteronomy), most likely were written around 1400 B.C.[2] As the books describe events from thousands of years prior, however, it is almost certain that many oral and written sources underlie our current text. Of course, Moses' selection or editing of such sources took place under God's superintendence. The last book in the Old Testament, Malachi, was written around 430 B.C. So, the thirty-nine books of the Old Testament were composed more than a thousand-year span by about forty different authors. (Some books in the Old Testament were written by the same author—Jeremiah and Lamentations, for example. Other books, such as 1 and 2 Kings, do not explicitly cite an author. Still other books, such as the Psalms or Proverbs, cite multiple authors for various portions.) The Old Testament was written in Hebrew with a few small portions in Aramaic (Ezra 4:8–6:18; 7:12–26; Dan. 2:4b–7:28; Jer. 10:11).[3]

The first book of the New Testament (possibly James or Galatians) likely was written in A.D. mid- to late 40s. Most of the books in the New Testament were written in the 50s and 60s. The last book of the New Testament, the book of Revelation, also called the Apocalypse of John, probably was written

---

1. John R. W. Stott, *John Stott on the Bible and the Christian Life: Six Sessions on the Authority, Interpretation, and Use of Scripture* (Grand Rapids: Zondervan, 2006). The quote is from the first DVD lecture, "The Authority of Scripture."
2. Some scholars think Job predates the books of Moses.
3. Also, two words in Genesis 31:47 are in Aramaic—*Jegar-sahadutha* ("heap of witness").

around A.D. 90. The New Testament was written in Greek, the *lingua franca* of its day, though it contains a few transliterated Aramaic and Latin words.

FIGURE 1: TIME LINE OF BIBLICAL EVENTS AND BOOKS	
Adam and Eve	*l.t.a.*[4]
Noah	*l.t.a.*
The calling of Abraham	2000 B.C.
The exodus	1446 B.C. (first books of the Bible written by Moses)
The monarchy begins	1050 B.C. (God chooses Saul)
King David	1010–970 B.C.
King Solomon	970–930 B.C.
The divided kingdom	931 B.C. (Israel and Judah divided)
The Assyrian exile	722 B.C. (destruction of Samaria)
The Babylonian exile	586 B.C. (destruction of Jerusalem)
The Persian period	537 B.C. (return of Jews under Cyrus)
Second temple finished	515 B.C.
Nehemiah/Ezra	mid-400s B.C.
Malachi (last Old Testament book)	430 B.C.
Intertestamental period	430 B.C.–A.D. 45
Jesus' birth	7–4 B.C.
Jesus' ministry	A.D. 27–30
Jesus' crucifixion	A.D. 30
First New Testament book(s) written	A.D. 45
Revelation written	A.D. 90 (last book of the New Testament)

---

4. *L.t.a.* stands for "long time ago." While I believe that Adam and Eve were historical persons, I will not venture to guess the year that God created them. It was (we can all agree) a long time ago.

REFLECTION QUESTIONS

1. What is one new thing that you learned about the Bible? (Or, possibly note a previously known fact that struck you afresh.)

2. One purpose of the Bible is to bring persons into a saving relationship with God through Jesus Christ. Has that purpose been accomplished in your life? How do you know?

3. How would you rank your knowledge of the Bible on a scale of 1 to 10? How did you learn about the Bible? (Or, why do you not know much about the Bible?)

4. Have you read the entire Bible? If not, consider committing to do so over the next year.

5. Do you have a general question about the Bible that this section failed to answer? What is it?

FOR FURTHER STUDY

The Bible. (There is no better way to learn about the Bible than to read it for yourself. See question 7 for suggestions of which English translation to read.)

Carson, D. A. *For the Love of God: A Daily Companion for Discovering the Riches of God's Word.* Vols. 1 and 2. Wheaton, IL: Crossway, 1998, 1999. (These devotional books include one-page readings for each day and a Bible-reading plan that takes you through the Old Testament once and the New Testament twice in one year. Carson's writing is faithful and insightful, though challenging for persons with little biblical knowledge.)

How Is the Bible Organized?

Maybe you grew up in a church where the children participated in competitions to memorize the locations of the books in the Bible. Or perhaps you are unsure of the order of the books of the Bible and feel intimidated when asked to look up a verse. Is there any discernible order or logic in the way the books in the Bible are arranged? When were chapter and verse divisions added? These are some of the questions we will answer in this section.

The Basic Division—The Testaments

The first three-fourths of the Bible was written between 1400 B.C. and 430 B.C. It includes thirty-nine books in the Hebrew language (Daniel and Ezra have a few small portions in Aramaic, a related Semitic language).[1] This part of the Bible is called the Old Testament. Non-Christian Jews, of course, simply refer to these books as their Scripture, or TANAK (Hebrew acrostic for Law, Prophets, and Writings). Jews who reject Jesus as Messiah do not recognize the New Testament as inspired.

The word *testament* comes from the Latin word *testamentum*, meaning "covenant" or "agreement." Apparently the first person to use this term to describe the divisions of the Bible was the early Christian apologist Tertullian (A.D. 160–225).[2] The idea of the Bible being organized around two covenants between God and humanity was not new to Tertullian, however, but is found explicitly in several biblical texts.

Jeremiah 31:31–33, written between 626 and 580 B.C., predicts the coming of the Messiah with explicit reference to a new covenant.

---

1. Jeremiah 10:11 is also in Aramaic, as are two words in Genesis 31:47, *Jegar-sahadutha* ("heap of witness").
2. *Against Marcion* 3.14; 4.6.

"The time is coming," declares the LORD, "when I will make a *new covenant* with the house of Israel and with the house of Judah. It will not be like the *covenant* I made with their forefathers when I took them by the hand to lead them out of Egypt, because they broke my *covenant*, though I was a husband to them," declares the LORD. "This is the *covenant* I will make with the house of Israel after that time," declares the LORD. "I will put my law in their minds and write it on their hearts. I will be their God, and they will be my people." (my emphasis)

In instituting the Lord's Supper on the night he was betrayed, Jesus alluded to the fulfillment of Jeremiah's prophecy in his death, saying, "This cup is the *new covenant* in my blood, which is poured out for you" (Luke 22:20, my emphasis). Because Jesus taught that his death and resurrection instituted God's promised new covenant, it was only natural for books that witnessed to and expounded on this reality to be referred to as the New Testament. Thus, Christians call the twenty-seven inspired books that came from Jesus' apostles and their companions the New Testament. These books, which make up the latter one-fourth of the Bible, were written between A.D. 45 and 90.

Number and Order of the Old Testament Books
The Old Testament includes thirty-nine individual books. These books vary in literary genre from historical narrative to romantic poetry. As they stand currently in our English Bible, they are organized somewhat topically (see figure 2).

FIGURE 2: THE OLD TESTAMENT			
LAW	**HISTORICAL BOOKS**	**WISDOM BOOKS**	**PROPHETICAL BOOKS**
			MAJOR PROPHETS
Genesis	Joshua	Job	Isaiah
Exodus	Judges	Psalms	Jeremiah
Leviticus	Ruth	Proverbs	Lamentations
Numbers	1–2 Samuel	Ecclesiastes	Ezekiel
Deuteronomy	1–2 Kings	Song of Solomon	Daniel
	1–2 Chronicles	(Song of Songs)	
	Ezra		MINOR PROPHETS
	Nehemiah		Hosea—Malachi
	Esther		(The Twelve)

- *Law (Genesis–Deuteronomy).* These five books are also called the Books of Moses or the Pentateuch. (*Pentateuch* is a Greek word meaning "the five books.") These books describe the origin of the world, the beginnings of the nation of Israel, God's choosing of Israel, the giving of his laws to them, and his bringing them to the border of the Promised Land.

- *The Historical Books (Joshua–Esther).* These twelve books recount God's dealings with Israel, primarily through historical narrative.

- *Wisdom and Songs (Job–Song of Solomon).* These five books include proverbs, other ancient wisdom literature, and songs.

- *The Major Prophets (Isaiah–Daniel).* These five books are called the major prophets because they are longer, not because they are more important. These books witness to God's many warnings, instructions, and promises that he sent to Israel through his divine spokesmen, the prophets.

- *The Minor Prophets (Hosea–Malachi).* These prophetic books are shorter and are thus called the minor ones. In the ancient Jewish collection of Scriptures, they were counted as one book, called The Book of the Twelve (that is, the twelve prophetic books).

If one were to visit a modern-day Jewish synagogue ("temple") and pick up a copy of the Hebrew Scriptures, it would include exactly the same contents as the Christian Old Testament but in a different arrangement. From ancient times, the Jews have organized their holy writings in three main divisions—Law (*Torah*), Prophets (*Nebi'im*), and Writings (*Kethubim*). The first five books of the Hebrew Bible are the same as the Christian Old Testament—the books of Moses, or the Law. After that, however, the order changes noticeably, and sometimes multiple books are grouped together. The last book in the Hebrew Bible is 2 Chronicles.

Jesus possibly alludes to the traditional Jewish order of the Hebrew Scriptures in Luke 11:49–51, where he says,

> Because of this, God in his wisdom said, "I will send them prophets and apostles, some of whom they will kill and others they will persecute." Therefore this generation will be held responsible for the blood of all the prophets that has been shed since the beginning of the world, from the blood of Abel to the blood of Zechariah, who was killed between the altar and the sanctuary. Yes, I tell you, this generation will be held responsible for it all.

According to the Jewish canonical order, the Hebrew Bible begins with Genesis and ends with 2 Chronicles. Thus, Abel is the first martyr (Gen.

4:8), and Zechariah is the last (2 Chron. 24:20–22). Jesus also references the
threefold division of the Jewish canon when he speaks of "the Law of Moses,
the Prophets and the Psalms" (Luke 24:44). (Sometimes the Writings section
was simply referred to with the most prominently used book in that section—
the Psalms.)[3] When the Hebrew Bible was translated into Greek and Latin,
the books began to appear in a more topical arrangement, from which we
ultimately derive our order in the English Bible. Even so, there is not complete uniformity of book order among early Greek and Latin manuscripts or
later translations. Knowing of this variety in the manuscripts should prevent
modern interpreters from claiming divine sanction or meaning for any particular order of books in our current English Bible.

Number and Order of the New Testament Books

During Jesus' earthly ministry, he used a variety of striking mnemonic devices (e.g., rhyme, unexpected details, and captivating stories). Furthermore,
he promised his disciples that the Holy Spirit would bring his teaching to their
memory (John 14:26). Following Jesus' resurrection and ascension, the stories
of Jesus apparently were told for some time primarily as oral tradition that
was carefully safeguarded and transmitted by eyewitnesses (Luke 1:1–4). Over
time, authoritative collections of these stories were written and recognized by
the church as having apostolic sanction—the four Gospels: Matthew, Mark,
Luke, and John. Luke also wrote a second volume, Acts, explaining how the
Holy Spirit came as predicted and propelled the early church outwards to testify about Jesus the Messiah.

As the apostles started churches all over the ancient Roman Empire, they
continued instructing those communities through letters. From the earliest
time, these apostolic letters were copied, circulated, and recognized as time-
lessly authoritative for the life of the church (Col. 4:16; 2 Peter 3:15–16).
Thirteen of the letters in the New Testament were written by the apostle Paul
(Romans–Philemon). Paul's letters are organized in the New Testament by
decreasing order of size, first to communities and then to individuals.[4] If more
than one letter was written to the same community or individual, the letters are kept together. The anonymous letter "to the Hebrews" (i.e., to Jewish

---

3. Paul D. Wegner notes that even in the tenth century, Arab historian al-Masudi refers to
the Jewish canon as "the Law, the Prophets, and the Psalms, which are the 24 books" (*The
Journey from Texts to Translations: The Origin and Development of the Bible* [Grand Rapids:
Baker, 1999], 109).

4. One exception is Galatians, which, although it is slightly shorter than Ephesians, "may
have been placed before Ephesians as a frontispiece to the collection of the Prison Epistles
(Ephesians, Philippians, Colossians) because of its use of the term *kanōn* or 'rule' (Gal
6:16)" (William W. Klein, Craig L. Blomberg, and Robert L. Hubbard, *Introduction to
Biblical Interpretation*, rev. ed. [Nashville: Thomas Nelson, 2004], 114).

Christians) was apparently included after Paul's letters because some people in the early church believed Paul or a Pauline companion wrote the letter.

Other New Testament letters were written by James, Peter, John, and Jude. Perhaps these letters are arranged in a decreasing order of prominence of the authors. Paul mentions "James, Cephas [Peter], and John" as Jerusalem church "pillars" in Galatians 2:9. This Pauline list mirrors the order of their respective letters in the New Testament (James, 1 Peter, 2 Peter, 1 John, 2 John, 3 John). The letter of Jude, a half-brother of Jesus, appears next. The final book of the New Testament, the Revelation or Apocalypse of John, is a mixed genre, including letters, prophecy, and apocalypse. As much of the book is made up of visions and symbolic images that point to the end of the world, it is fitting as the last book of the twenty-seven-book New Testament canon (see figure 3).

FIGURE 3: THE NEW TESTAMENT		
GOSPEL AND ACTS	**PAULINE LETTERS**	**GENERAL LETTERS AND REVELATION**
Matthew	Romans	Hebrews
Mark	1–2 Corinthians	James
Luke	Galatians	1–2 Peter
John	Ephesians	1–3 John
Acts	Philippians	Jude
	Colossians	Revelation
	1–2 Thessalonians	
	1–2 Timothy	
	Titus	
	Philemon	

It is worth noting that the practice of including multiple literary works within one book is not widely attested until at least the second century A.D. Prior to this time, most books in the Bible would have circulated as individual scrolls. A community of believers likely would have had a cabinet in which they kept the various scrolls with tags on the end to identify their contents. In the second and third century, however, books with multiple leaves (i.e., codices) began to appear with greater frequency. Some scholars have suggested that the canonical impulse of early Christians was the force behind the creation of the codex.

Chapter Divisions

Early Christians and Jews often cited Scripture with reference to a book, author, or textual event but with little further specificity. Jesus, for example, in referencing the account of Moses, refers to the text simply with the phrase "at the bush [passage]" (Mark 12:26; Luke 20:37, my translation). As biblical texts came to be copied, read, and commented on, some made various attempts to further subdivide and label them. For example, Eusebius (ca. A.D. 260–340), a prominent historian in the early church, divided the four Gospels into a number of canons, or divisions. Eusebian canons are included in such ancient manuscripts as Codex Vaticanus. Likewise, ancient Jewish rabbis applied various organizational subdivisions to the text.

Our current chapter divisions were added to the Old and New Testament by Stephen Langton (1150–1228), Archbishop of Canterbury in the early thirteenth century, while he was lecturing at the University of Paris.[5] Langton added the divisions to the Latin text, and subsequent publications came to follow his format. Langton's chapter divisions were inserted in modified form to the Hebrew text by Salomon ben Ishmael around A.D. 1330.[6] In light of this background, it seems unwise to claim any divine meaning behind Langton's chapter divisions, which are widely recognized to break the text unnaturally at some points. For example, the division between chapters 10 and 11 of 1 Corinthians introduces an unnatural split in Paul's thought.

Verse Divisions

Verse divisions in our modern English Old Testament are based on the versification standardized by the Ben Asher family (Jewish scribes) around A.D. 900. When Langton's chapter divisions were added to the Hebrew Bible at a later date (see above), the chapter divisions were sometimes adjusted to fit the Ben Asher scheme.[7] Thus, there are sometimes slight differences between the chapter and verse numbers of Hebrew and English Bibles. Scholars generally recognize the superiority of the Hebrew divisions in keeping together thought units.

Verse divisions in the New Testament were added to a Latin/Greek diglot text in 1551 by Robert "Stephanus" Estienne, a printer from Paris. Drawing from an obscure comment by Estienne's son, some scholars have claimed that the printer made the verse divisions while riding horseback on a journey from Paris to Lyons (thus explaining the sometimes unnatural breaks). More likely, Estienne's son intended to say that his father divided the text while resting at inns during the trip.[8]

Prior to Estienne's verse divisions, biblical scholars were forced to refer to texts with phrases such as "halfway through chapter 4 in Galatians." However

---

5. Bruce M. Metzger, *Manuscripts of the Greek Bible: An Introduction to Palaeography* (New York: Oxford University Press, 1981), 41.
6. Wegner, *Journey from Texts to Translations*, 176.
7. Ibid.
8. Metzger, *Manuscripts of the Greek Bible*, 41n.106.

flawed, Estienne's versification was a major advance in allowing for specificity in citation. The first English Bible to have verse divisions was the Geneva Bible of 1560. Though Estienne is still criticized for some of his segmentations, it is virtually unthinkable that any other scheme will ever challenge the universal acceptance of his system. Again, knowing the history of our current verse divisions should prevent us from engaging in creative biblical mathematics, claiming divine meaning behind current verse numbers.

REFLECTION QUESTIONS

1. When you have spoken of the Old Testament and New Testament, have you thought of the term *testament* as meaning "covenant"? How does viewing the Bible as based on covenants between God and humanity affect your reading?

2. Prior to reading the material above, where did you think the chapter and verse divisions in the Bible originated?

3. What is one new fact that you learned about the Bible in the section above?

4. Has this section raised any new questions for you?

5. Can you recite the Old Testament and New Testament books in order? If not, make it your goal to learn them over the next week.

FOR FURTHER STUDY

Patzia, Arthur G. *The Making of the New Testament: Origin, Collection, Text and Canon.* Downers Grove, IL: InterVarsity Press, 1995.
Wegner, Paul D. *The Journey from Texts to Translations: The Origin and Development of the Bible.* Grand Rapids: Baker, 1999.

Who Wrote the Bible—Humans or God?

"God said it. I believe it. That settles it." So goes a popular fundamentalist mantra about the Bible. But if God wrote the Bible, why does Paul say in his letter to Philemon, "I, Paul, am writing this with my own hand" (Philem. 19)? Or, at the end of John's Gospel, we read, "This is the disciple who testifies to these things and who wrote them down" (John 21:24). So, who did write the Bible—humans or God?

Theories of Inspiration

Everyone who claims the name "Christian" would agree that the Scriptures are inspired. Yet, a wide variety of meanings are attached to the adjective "inspired." What are some of the main theories of inspiration?

- *The Intuition Theory.* According to this view, the writers of the Bible exhibit a natural religious intuition that is also found in other great philosophical or religious thinkers, such as Confucius or Plato. Obviously, the absolute truth claims of Scripture are denied by those holding this view of inspiration.

- *The Illumination Theory.* This view holds that the Spirit of God in some way did objectively impress himself upon the consciousness of the biblical writers but not in a way that is essentially different from the way the Spirit communicates with all humanity. Only in degree is the Spirit's influence different, not in kind.

- *The Dynamic Theory.* This view asserts that God gave definite, specific impressions or concepts to the biblical authors but that allowed the writers to communicate those concepts in their own words. That is, the exact phrasing of Scripture is due to human choice, while the main tenor of the content is determined by God.

- *The Dictation Theory.* This view holds that God dictated the exact words to the human authors. Like court stenographers, the authors of Scripture exercised no human volition in the composition of their writings. Sometimes those holding the verbal plenary theory (see below) are wrongly accused of believing in such mechanical dictation.

- *The Verbal Plenary Theory.* This view (the biblical one, I believe) asserts that there is a dual authorship to the Scriptures. While the authors of the Bible wrote as thinking, feeling human beings, God so mysteriously superintended the process that every word written was also the exact word he wanted to be written—free from all error. This view is sometimes called the verbal theory. It will be explored in greater detail in the following sections.[1]

The Dual Authorship of Scripture

When writing a letter to the Corinthians, Paul did not enter an ecstatic state, recite the letter to a secretary, and then, when finished, pick up the completed composition and say, "Let's see what God wrote!" Yet, as an apostle, Paul expected his teaching to be fully obeyed and believed—received, in fact, as the very word of God (1 Cor. 7:40; 14:36–37; 2 Cor. 2:17; 4:2; Col. 1:25; 1 Thess. 2:13; 2 Thess. 3:14). Similarly, Psalm 95 is clearly written by an ancient Israelite leading other ancient Israelites in worship. The psalm begins, "Come, let us sing for joy to the LORD; let us shout aloud to the Rock of our salvation. Let us come before him with thanksgiving and extol him with music and song" (Ps. 95:1–2). Yet, hundreds of years later, the author of Hebrews can quote Psalm 95 with the introductory citation, "The Holy Spirit says" (Heb. 3:7). Such apparent inconsistencies (Paul as author and his communication as the word of God; an ancient Israelite and the Holy Spirit as the author of the same psalm), in fact, convey a profound truth about Scripture—it is dually authored. Each word in the Bible is the word of a conscious human author and at the same time the exact word that God intends for the revelation of himself.

Variation within Dual Authorship

As is clear from a cursory glance at the Bible, God revealed himself "at many times and in various ways" (Heb. 1:1). Some Old Testament prophets

---

1. This five-theory summary is derived from Millard J. Erickson, *Christian Theology*, 2nd ed. (Grand Rapids: Baker, 1998), 231–33. Erickson calls the verbal plenary theory the "verbal theory."

gave oral denouncements, often with the repeated introductory phrase, "Thus says the Lord" (e.g., Isa. 7:7; Ezek. 2:4; Amos 1:3; Obad. 1:1; Mic. 2:3; Nah. 1:12; Hag. 1:5; Zech. 1:3; Mal. 1:4). Elsewhere, God's revelatory servants were given visions and prophecies, sometimes as the prophets themselves admitted their ignorance of all the meanings of their proclamations (Dan. 12:8–9, cf. 1 Peter 1:10–12). In other genres, the author's conscious role in composing or selecting the material is more on the surface of the text. For example, at the beginning of his Gospel, Luke writes,

> Many have undertaken to draw up an account of the things that have been fulfilled among us, just as they were handed down to us by those who from the first were eyewitnesses and servants of the word. Therefore, since I myself have carefully investigated everything from the beginning, it seemed good also to me to write an orderly account for you, most excellent Theophilus, so that you may know the certainty of the things you have been taught. (Luke 1:1–4)

Note, Luke does not say, "I prayed and the Holy Spirit brought to my mind the stories of Jesus to write." Luke was a historian—engaged in real historical research. Yet, as an inspired companion of the apostles, Luke was also God's revelatory agent. Similarly, Paul's role in composing his own letters is undeniably on the surface of the text. For example, in Galatians 4:19–20, Paul is exasperated with the Galatians for their implicit denial of the gospel he preached to them. He writes, "My dear children, for whom I am again in the pains of childbirth until Christ is formed in you, how I wish I could be with you now and change my tone, because I am perplexed about you!" Undoubtedly, depending on the situation, authors were more or less conscious of relating divine revelation (for example, relaying a "Thus says the Lord" prophetic message versus the writing of a personal letter).

Much of the Bible comes as situational literature (documents addressed to specific persons facing particular historical situations), so it is worth asking how this situational literature can be the timeless Word of God. Muslims, for example, have in the Qur'an mostly abstract poetry that praises the attributes of Allah. Such poetry came to Mohammad, Muslims claim, in ecstatic utterance. The Bible, by contrast, testifies to God revealing himself in history through repeated, consistent, and anticipatory ways. That is, God spoke repeatedly to his people; he was consistent in his message; and, while God addressed the people in their current situation, his earlier revelation anticipates and points to a climactic intervention that ultimately came in Christ's life, death, and resurrection. Yet, it is not in abstract poetry but in the reality of daily life that God's Word came. Strikingly, when the Word of God became flesh (the incarnation), it was also in the seeming ordinariness of life that he appeared.

Some Implications of Dual Authorship

The fact that the Bible presents itself as a dually authored book has a number of implications for the way we approach it.

1. The clear purpose of the human author is a good place to start in understanding the Bible. The Scripture cannot mean *less* than the human authors consciously intended. Admittedly, there are a few places where the human author confesses his ignorance of the revelation given to him (e.g., Dan. 12:8–9), but these are exceptions. The human authors usually seem acutely aware of conveying timely messages to their current audiences.

2. God, as the Lord of history and revelation, included patterns or foreshadowing of which the human authors were not fully aware. Under God's sovereign hand, his prior historical interventions were in themselves prophetic—pointing forward to Christ. About the Old Testament regulations given to Israel, the author of Hebrews says, "The law is only a shadow of the good things that are coming—not the realities themselves" (Heb. 10:1). Similarly, Paul notes that the inclusion of the Gentiles and Jews together under the saving work of Christ was a "mystery" present in the Scriptures but not fully revealed until the Spirit declared this truth through the New Testament prophets and apostles (Eph. 3:3–6). We should seek explicit statements in later revelation to clarify any such divine intentionality. One should be forewarned against finding symbolic or prophetic details in the Old Testament when no New Testament author has provided authoritative interpretation of the text.

3. Sometimes it is asserted that the Bible can never mean something of which the human author was not consciously aware as he was writing. It is possible, however, to affirm a hermeneutical approach based on authorial intent without affirming the above statement. The biblical authors were conscious of being used by God to convey his word and believed that their revelation was part of a grand scheme of history. The Old Testament authors knew they were somewhere along the stair steps of revelation, but few, if any, knew how close they were to the top of the stairs (i.e., Christ). Though they could not know all the future events, the prophets certainly would not deny God's providential control of history, which exceeded their conscious reflection (see question 24, "How do we interpret prophecy? [Typology]").

Inspiration and the Incarnation

It is often noted that the divine-human dual authorship of Scripture can be compared with the Lord Jesus Christ, who is both fully human and fully

God. To some degree, this comparison can be helpful. Just as no one can explain exactly how both human and divine natures can be fully present in the one person of Jesus, neither can one explain fully how God so superintended the writing of Scripture so that each word is divinely inspired and yet also a word chosen by a human author. To affirm the divine and human natures of Christ and the divine-human authorship of Scripture, one need not be able to explain fully the mystery of these revealed truths.

T. C. Hammond's insightful comparison between inspiration and incarnation is worth quoting at length.

> The living Revelation was mysteriously brought into the world without the intervention of a human father. The Holy Spirit was the appointed Agent. The written revelation came into being by a similar process without the aid of human philosophical abstractions. The Holy Spirit was again the appointed Agent. The mother of our Lord remained a human mother and her experiences throughout would appear to have been those of every other mother— except that she was made aware that her child was to be the long-expected Redeemer of Israel. The writers of the biblical books remained human authors, and their experiences appear to have been similarly natural, though they were sometimes aware that God was giving to the world through them a message of no ordinary importance (e.g., "For I received from the Lord what I also delivered to you . . ." 1 Cor. 11:23). Mary, the mother of our Lord, probably brought into the world other children by the normal process of birth. The writers of the biblical books probably wrote other purely personal letters which were not necessarily of canonical importance. More important still, no student should fail to grasp the fact that the divine-human personal life of our Lord is one and indivisible by any human means of analysis. On no recorded occasions can we say that in the one instance there was *purely divine* thought, and in the other a *purely human* thought. The two natures were united in one indissoluble Person. From the manger to the cross, the Lord must always be thought of and described from that point of view. Similarly, though the parallel is not quite complete, the student will be saved much unsound thinking, unnecessary confusion and, injury to his faith, by observing that in the Scriptures the divine and human elements are blended in such a way that in few cases can we, with any certainty, analyse the record to demonstrate purely human elements.[2]

One also should note that the divine-human dimension of the Bible concerns its authorship, *not* its very nature. We listen reverently to the Bible

---

2. T. C. Hammond, *In Understanding Be Men: An Introductory Handbook of Christian Doctrine*, rev. and ed. David F. Wright, 6th ed. (Leicester: Inter-Varsity Press, 1968), 34–35. I have retained the author's nonstandard capitalization.

as the written Word of God, but we worship Jesus as the incarnate Son of God.

REFLECTION QUESTIONS

1. How can a letter from a dead man to dead people (Paul's letter to the Galatians, for example) be of significance to modern people?

2. Besides the Bible verses cited above, can you list other verses that point to the dual authorship of Scripture?

3. Is anything lost in ignoring or denying the human element in the writing of the Bible? Is it too simplistic to just say, "God wrote it"?

4. If one affirms the dual authorship of Scripture, what controls are left to prevent the finding of hidden "divine meanings" everywhere?

5. In what ways are Jesus' human and divine natures similar to and different from the divine-human authorship of Scripture?

FOR FURTHER STUDY

Carson, D. A. "Approaching the Bible." In *The New Bible Commentary: 21st Century Edition*, edited by D. A. Carson et al., 1–19. Downers Grove, IL: InterVarsity Press, 1994.

Erickson, Millard J. *Christian Theology*. 2nd ed. Grand Rapids: Baker, 1998. (See chap. 10, "The Preservation of Revelation: Inspiration," 224–45).

Marshall, I. Howard. *Biblical Inspiration*. Grand Rapids: Eerdmans, 1982. This book has been republished by Regent College Publishing.

Does the Bible Contain Error?

It is not uncommon to encounter people who assert that the Bible has errors in it. Such a view, however, does not square with the Bible's claims about itself or the historic view of the Christian church. What do we mean when the say the Bible is inerrant, and how can we support that assertion in light of alleged discrepancies in the Bible?

The Vocabulary of Inerrancy

Up until the mid-seventeenth century, essentially all persons who claimed the name of Christian accepted that the Bible was completely truthful in all matters that it asserted. With the elevation of human reason in the Enlightenment, however, some people began to have a more skeptical view of previously sacrosanct texts. People started to judge revelation (that is, the Bible) on the basis of their own human reason, rejecting and criticizing various portions, based on what seemed reasonable or probable to them. Many of these critics wanted to maintain some connection with the Christian church while at the same time making themselves the final arbiters of truth. Of course, the historic witness of the church to the complete truthfulness of Scripture has continued in spite of challenges, but the critics of it also have continued until this day.[1]

Within the last fifty years, due to increased Christian debates over the truthfulness of Scripture, a vocabulary has evolved to summarize various claims about the Bible's truthfulness. Below are some of the terms that are regularly used.

---

1. New challenges against inerrancy continue to appear. For a modern defense of inerrancy against recent detractors, see G. K. Beale, *The Erosion of Inerrancy in Evangelicalism: Responding to New Challenges to Biblical Authority* (Wheaton, IL: Crossway, 2008).

- *Inerrant/Inerrancy.* The doctrine of inerrancy, or the claim that the Scriptures are inerrant, means that the Bible is completely truthful in all things that the biblical authors assert—whether in geographic, chronological, or theological details. Advocates of inerrancy affirm a verbal plenary view of inspiration. That is, although the human authors of Scripture were thinking composers, God so superintended the writing process such that *every word* written was according to his will. The words were divinely guarded from all error. Wayne Grudem provides this helpful definition of inerrancy: "The inerrancy of Scripture means that Scripture in the original manuscripts does not affirm anything that is contrary to fact."[2] Similarly, Kenneth Kantzer writes, "Put quite simply, . . . inerrancy holds that the Bible tells us truth and never says what is not so."[3]

- *Infallible/Infallibility.* Infallible, according to modern dictionaries, also means "incapable of error."[4] However, the word has taken on more narrow connotations in current debates over the Bible. To claim the Scriptures as infallible is to assert that they are error-free *in* matters of theology or faith. This view is sometimes also called limited inerrancy. Advocates of full inerrancy certainly would affirm that the Scriptures are infallible, but not all persons who affirm the Bible's infallibility also would affirm full inerrancy. The word *infallible* is weaker in connotation and does not include within it the claim that the Bible is free from *all* error (intentional or unintentional, theological or nontheological). Those less familiar with the narrow connotations of the term *infallible* may unwittingly use it as a synonym for *inerrant*.

- *Inspired/Inspiration.* To claim the Bible as divinely inspired is to assert that God was somehow behind its writing. Without further clarification, this assertion is more ambiguous than the terms above. Some who claim the Bible as inspired also would maintain that nonbiblical documents also are inspired or that God continues to inspire people in the same way today. Advocates of inerrancy claim that the Bible is inspired in a unique, verbal plenary way. See question 3 ("Who wrote the Bible—humans or God?") for a brief discussion of competing views of inspiration.

- *Neo-orthodox/Neo-orthodoxy.* Neo-orthodoxy literally means "new orthodoxy" and is a term used to describe a theological movement of

---

2. Wayne Grudem, *Systematic Theology: An Introduction to Biblical Doctrine* (Grand Rapids: Zondervan; Leicester: Inter-Varsity Press, 1994), 90.
3. Kenneth S. Kantzer, foreword to *Encyclopedia of Bible Difficulties, by* Gleason L. Archer (Grand Rapids: Zondervan, 1982), 7.
4. This is the first definition of *infallible* in the Merriam-Webster Online Dictionary, www.merriam-webster.com (accessed March 31, 2008).

the 1920s to the 1960s. Neo-orthodox scholars generally affirm that God revealed himself in history through mighty acts but that fallible human beings recorded these acts imperfectly. According to neo-or-thodox theologians, these writings become the Word of God as they are newly proclaimed and people have an existential encounter with the living God. Though neo-orthodoxy is no longer a recognizable movement, the works of neo-orthodox theologians (e.g., Karl Barth, Emil Brunner) continue to exercise influence.

- *Trustworthy/True/Authoritative.* Sometimes critics charge that words like *inerrant* and *infallible* are not found in Scripture and wrongly focus on negation (that is, *no* error). Would it not be better, they ask, to use positive and historic terms such as *true, trustworthy,* or *authoritative*? While such positive affirmations admittedly are beneficial, modern de-bate over the Scripture has necessitated the precision of words such as *inerrant* (along with further explanatory comments on what *iner-rant* means and does not mean). A glance at the history of Christian theology shows that new summary terms and qualifications often are required to combat theological error.

Scripture's Claims About Itself

Within the Bible itself, we find numerous claims and assumptions that the Scriptures are completely truthful in all that they assert (intentional or unin-tentional claims, theological or nontheological information). Below is a brief sampling of such Scriptures with a few explanatory comments.

- *Numbers 23:19:* *"God is not a man, that he should lie, nor a son of man, that he should change his mind. Does he speak and then not act? Does he promise and not fulfill?"* If God is completely truthful and the Bible is God's communication to humanity (Heb. 1:1–3), then it follows that the Bible, as God's Word, is completely truthful.

- *Psalm 12:6:* *"And the words of the* LORD *are flawless, like silver refined in a furnace of clay, purified seven times."* Psalms and Proverbs are filled with re-peated praises of the perfections of God's Word. See especially Psalm 119.

- *2 Timothy 3:16:* *"All Scripture is God-breathed and is useful for teaching, rebuking, correcting and training in righteousness."* This verse asserts that while the Bible has human authors, the words they wrote must be attributed ultimately to the divine in-breathing (inspiration) of God.

- *2 Peter 1:21:* *"For prophecy never had its origin in the will of man, but men spoke from God as they were carried along by the Holy Spirit."*

Again, this verse reminds us that each word written in the Bible is the exact word God intended to be written.

- *John 10:35: "The Scripture cannot be broken."* In his teachings and debates, Jesus repeatedly appealed to the Old Testament Scriptures, with the clear assumption that those texts were completely true in all they reported. Jesus referenced many persons and incidents of the Old Testament, assuming the factuality of all details. While Jesus frequently criticized distorted understandings of the Bible, he never questioned the veracity of the Scriptures themselves.[5] Like Jesus (as recorded in the Gospels), all the New Testament authors are unified in their citation of the Old Testament as a historically accurate work.[6]

- *Hebrews 1:1–2: "In the past God spoke to our forefathers through the prophets at many times and in various ways, but in these last days he has spoken to us by his Son, whom he appointed heir of all things, and through whom he made the universe."* If the prior anticipatory revelation of God (the Old Testament) was completely truthful ("God spoke"), how much more then should the culmination of God's revelation in Christ be received as completely trustworthy and authoritative.

The Historic View of the Christian Church

During the late nineteenth and twentieth centuries, the issue of the truthfulness of Scripture became a major dividing line between Christians in the United States. Denominations divided, and new denominations, schools, and mission agencies were founded as a result of this debate. Some noninerrantists claimed that the so-called doctrine of inerrancy was really the creation of modern conservative Protestants, not the historic witness of the Christian church.[7] In response, overwhelming evidence has been presented to prove the contrary. While the exact term *inerrancy* (or non-English equivalents of this term) may not be found in early, medieval, or reformational church history, the *concept* or *idea* of inerrancy is the historic position of the church in all ages.[8] From 1977 to 1988, supporters of inerrancy worked through

---

5. See the definitive study by John Wenham, *Christ and the Bible*, 3rd ed. (Grand Rapids: Baker, 1994).
6. See Grudem's list of references outside the four Gospels *(Systematic Theology*, 94).
7. See Jack B. Rogers and Donald K. McKim, *The Authority and Interpretation of the Bible: An Historical Approach* (San Francisco: Harper & Row, 1979); or, similarly, Russell H. Dilday, *The Doctrine of Biblical Authority* (Nashville: Convention Press, 1982), 57–59.
8. See John D. Woodbridge, *Biblical Authority: A Critique of the Rogers and McKim Proposal* (Grand Rapids: Zondervan, 1982). Erickson agrees: "The church throughout its history has believed in the freedom of the Bible from any untruths" (Millard J. Erickson, *Christian Theology*, 2nd ed. [Grand Rapids: Baker, 1998], 252). Also, see Article XVI of the Chicago

the International Council on Biblical Inerrancy and produced three formal, signed statements on inerrancy and interpretation.[9] The most significant of these documents, the "Chicago Statement on Biblical Inerrancy" (1978), continues to serve as a touchstone for the definition of inerrancy.

Qualifications of Inerrancy

The doctrine of inerrancy must be properly explained and qualified to prevent misunderstanding. A number of important qualifications are listed below.

1. *Inerrancy applies only to the autographs (original copies of Scripture).*[10] No one denies that there are some copying errors in *every* Hebrew and Greek manuscript of the Bible (particularly with numbers, for example). Yet, with the vast number of Greek and Hebrew manuscripts and their careful transmission, we are able to reconstruct the original wording of the Old and New Testament with extreme accuracy.[11] For more detail on manuscript accuracy, see question 5 ("Were the ancient manuscripts of the Bible transmitted accurately?").

2. *Inerrancy respects the authorial intent of the passage and the literary conventions under which the author wrote.* If the author intended an

---

Statement on Biblical Inerrancy: "We affirm that the doctrine of inerrancy has been integral to the Church's faith throughout its history. We deny that inerrancy is a doctrine invented by scholastic Protestantism, or is a reactionary position postulated in response to negative higher criticism."

9. According to a 1980 publication by the International Council on Biblical Inerrancy, "The International Council on Biblical Inerrancy is a California-based organization founded in 1977. It has as its purpose the defense and application of the doctrine of biblical inerrancy as an essential element for the authority of Scripture and a necessity for the health of the church. It was created to counter the drift from this important doctrinal foundation by significant segments of evangelicalism and the outright denial of it by other church movements" (from inside the front cover of R. C. Sproul, *Explaining Inerrancy: A Commentary*, ICBI Foundation Series, vol. 2 [Oakland, CA: International Council on Biblical Inerrancy, 1980]).

10. Article X of the Chicago Statement on Biblical Inerrancy reads: "We affirm that inspiration, strictly speaking, applies only to the autographic text of Scripture, which in the providence of God can be ascertained from available manuscripts with great accuracy. We further affirm that copies and translations of Scripture are the Word of God to the extent that they faithfully represent the original. We deny that any essential element of the Christian faith is affected by the absence of the autographs. We further deny that this absence renders the assertion of biblical inerrancy invalid or irrelevant."

11. Grudem writes, "For over 99 percent of the words of the Bible, we know what the original manuscript said" (*Systematic Theology*, 96). D. A. Carson lists 96–97 percent for the New Testament ("Who Is This Jesus? Is He Risen?" a documentary film hosted by D. James Kennedy and Jerry Newcombe [Fort Lauderdale, FL: Coral Ridge Ministries, 2000]). No doctrinal issue is left in question by textual variations.

assertion literally, we should understand it so. If the passage is figurative, likewise, we should interpret it accordingly. We must respect the level of precision intended, as well as the writing conventions of that day. For example, in Mark 1:2–3, Mark cites three different Old Testament texts (Exod. 23:30; Isa. 40:3; Mal. 3:1) with the introductory phrase, "As it is written in Isaiah the prophet." Assuming our modern conventions of citation, this is an error because part of the quotation is from Exodus and Malachi. But, as early Jews sometimes cited only one prophetic spokesman when quoting amalgamated texts, we should respect the literary conventions of Mark's day.[12]

3. As another example we can consider the order of events in the Synoptic Gospels. It is clear that the Gospel authors are not intending to give a strict chronological account of Jesus' ministry.[13] The material is frequently arranged topically. Thus, it should not surprise us to find a different order to Jesus' temptations in Luke 4:1–13 and Matthew 4:1–11. As the temple is a motif in Luke (e.g., Luke 1:9; 18:10; 23:45; 24:53; Acts 2:46; 5:20; 26:21), it appears that Luke has rearranged Jesus' temptations to place the pinnacle of the temple as the climactic temptation.[14] Or, possibly, as mountains are often of symbolic value in the Gospel of Matthew (5:1; 8:1; 14:23; 15:29; 17:1; 28:16), Matthew has done the rearranging. Part of faithful interpretation is respecting the individual emphases and purposes of the different authors and faithfully allowing those original emphases to come through in our teaching and preaching.

4. *Inerrancy allows for partial reporting, paraphrasing, and summarizing.* The words of a speaker, for example, might be summarized or paraphrased rather than given verbatim. As long as the meaning of the speaker is accurately conveyed, this reporting is completely truthful.

---

12. J. Marcus writes, "Such conflation of OT texts is familiar from postbiblical Judaism, especially from the Dead Sea Scrolls" (*Mark 1–8: A New Translation with Introduction and Commentary*, AB 27 [New York: Doubleday, 2000], 147).

13. Even Papias (ca. A.D. 70–155), notes, "And the elder [the apostle John?] used to say this: 'Mark, having become Peter's interpreter, wrote down accurately everything he remembered, though not in order, of the things either said or done by Christ. For he neither heard the Lord nor followed him, but afterward, as I said, followed Peter, who adapted his teachings as needed but had no intention of giving an ordered account of the Lord's sayings. Consequently Mark did nothing wrong in writing down some things as he remembered them, for he made it his one concern not to omit anything that he heard or to make any false statement in them'" (*Fragments of Papias* 3.15 in *The Apostolic Fathers: Greek Texts and English Translations*, ed. and trans. Michael W. Holmes, 3rd ed. [Grand Rapids: Baker, 2007], 739–41).

14. The word *temple* occurs 46 times in Luke–Acts (NIV).

Also, just as modern writers may choose to leave out certain details or emphasize other points, biblical writers did the same as they reported on the same events from different vantage points. For example, John reports more of Jesus' ministry in Jerusalem, while Matthew, Mark, and Luke focus on his itinerant Galilean ministry.

5. *Inerrancy allows for phenomenological language (that is, the description of phenomena as they are observed and experienced).* Humans often report events they see from their experiential vantage point rather than providing an objective scientific explanation. Thus, we would no more charge a biblical author with error when speaking of the sun rising (Ps. 19:6) than we would chastise a modern meteorologist for speaking of the anticipated time of tomorrow's sunrise. Neither the psalmist nor the meteorologist is intending to deny a heliocentric (sun-centered) solar system.

6. *Inerrancy allows the reporting of speech without the endorsement of the truthfulness of that speech (or the implication that everything else said by that person is truthful).* Psalm 14:1 says, "There is no God." Of course, in broader context, the passage reads, "The fool says in his heart, 'There is no God.'" Obviously, in reporting the speech of "the fool," the psalmist does not agree with him. Similarly, in quoting from pagan authors in his speech before the Athenians (Acts 17:22–31), Paul (and by extension, Luke, who records the speech) is not intending to endorse the truthfulness of everything written by Epimenides or Aratus (Acts 17:28).

7. *Inerrancy does not mean that the Bible provides definitive or exhaustive information on every topic.* No author in the Bible, for example, attempts a classification of mollusks or lessons in subatomic physics. The Bible tangentially touches on these subjects in asserting that God is the creator of all things, marine or subatomic, but one must not press the Scriptures to say more than they offer. If you want to learn how to bake French pastries, for example, there is no biblical text I can suggest. I can, however, exhort you to do all things diligently for God's glory (Col. 3:17) and not to engage in gluttony (Prov. 23:20). And I would be happy to sample any of the pastries you make.

8. *Inerrancy is not invalidated by colloquial or nonstandard grammar or spelling.* Spelling and grammar vary within various linguistic, cultural, geographical, and economic groups without impinging on the truthfulness of the actual communication. As Wayne Grudem notes, "An uneducated backwoodsman in some rural area may be the most

trusted man in the country even though his grammar is poor, because he has earned a reputation for never telling a lie. Similarly, there are a few statements in Scripture (in the original languages) that are ungrammatical (according to current standards of proper grammar at that time) but still inerrant because they are completely true. The issue is *truthfulness* of speech."[15]

Recommendations for Dealing with Difficult Texts in the Bible

Below are a few recommendations for dealing with alleged discrepancies in the Bible.

1. *Be sure that you are interacting with real texts.* Do not allow another person's uninformed skepticism to poison your own intellect.

2. *Approach the text in trust, not as a skeptic.* Investigating the truthfulness of Christianity is to be encouraged.[16] Christianity has nothing to fear from the facts. However, there comes a point when one realizes that the Bible is internally consistent and its claims are frequently confirmed by externally verifiable data (that is, by other ancient sources, archeology, etc.). Just as in a healthy marriage one trusts his or her spouse and does not live in constant doubt or suspicion, likewise a Christian trusts the biblical text in areas that cannot be confirmed by external criteria. For example, we have no external records confirming the visit of the magi to Herod (Matt. 2:1–12). Yet the jealous, distrustful behavior of Herod the Great in the Gospel of Matthew certainly agrees with extrabiblical accounts of his character (see Josephus, *Antiquities* 17.6.5).

3. *Pray about a difficult text.* God is a loving Father who cares for his children. Jesus taught,

> Ask and it will be given to you; seek and you will find; knock and the door will be opened to you. For everyone who asks receives; he who seeks finds; and to him who knocks, the door will be opened. Which of you, if his son asks for bread, will give him a stone? Or if he asks for a fish, will give him a snake? If you, then, though you are evil, know how to give good gifts to your children, how much more

---

15. Grudem, *Systematic Theology*, 92.
16. See, for example, Lee Strobel, *The Case for Faith: A Journalist Investigates the Toughest Objections to Christianity* (Grand Rapids: Zondervan, 2000); Craig A. Evans, *Fabricating Jesus: How Modern Scholars Distort the Gospels* (Downers Grove, IL: InterVarsity Press, 2008); and J. P. Moreland, *Scaling the Secular City: A Defense of Christianity* (Grand Rapids: Baker, 1987).

will your Father in heaven give good gifts to those who ask him!
(Matt. 7:7–11)

4. *Keep in mind the "Qualifications of Inerrancy" when dealing with difficult texts (see above).* Don't demand that ancient writers conform to your expected standards (demanding perfectly parallel, verbatim quotations, for example).

5. *Seek counsel when dealing with difficult texts.* Tell a Christian friend, pastor, or professor about your question. Sometimes the serpent of apparent error is defanged in articulating one's question. Consult the best evangelical commentaries on the subject.[17]

6. *Be willing to set a text aside for further consideration rather than force harmonization.* Augustine (A.D. 354–430) speaks of his trusting and patient approach to the canonical Scriptures:

> I have learned to yield this respect and honour only to the canonical books of Scripture: of these alone do I most firmly believe that the authors were completely free from error. And if in these writings I am perplexed by anything which appears to me opposed to truth, I do not hesitate to suppose that either the [manuscript] is faulty, or the translator has not caught the meaning of what was said, or I myself have failed to understand it.[18]

REFLECTION QUESTIONS

1. Has anyone ever presented you with an alleged error in the Bible as an argument as to why it is not true? What was your response?

2. What is the most puzzling text in the Bible to you?

3. Why do people disagree on their assessment of the Bible's truthfulness— some seeing it as the inerrant Word of God and others viewing it as an unreliable collection of contradictory documents?

---

17. For suggestions on the best commentaries, see Tremper Longman, *Old Testament Commentary Survey*, 4th ed. (Grand Rapids: Baker, 2007); and D. A. Carson, *New Testament Commentary Survey*, 6th ed. (Grand Rapids: Baker, 2007). Also, you can consult reference works such as Gleason L. Archer's *Encyclopedia of Bible Difficulties* or an evangelical study Bible, such as *The Zondervan NIV Study Bible*, ed. Kenneth Barker et al., rev. ed. (Grand Rapids: Zondervan, 2008); or *The ESV Study Bible* (Wheaton, IL: Crossway, 2008).
18. Augustine, *Letter* 82.3. Translation by J. G. Cunningham, *NPNF1* 1:350.

4. If a neighbor were to tell you that he didn't believe the Bible because it is "full of errors," how would you respond?

5. Have you ever met an "ungodly inerrantist" (someone with a verbal affirmation of the Bible's truthfulness but otherwise ungodly behavior)? What does the Bible say about this situation?

FOR FURTHER STUDY

Archer, Gleason L. *A Survey of Old Testament Introduction.* Rev. ed. Chicago: Moody Press, 1994.

_____. *New International Encyclopedia of Bible Difficulties.* Grand Rapids: Zondervan, 2001.

Beale, G. K. *The Erosion of Inerrancy in Evangelicalism: Responding to New Challenges to Biblical Authority.* Wheaton, IL: Crossway, 2008.

Blomberg, Craig L. *Making Sense of the New Testament: Three Crucial Questions.* Grand Rapids: Baker, 2004.

Bruce, F. F. *The New Testament Documents: Are They Reliable?* 6th ed. Downers Grove, IL: InterVarsity Press; Grand Rapids: Eerdmans, 1981.

Geisler, Norman L., and Thomas Howe. *The Big Book of Bible Difficulties: Clear and Concise Answers from Genesis to Revelation.* Grand Rapids: Baker, 2008.

Kaiser, Walter C., Jr., Peter H. Davids, F. F. Bruce, and Manfred T. Brauch. *Hard Sayings of the Bible.* Downers Grove, IL: InterVarsity Press, 1996.

Kitchen, K. A. *On the Reliability of the Old Testament.* Grand Rapids: Eerdmans, 2003.

See the entry for "Chicago Statement on Biblical Inerrancy" at www.wikipedia. org for a link to the full text of the statement.

Were the Ancient Manuscripts of the Bible Transmitted Accurately?

When discussing the Bible with non-Christians, one might hear the objection: "Yes, the Bible reads that way *now*, but everyone knows that it has been changed."[1] Does this objection have any substance to it? How do we know that the Bible in our hands is a faithful transmission of the words that the inspired authors originally wrote?

Overview of Textual Issues

The Old Testament originally was written in Hebrew (with a few Aramaic portions) between 1400 and 430 B.C. The New Testament was written in Greek between A.D. 45 and 90. The original copies of ancient documents are called the autographs (or *autographa*). All autographs of biblical books have been lost or destroyed, though we have thousands of ancient copies. The process of comparing and studying these copies to reconstruct the wording of the originals is called textual criticism. Textual criticism began to flourish in sixteenth-century Europe for a number of reasons. First, the printing press had been introduced in the mid-fifteenth century, which allowed for multiple exact copies of the same book—ideal for the collation and comparison of variant manuscripts.[2]

---

1. In fact, Muslim apologists explain Muhammad's apparent acceptance of the Old and New Testaments (Sūrah 3:3) by arguing that the biblical texts were subsequently corrupted. Of course, we have complete manuscripts of the Old and New Testament that predate Muhammad (ca. A.D. 570–632) by two centuries. Such manuscripts, while containing variants, are in fundamental agreement with the textual basis of modern Bible translations.
2. The first printed (with a printing press) Hebrew Old Testament appeared in 1488. The printed Greek New Testament produced under the auspices of Cardinal Ximenes (the Complutensian Polyglot) was completed in 1514. The first printed Greek New Testament to be published was the work of Erasmus in 1516. See Paul D. Wegner, *The Journey from Texts to Translations: The Origin and Development of the Bible* (Grand Rapids: Baker, 1999), 266–67.

Second, there was a revival of learning in Europe, resulting in a great interest in ancient languages, cultures, and texts. Third, the Protestant Reformation and Catholic Counter-Reformation focused scholarly attention on the Bible.

The science of textual criticism continued to develop, reaching new heights with the discovery of many ancient manuscripts in the nineteenth and twentieth centuries. As with any science, the particulars of textual criticism are very complex. (For example, consider the archaeological, paleographic, and linguistic expertise needed to accurately date and decipher just one ancient manuscript.) At the same time, most scholars, both liberal and conservative, agree that text criticism has served to confirm the reliable transmission of the Old and New Testament manuscripts. A leading biblical scholar, D. A. Carson, notes that the New Testament autographs can be reconstructed with roughly 96–97 percent accuracy.[3] Furthermore, no text in question affects Christian doctrine. That is, all Christian doctrines are firmly established without appealing to debated texts. Most unsolved textual issues have little or no doctrinal significance.

Modern translations of the Bible (for example, ESV, NIV, NLT, etc.) include footnotes of significant variants. For example, at the bottom of the page, one will notice comments such as "Some manuscripts say . . ." or "Most early manuscripts do not include . . ." By quickly skimming these footnotes, one can get a sense of what debated textual issues remain.

The Copying of Ancient Texts

Because our modern culture is so accustomed to technologically advanced methods of communication, we sometimes exhibit suspicion toward more ancient methods of literature production. Nevertheless, it should be noted that ancient Jewish rabbis and early Christian scribes usually exercised great precision in the copying of biblical texts. Jewish scribes followed detailed systems for counting letters in manuscripts and checking for accidental variations.[4] Likewise, Christian scribes showed great caution, often having multiple correctors read through their copies to check for errors. Inevitably, all hand-copied manuscripts have some variations, but striking accuracy is evidenced in most ancient copies of our Old and New Testaments.

---

3. Carson says, "Almost all text critics will acknowledge that 96, even 97 percent, of the Greek New Testament is morally certain. It's just not in dispute" ("Who is This Jesus? Is He Risen?" a documentary film hosted by D. James Kennedy and Jerry Newcombe [Fort Lauderdale, FL: Coral Ridge Ministries, 2000]). Klein, Blomberg, and Hubbard make a similar assessment: "Estimates suggest between 97 and 99 percent of the original New Testament can be reconstructed from the existing manuscripts beyond any measure of reasonable doubt. The percentage for the Old Testament is lower, but at least 90 percent or more" (William W. Klein, Craig L. Blomberg, and Robert L. Hubbard, *Introduction to Biblical Interpretation*, rev. ed. [Nashville: Thomas Nelson, 2004], 122).
4. See Wegner, *Journey from Texts to Translations*, 167, 171–72.

The Old Testament

In 1947, the first part of a cache of ancient Jewish documents was discovered in caves near the Dead Sea. According to one story, a young Arab goat herder investigated a cave after throwing a rock in and hearing a piece of pottery (a scroll jar) break. The documents discovered in these caves apparently belonged to a Jewish sect, the Essenes, who lived in a separatist community in the Judean desert near the Dead Sea. When the Essenes fled from the attacking Romans around A.D. 70, they left a treasure trove of manuscripts for modern-day text critics. In addition to many interesting sectarian documents and other extrabiblical literature, scholars have found portions of all Old Testament books except Esther and Nehemiah. These manuscripts have come to be called the Dead Sea Scrolls. The documents represent manuscripts and copies of manuscripts from roughly 250 B.C. to A.D. 50. Prior to the discovery of the Dead Sea Scrolls, the most significant extant Hebrew Old Testament manuscripts were the Leningrad Codex (A.D. 1008) and Aleppo Codex (ca. A.D. 900). The Dead Sea Scrolls pushed the Hebrew manuscript evidence back a millennium earlier.[5]

While not without some textual puzzles, the Dead Sea Scrolls have confirmed that the Hebrew books of the Bible were meticulously and faithfully copied. The Old Testament preserved in the Leningrad Codex (A.D. 1008) and Dead Sea Scrolls (250 B.C.–A.D. 50) is fundamentally the same Hebrew base text used for modern English translations today. Any significant text variations will be noted in the footnotes of modern translations, sometimes after the abbreviation "DSS" (Dead Sea Scrolls). Even when considering all known Old Testament manuscripts and variations, Shemaryahu Talmon of The Hebrew University of Jerusalem, avers, "It should . . . be stressed that these errors and textual divergences between the versions materially affect the intrinsic message only in relatively few instances."[6]

In addition to ancient Hebrew texts, we also have ancient copies of the Old Testament translated into several other languages—Greek, Latin, Syriac, etc. Ancient translations of the Old Testament sometimes can help in the deciphering of a difficult Hebrew word or phrase. More importantly, these texts sometimes can serve as helpful witnesses to variant readings in the ancient Hebrew (that is, they were translated from a Hebrew text that varied from the one we currently know). If translators suspect that an early translation may best preserve the original Hebrew wording, they may follow that wording in their English translation or footnote the variant. Again, see any pertinent Bible footnotes to see whether the Masoretic (Hebrew), Dead Sea Scrolls,

---

5. We do, however, have many copies of the Septuagint (Greek translation of the Old Testament), which predate the Leningrad and Aleppo Codices by centuries.

6. Shemaryahu Talmon, "The Old Testament Text," in *The Cambridge History of the Bible: From the Beginnings to Jerome*, ed. P. R. Ackroyd and C. F. Evans (Cambridge: Cambridge University Press, 1970), 1:162.

Greek (Septuagint), or Syriac manuscripts are being followed. If your Bible lacks such notes, see the extensive translator footnotes for the free online NET Bible (New English Translation) at www.bible.org.

The New Testament

Even within the Bible itself, we find evidence of New Testament documents being hand-copied and circulated (Col. 4:16; 1 Thess. 5:27; 2 Peter 3:15–16). As these copies continued to increase and copies were made of copies, certain uniform scribal tendencies came to be embodied in various text families, usually classified according to geographic provenance—Western, Alexandrian, Byzantine, and Caeasarean. The Greek-speaking Byzantine Empire was a region that continued to need and produce more Greek copies of the New Testament, so the Byzantine text family was copied the most. Yet most scholars agree that the Byzantine text family usually does not represent the oldest or most reliable reading.

By comparing ancient witnesses within the various text traditions, we can approach with amazing accuracy the wording of the autographs. In speaking of text families and manuscript variations, the unstudied reader can jump to wrong conclusions about the amount or significance of variations in the ancient manuscripts. Most variations have little or no effect on the overall unified message of the New Testament. As a professor who teaches text criticism to intermediate-level Greek students, I have found that a detailed study of text criticism serves to increase students' trust in the Bible.

We have nearly six thousand ancient manuscripts or portions of manuscripts of the New Testament.[7] (For a photograph of one of the most famous manuscripts, see figure 4.) The oldest extant fragment of the New Testament comes from about A.D. 130.[8] No other ancient text comes even close to having this amount of early textual evidence. The classically trained F. F. Bruce once compared the textual evidence for the New Testament to other well-known ancient Greco-Roman literature, noting:

> Perhaps we can appreciate how wealthy the New Testament is in manuscript attestation if we compare the textual material for other ancient historical works. For Caesar's *Gallic War* (composed between 58 and 50 B.C.) there are several extant MSS (manuscripts), but only nine or ten are good, and the oldest is some 900 years later than Caesar's day. Of the 142 books of the *Roman History* of Livy (59 B.C.–A.D. 17) only thirty-five survive; these

---

7. The most recent count is 5,752 manuscripts, with the number increasing yearly (Daniel B. Wallace, "Challenges in New Testament Textual Criticism for the 21st Century," plenary address at the sixtieth annual meeting of the Evangelical Theological Society, Providence, Rhode Island, November 20, 2008). Wallace serves as executive director of The Center for the Study of New Testament Manuscripts (www.csntm.org).
8. The John Rylands fragment of John 18:31–33, 37–38.

are known to us from not more than twenty MSS of any consequence, only one of which, and that containing fragments of Books iii–vi, is as old as the fourth century. Of the fourteen books of the *Histories* of Tacitus (*c.* A.D. 100) only four and a half survive; of the sixteen books of his *Annals*, ten survive in full and two in part. The text of these extant portions of his two great historical works depends entirely on two MSS, one of the ninth century and one of the eleventh. The extant MSS of his minor works (*Dialogus de Oratoribus, Agricola, Germania*) all descend from a codex of the tenth century. The *History* of Thucydides (*c.* 460–400 B.C.) is known to us from eight MSS, the earliest belonging to *c.* A.D. 900, and a few papyrus scraps, belonging to about the beginning of the Christian era. The same is true of the *History* of Herodotus (*c.* 488–428 B.C.). Yet no classical scholar would listen to an argument that the authenticity of Herodotus or Thucydides is in doubt because the earliest MSS of their works which are of any use to us are over 1,300 years later than the originals.[9]

FIGURE 4: THE BEGINNING OF THE GOSPEL OF JOHN FROM CODEX SINAITICUS.

Codex Sinaiticus is a late fourth century manuscript. To view the entire manuscript, go to the following Web site: www.codexsinaiticus.org.

---

9. F. F. Bruce, *The New Testament Documents: Are They Reliable,* 6th ed. (Downers Grove, IL: InterVarsity Press; Grand Rapids: Eerdmans, 1981), 11.

Samples of Textual Variants

To provide a better sense for the kind of variations that occur in ancient manuscripts, a few samples will be given below. The examples will be drawn from the New Testament, though similar examples could be given from the Old Testament.[10]

Unintentional Errors

According to one reckoning, 95 percent of textual variants are accidental—the unintentional variations introduced by tired or incompetent scribes.[11] Such variants include the following:[12]

1. *Errors of Sight.* Scribes sometimes copied texts by looking back and forth to the originals. By this method, they inevitably made a number of errors of sight. For example, they confused letters that looked similar in appearance, divided words wrongly (the oldest Greek manuscripts of the Bible have no spaces between words), repeated words or sections (that is, copied the same thing twice), accidentally skipped letters, words, or sections, or changed the order of letters in a word or words in a sentence.

2. *Errors of Hearing.* When scribes copied manuscripts through dictation (that is, scribes wrote as a manuscript was being read), errors of hearing were made. For example, vowels, diphthongs, or other sounds were misheard. (We make similar mistakes in English, for example, writing "night" when someone says "knight.")

3. *Errors of Writing.* Sometimes scribes introduced errors into texts simply by writing the wrong thing. For example, a scribe might accidentally add an additional letter to the end of a word, resulting in a different meaning.

4. *Errors of Judgment.* Sometimes scribes exercised poor judgment through incorporating marginal glosses (ancient footnotes) into the body of the text or similar unintentional corrupting influences.

Intentional Errors

The remaining 5 percent of textual variants resulted from intentional activity on the part of scribes. Such changes included:

---

10. For a similar list of examples from the Old Testament, see Wegner, *Journey from Texts to Translations*, 180–81.
11. Arthur G. Patzia, *The Making of the New Testament: Origin, Collection, Text and Canon* (Downers Grove, IL: InterVarsity Press, 1995), 138.
12. The material below is drawn from Patzia, *The Making of the New Testament*, 138–46.

1. *Revising Grammar and Spelling.* In an attempt to standardize grammar or spelling, scribes sometimes corrected what they perceived as orthographic or grammatical errors in the text they were copying.

2. *Harmonizing Similar Passages.* Scribes had a tendency to harmonize parallel passages and introduce uniformity to stylized expressions. For example, details from the same incident in multiple Gospels might be included when copying any one Gospel. As a professor of intermediate Greek, I have found it interesting that students sometimes unintentionally insert *Lord* or *Christ* when translating a passage with the name *Jesus*. Students, of course, are not intending to promote a higher Christology; they are simply conforming their speech to a stylized reference to the Savior. Ancient scribes behaved in a similar way.

3. *Eliminating Apparent Discrepancies and Difficulties.* Scribes sometimes fix what they perceived as a problem in the text. For example, in Mark 1:2–3, some manuscripts cite the amalgamated text as from "the prophets" rather than "Isaiah," as Mark wrote. See question 4 ("Does the Bible contain error?") for a further discussion of this text and the issue of discrepancies.

4. *Conflating the Text.* Sometimes when a scribe knew of variant readings in the manuscript base from which he was copying, he would include both variants within his copy, conflating them together.

5. *Adapting Different Liturgical Traditions.* In a few isolated places, it is possible that church liturgy (that is, stylized prayers or praises) influenced some textual additions or wording changes (for example, Matthew 6:13, "For yours is the kingdom, and the power, and the glory forever, Amen").

6. *Making Theological or Doctrinal Changes.* Sometimes scribes made theological or doctrinal changes—either omitting something they saw as wrong or making clarifying additions. For example, in Matthew 24:36, some manuscripts omit the reference to the Son's ignorance of the day of his return—a passage that is obviously difficult to understand.[13]

Of course, with so many ancient texts at their disposal, text critics can

---

13. In this text, as in a few other places (e.g., John 4:6), Scripture seems to speak of Jesus from the perspective of his human nature, not intending to deny the omniscience or omnipotence of his divine nature. Others have explained this passage by claiming that prior to his exaltation, Jesus emptied himself of certain divine prerogatives (i.e., the kenotic theory).

dismiss most of the variants listed above, and therefore there is no need to cite the majority of variants in modern English translations. For the curious, more detailed discussions of manuscript variations can be found in reference works for text critics, critical editions of the Old and New Testaments, and scholarly commentaries (see question 13, "What are some helpful books or tools for interpreting the Bible?").

Early Christian Orthodoxy and Other Ancient Manuscripts

Some sensationalistic writings have asserted that the Old and New Testaments show only the beliefs of those who won the doctrinal battles of ancient Judaism and early Christianity. In other words, there existed a plurality of competing religious views in ancient Judaism and early Christianity. As one view won out (monotheistic Judaism or orthodox Christianity), the winners rewrote history so that the losers never appeared to have a stake in the game. At a scholarly level, this view is represented by Walter Bauer's *Orthodoxy and Heresy in Earliest Christianity* (German original: 1934). On a popular level, this approach is embodied by the conspiracy-laden works of Dan Brown (*The Da Vinci Code*) and Bart Ehrman (*Misquoting Jesus*). Underlying such approaches is an extreme skepticism toward the Bible that will not hold up under more objective evaluation. A full-scale rebuttal of such aberrant views exceeds the parameters of this book, but for further study, the reader is referred to Darrell L. Bock's *The Missing Gospels* (in reply to Bauer or Brown), Timothy Paul Jones's *Misquoting Truth* (in reply to Ehrman's *Misquoting Jesus*), and Craig Evans's *Fabricating Jesus*.[14]

REFLECTION QUESTIONS

1. Before reading this question, had you ever considered the transmission of the ancient copies of our Old and New Testaments? If so, what prompted your interest?

2. When reading the Bible, do you look at the footnotes that deal with text variants? Why or why not?

3. What is something new that you learned about the transmission of biblical manuscripts?

---

14. Darrell L. Bock, *The Missing Gospels: Unearthing the Truth Behind Alternative Christianities* (Nashville: Thomas Nelson, 2006); Timothy Paul Jones, *Misquoting Truth: A Guide to the Fallacies of Bart Ehrman's Misquoting Jesus* (Downers Grove, IL: InterVarsity Press, 2007); and Craig A. Evans, *Fabricating Jesus: How Modern Scholars Distort the Gospels* (Downers Grove, IL: InterVarsity Press, 2008).

4. Have you ever read a book by Bart Ehrman (*Misquoting Jesus*) or Dan Brown (*The Da Vinci Code*), or have you encountered other persons influenced by their works?

5. Do you have any remaining questions about textual variants or text criticism?

FOR FURTHER STUDY

Bock, Darrell L. *The Missing Gospels: Unearthing the Truth Behind Alternative Christianities*. Nashville: Thomas Nelson, 2006.

Bruce, F. F. *The New Testament Documents: Are They Reliable?* 6th ed. Downers Grove, IL: InterVarsity Press; Grand Rapids: Eerdmans, 1981.

Evans, Craig A. *Fabricating Jesus: How Modern Scholars Distort the Gospels*. Downers Grove, IL: InterVarsity Press, 2008.

Jones, Timothy Paul. *Misquoting Truth: A Guide to the Fallacies of Bart Ehrman's Misquoting Jesus*. Downers Grove, IL: InterVarsity Press, 2007.

Kaiser, Walter C. *The Old Testament Documents: Are They Reliable and Relevant?* Downers Grove, IL: InterVarsity Press, 2001.

Wegner, Paul D. *The Journey from Texts to Translations: The Origin and Development of the Bible*. Grand Rapids: Baker, 1999.

Who Determined What Books Would Be Included in the Bible?

The canon is the closed list of books that Christians view as uniquely authoritative and inspired. The Greek term *kanōn* originally meant "reed" or "measuring rod" and only later "norm" or "rule."[1] While the concept of a limited canon is ancient (Deut. 31:24–26; Dan. 9:2), the first person to use the Greek word *kanōn* to refer to Christianity's restricted list of inspired books was apparently Athanasius, bishop of Alexandria (ca. A.D. 352, *Decrees of the Synod of Nicea* 5.18).[2] The first church council to use the word *kanōn* in this way was the Synod of Laodicea (A.D. 363).[3] Very quickly, the term came to be widely used and accepted.[4]

For Protestant Christians, the canon is not an authorized collection of writings (in that the church conferred its authority or approval upon a list of books). Rather, the canon is a collection of authoritative writings. The biblical writings have an inherent authority as works uniquely inspired by God. Canonization is the process of recognizing that inherent authority, not bestowing it from an outside source.

Most Christians take the canon for granted without thinking about the process of the books' recognition. Oftentimes, only when a Christian encounters a

---

1. *Kanōn* is derived from the Hebrew word for reed or stalk, *qāneh*. See H. W. Beyer, "κανών," in *TDNT*, 3:596–602.
2. As cited in R. K. Harrison, *Introduction to the Old Testament* (Grand Rapids: Eerdmans, 1969; Peabody, MA: Prince (Hendrickson), 1999), 261.
3. While the synod's list of canonical New Testament books matches our own (except for the omission of Revelation), most scholars believe this list is a later addition (Bruce M. Metzger, *The Canon of the New Testament: Its Origin, Development, and Significance* [Oxford: Oxford University Press, 1987], 210).
4. David S. Dockery, *Christian Scripture: An Evangelical Perspective on Inspiration, Authority and Interpretation* (Nashville: Broadman & Holman, 1995), 89.

person who rejects the canon outright (a non-Christian) or one who endorses a variation of the canon (a Roman Catholic who accepts the Apocrypha, for example) does he begin to think more deeply about this issue. Who determined that thirty-nine books would be in the Old Testament canon and twenty-seven books in the New Testament canon? Why and when did they choose these books and not other books? Is the canon closed, or can additional books be added?

Old Testament Canon

The thirty-nine books in the Old Testament canon were written between 1400 and 430 B.C. We do not have detailed information about the discussion that likely surrounded the inclusion or rejection of writings into the Old Testament. It seems that some books were recognized instantly as authoritative on the basis of their self-authenticating nature or a prophetic word being fulfilled (Exod. 24:3–7; Deut. 18:15–22; Dan. 9:2). Other books may have taken some time to be edited or fully recognized (Isa. 30:8; Prov. 25:1). Walter Kaiser summarizes the apparent history of the Old Testament canon: "[There was a] *progressive recognition* of certain books as being canonical right from their inception by readers and listeners who were contemporaries with the writers and who are thereby in the best position to determine the claims of the writers."[5] It seems clear that by the time of Jesus, most Jews were in agreement as to their own canon—a list that matches our current Old Testament in content.

The Samaritans (half-Jews) of Jesus' day recognized only an edited copy of the Pentateuch (the first five books of the Old Testament) as their Scripture, but Jews never viewed the Samaritans as legitimate descendents of Abraham (Matt. 10:5–6; Luke 17:18). A small but more mainstream Jewish party in Jesus' day, the Sadducees, viewed books outside the Pentateuch as less authoritative or inspired (Matt. 22:23; Acts 23:8). Jesus rejected the Sadducees' views, endorsing the threefold Jewish canon (Law, Prophets, Writings) as it stood in his day (Luke 24:44; note that the Psalms, as the largest of the Writings section, was sometimes used to refer to the whole section). For Christians, accepting the thirty-nine–book Old Testament canon is relatively easy. One might say, "Jesus and his apostles affirmed the Jewish canon of the Hebrew Scriptures in their day. As a follower of Jesus, I affirm the same."

In recent history, some Old Testament scholars have claimed that the Jewish canon was not closed until the so-called Jewish Council of Jamnia(or Jabneh) in A.D. 90.[6] The term *council* and a specific date are misleading,

---

5. Walter C. Kaiser Jr., *The Old Testament Documents: Are They Reliable and Relevant?* (Downers Grove, IL: InterVarsity Press, 2001), 31.
6. H. H. Graetz is apparently the originator of this idea (*Kohélet oder der Salominishe Prediger* [Leipzig: Winter, 1871], 160–63), followed by H. E. Ryle, *The Canon of the Old Testament* (London: Macmillan, 1892). More recently, see, for example, Bernhard Anderson, *Understanding the Old Testament*, 4th ed. (Englewood Cliffs, NJ: Prentice-Hall, 1986), 641.

however. In actuality, following the destruction of the Jerusalem temple by the Romans in A.D. 70, rabbinic discussions continued on a variety of subjects in Jamnia for the next six decades.[7] Subsequent reexamination of the rabbinic discussion at Jamnia favors the traditional Christian view that the canon was long settled for the majority of Jews by the first century.[8] Jamnia provided a venue for the discussion of challenging Old Testament texts, but no binding canonical decisions were proclaimed.[9] Josephus claimed that the Jewish canon, which matches in content our modern Old Testament, had been settled from the time of the Persian King Artaxerxes (465–423 B.C.). The Jews in Josephus's and Jesus' day ordered their Hebrew Scriptures differently, resulting in twenty-four books, equaling our current number of thirty-nine books (see figure 5).[10] Josephus's statement on the closure of the Hebrew canon (see the box on the next page) is particularly striking. It is difficult to see why we should dismiss his unambiguous claims in favor of tenuous modern reconstructions.

New Testament Canon

Compared with the Old Testament canon, we know much more about the formal recognition of the books in the New Testament. In discussing the canon, the early church insisted that recognized books be:

- *Apostolic:* written by or tied closely to an apostle (an authorized eyewitness of Jesus).

Liberal theories of canonical formation also date the books of the Old Testament much later.

7. Jack P. Lewis, "Jamnia (Jabneh), Council of," *ABD* 3:635–36.
8. Jack Lewis writes, "It would appear that the frequently made assertion that a binding decision was made at [Jamnia] covering all scripture is conjectural at best" ("What Do We Mean by Jabneh?" *JBR* 32 [1964]: 132). According to Sid Leiman, "The widespread view that the Council of Jamnia closed the biblical canon, or that it canonized any books at all, is not supported by the evidence and need no longer be seriously maintained" ("The Canonization of Hebrew Scripture: The Talmudic and Midrashic Evidence," *Transactions of the Connecticut Academy of Arts and Sciences* 47 [Hamden, CT: Archon, 1976], 124).
9. Admittedly, a minority of Jews did question the appropriateness of some texts or books (e.g., Song of Songs, Ecclesiastes), but such questioning continued, and, in fact, continues even among some Jewish scholars today. Giving Jamnia the most credit it could merit, Bruce writes, "The books which [the participants at Jamnia] decided to acknowledge as canonical were already generally accepted, although questions had been raised about them. Those which they refused to admit had never been included. They did not expel from the canon any book which had previously been admitted. The Council of Jamnia, as J. S. Wright puts it, 'was the confirming of public opinion, not the forming of it'" (F. F. Bruce, *The Books and the Parchments*, rev. ed. [London: Marshall Pickering, 1991], 88–89).
10. Josephus counts Judges–Ruth as one book and Jeremiah–Lamentations as one book, reducing the total number to twenty-two books.

- *Catholic:*[11] widely, if not universally, recognized by the churches.

- *Orthodox:* not in contradiction to any recognized apostolic book or doctrine.

Josephus (A.D. 37–100), the non-Christian Jewish historian, wrote about the discussions on the Hebrew canon:

For we have not an innumerable multitude of books among us, disagreeing from, and contradicting one another, [as the Greeks have], but only twenty-two books, which contain the records of all the past times; which are justly believed to be divine; and of them five belong to Moses, which contain his laws and the traditions of the origin of mankind till his death. This interval of time was little short of three thousand years; but as to the time from the death of Moses till the reign of Artaxerxes, king of Persia, who reigned after Xerxes, the prophets, who were after Moses, wrote down what was done in their times in thirteen books. The remaining four books contain hymns to God, and precepts for the conduct of human life. It is true, our history has been written since Artaxerxes very particularly, but has not been esteemed of the like authority with the former by our forefathers, because there has not been an exact succession of prophets since that time; and how firmly we have given credit to these books of our own nation, is evident by what we do; for, during so many ages as have already passed, no one has been so bold as either to add anything to them, to take anything from them, or to make any change in them; but it is natural to all Jews, immediately and from their very birth, to esteem these books to contain divine doctrines, and to persist in them, and, if occasion be, willingly to die for them. (*Against Apion* 1:38–42, Whiston's translation)

The first canonical list that matches exactly our twenty-seven–book New Testament is the list by Athanasius in his Easter letter (letter 39) of A.D. 367. Two

---

11. The word *catholic* means universal. Its use here should not be confused with the way the word is used to identify various strains of Christianity (e.g., The Roman Catholic Church).

early church councils (Hippo Regius, A.D. 393, and Carthage, A.D. 397) confirmed the twenty-seven–book list.

Though an oversimplification, T. C. Hammond presents a helpful summary of the recognition of the New Testament canon.

- The New Testament books were written during the period A.D. 45–100.

- They were collected and read in the churches A.D. 100–200.

- They were carefully examined and compared with spurious writings A.D. 200–300.

- Complete agreement was obtained A.D. 300–400.[12]

Sometimes students are troubled to discover that we do not have a canonical list of New Testament books that exactly matches our own until Athanasius's letter of A.D. 367. Several facts must be remembered, however. First, all the New Testament documents were viewed as authoritative and were circulating among the churches by A.D. 90 or 100 (Col. 4:16; 2 Peter 3:16). Second, from the earliest post-New Testament Christian writings (the apostolic fathers), it is clear that an implicit canon existed. By their frequency of citation, the apostolic fathers attribute unique authority to what came to be called the New Testament.[13] Third, in the absence of a unified ecclesiastical hierarchy and in a situation where documents were copied by hand, it is not surprising that we find churches debating what writings were truly apostolic. Eusebius (ca. A.D. 260–340) mentions three categories of books in his day—the universally confessed, the debated, and the spurious.[14] Fourth, one must keep in mind the large geographic distances between some early Christian communities, as well as the persecutions that made communication and gatherings of decision-making bodies virtually impossible until the conversion of the Roman emperor in the fourth century A.D.

The observation of Barker, Lane, and Michaels is fitting:

---

12. T. C. Hammond, *In Understanding Be Men: An Introductory Handbook of Christian Doctrine*, rev. and ed. David F. Wright, 6th ed. (Leicester: Inter-Varsity Press, 1968), 29. Hammond puts the books of the New Testament as written between A.D. 50 to 100, so I have adjusted his scheme by five years here. Also, canonical debates continued longer in the East.

13. John Barton writes, "The central importance of most of the writings that would come to form the New Testament is already established in the early second century" (*Holy Writings, Sacred Text: The Canon in Early Christianity* [Louisville, KY: Westminster John Knox, 1997], 64).

14. Eusebius, *Historia Ecclesiastica* 3.25.1–5.

FIGURE 5: ORDERING OF HEBREW SCRIPTURES IN THE FIRST CENTURY

JEWISH SCRIPTURE (24 BOOKS)	THE CHRISTIAN OLD TESTAMENT (39 BOOKS)
LAW	**HISTORICAL BOOKS**
Genesis	Genesis / Ruth
Exodus	Exodus / 1–2 Samuel
Leviticus	Leviticus / 1–2 Kings
Numbers	Numbers / 1–2 Chronicles
Deuteronomy	Deuteronomy / Ezra
	Joshua / Nehemiah
	Judges / Esther
PROPHETS	**WISDOM BOOKS**
FORMER PROPHETS	
Joshua	Job
Judges	Psalms
Samuel	Proverbs
Kings	Ecclesiastes
	Song of Solomon (Song of Songs)
LATTER PROPHETS	
MAJOR PROPHETS	
Isaiah	
Jeremiah	
Ezekiel	
MINOR PROPHETS	
Hosea—Malachi (The 12)	
WRITINGS	**PROPHETICAL BOOKS**
	MAJOR PROPHETS
Psalms	Isaiah
Job	Jeremiah
Proverbs	Lamentations
Ruth	Ezekiel
Song of Solomon (Song of Songs)	Daniel
Ecclesiastes	
Lamentations	
Esther	
	MINOR PROPHETS
Daniel	Hosea—Malachi (The 12)
Ezra—Nehemiah	
Chronicles	

The fact that substantially the whole church came to recognize the same 27 books as canonical is remarkable when it is remembered that the result was not contrived. All that the several churches throughout the Empire could do was to witness to their own experience with the documents and share whatever knowledge they might have about their origin and character. When consideration is given to the diversity in cultural backgrounds and in orientation to the essentials of the Christian faith within the churches, their common agreement about which books belonged to the New Testament serves to suggest that this final decision did not originate solely at the human level.[15]

Beyond the valid historical questions of canon formation, however, Christians approach the canon of the Bible with certain presuppositions. If God accurately preserved the prior revelation of himself in the Old Testament writings (as endorsed by Jesus), how likely is it that the culmination of that revelation—the person and teaching of his Son—would fail to be recorded and preserved (Heb. 1:1–2)? Indeed, Jesus promises his apostles the presence of the Holy Spirit in bringing his teaching accurately to their memory and conveying further necessary information to his followers (John 14:26).

The Apocrypha

Roman Catholic and Orthodox Christians (Eastern Orthodox, Russian Orthodox, Ethiopian Orthodox, etc.) have some additional books in their Old Testaments that Protestants do not consider Scripture[16] (see figure 6). Protestants refer to these books as the Apocrypha, though Roman Catholics call them the deuterocanonical books (literally, the "secondly canonical" books, because they were formally recognized as canonical at a later time—as opposed to the protocanonical, or "firstly canonical," books). These books were written by Jews in the roughly five-hundred-year period between the Old and New Testaments (430 B.C.–A.D. 40).

Protestants do not consider the Apocrypha as Scripture for a number of reasons.

1. The Jews who authored the books never accepted them into their canon. This is a weighty argument in that those who wrote and preserved these books put them in a different category from the recognized Hebrew Scriptures. Indeed, comments within the Apocrypha distinguish contemporary writers from the divinely inspired prophets, who had long been silent (1 Macc. 4:41–46; 9:27; 14:40).

---

15. Glenn W. Barker, William L. Lane, and J. Ramsey Michaels, *The New Testament Speaks* (New York: Harper & Row, 1969), 29.
16. See Hans Peter Rüger, "The Extent of the Old Testament Canon," *BT* 40 (1989): 301–8.

FIGURE 6: THE CANON IN VARYING CHRISTIAN TRADITIONS		
PROTESTANTISM	**ROMAN CATHOLICISM**	**GREEK ORTHODOXY**
OLD TESTAMENT	OLD TESTAMENT	OLD TESTAMENT
Pentateuch (Gen.—Deut.)	Pentateuch (Gen.—Deut.)	Pentateuch (Gen.—Deut.)
Prophets	Prophets	Prophets
Former (Josh.—Kings)	Former (Josh.—Kings)	Former (Josh.—Kings)
Latter	Latter	Latter
Major (Isa., Jer., Ezek.)	Major (Isa., Jer., Ezek.)	Major (Isa., Jer., Ezek.)
Minor (The Twelve)	Minor (The Twelve)	Minor (The Twelve)
Writings	Writings	Writings
	APOCRYPHA	APOCRYPHA
	Tobit	Tobit
	Judith	Judith
	Additions to Esther	Additions to Esther
	Wisdom of Solomon	Wisdom of Solomon
	Ecclesiasticus (Sirach)	Ecclesiasticus (Sirach)
	Baruch (+ Letter of Jeremiah)	Baruch (+ Letter of Jeremiah)
	Prayer of Azariah	Prayer of Azariah
	Susanna	Susanna
	Bel and the Dragon	Bel and the Dragon
	1 Maccabees	1 Maccabees
	2 Maccabees	2 Maccabees
		1 Esdras (or 3 Ezra)
		Prayer of Manasseh
		3 Maccabees
		4 Maccabees (appendix)
		Psalm 151
NEW TESTAMENT	NEW TESTAMENT	NEW TESTAMENT
Gospels	Gospels	Gospels
Acts	Acts	Acts
Paul (and Hebrews)	Paul (and Hebrews)	Paul (and Hebrews)
General Epistles	General Epistles	General Epistles
James—Jude	James—Jude	James—Jude
Revelation	Revelation	Revelation

2. The Apocrypha contains clear factual errors and, from the standpoint of Protestants, theological errors (such as praying for the dead, see 2 Macc. 12:43–45).[17]

3. The Roman Catholic Church did not officially recognize the books in the Apocrypha as canonical until the Council of Trent in 1546. In fact, Jerome (A.D. 340–420), the translator of the Vulgate (the official Roman Catholic Latin Bible for more than a millennium), claimed the books of the Apocrypha were edifying for Christians but were "not for the establishing of the authority of the doctrines of the church."[18] At the Council of Trent, Roman Catholics recognized the deutero-canonical books in reaction to Protestant leaders who called for a return to biblical Christianity, stripped of later accretions and distortions. Roman Catholics include the Apocryphal books within their Old Testament canon, sometimes adding whole books and sometimes combining apocryphal portions with books Protestants recognize as canonical (for example, three additions to Daniel—The Prayer of Azariah, Susanna, and Bel and the Dragon). These additions and combinations result in a forty-six-book Old Testament canon for Roman Catholics.[19]

4. While there are some debatable allusions to the Apocrypha in the New Testament, New Testament authors nowhere cite the Apocrypha as Scripture (that is, with a formula such as "The Scripture says"). Almost every book in the Old Testament is cited as Scripture.[20]

The Apocrypha is helpful for understanding the historical and cultural changes that lead up to the New Testament. For example, by reading 1 and 2 Maccabees, one can learn about the origins of the Feast of Dedication (mentioned in John 10:22). The Apocrypha also contains entertaining stories (for example, Tobit, which would make a great Disney movie, or Susanna or Bel and the Dragon, which read like detective stories). Other parts of the Apocrypha occasionally sound similar to the Psalms or Proverbs (e.g., Sirach). In fact, Protestants sometimes unwittingly sing hymns based upon Apocryphal texts

---

17. For examples of errors, see table 8.4 ("Inaccuracies in the Apocryphal Books") in Paul D. Wegner, *The Journey from Texts to Translations: The Origin and Development of the Bible* (Grand Rapids: Baker, 1999), 125.

18. Jerome, *Prologus Galeatus,* as cited in Gleason L. Archer, *A Survey of Old Testament Introduction,* rev. ed. (Chicago: Moody Press, 1994), 81n.8.

19. *Catechism of the Catholic Church* (Liguori, MO: Liguori Publications, 1994), 34.

20. Gleason Archer notes that every Old Testament book is quoted or alluded to in the New Testament except Ruth, Ezra, and Song of Songs (*A Survey of Old Testament Introduction,* 83n.16). Most Old Testament books are cited unambiguously as Scripture.

("It Came Upon a Midnight Clear," based on Wisdom of Solomon 18:14–15, and "Now Thank We All Our God," based on Sirach 50:22–24). Still, it is clear that the leaders of the Protestant Reformation were wise to return the church to its earliest understanding of the Apocrypha as interesting, sometimes beneficial, but uninspired literature.[21]

Is the Canon Closed?

According to the early church's categories for canonicity (apostolic, catholic, orthodox—see above), it would be impossible to have any additions to the canon. For example, even if a genuine and orthodox letter of the apostle Paul were discovered, that letter would not have had widespread usage in the early church (that is, it could never claim catholicity). The canon of Scripture is closed.

REFLECTION QUESTIONS

1. Prior to the reading above, had you ever investigated the canon? What prompted your interest in turning to this question?

2. Explain the difference between "an authorized collection of writings" and "a collection of authoritative writings." Is this an important distinction?

3. If a Roman Catholic neighbor were to ask you, "Why do you Protestants cut some books out of the Bible?" How would you reply?

4. Is it possible to be a Christian and yet have a wrong understanding of the canon (as say, an Ethiopian Orthodox person would)? Explain.

5. Does the survey of the canon above leave any questions unanswered for you?

FOR FURTHER STUDY

Archer, Gleason L. *A Survey of Old Testament Introduction*. Rev. ed. Chicago: Moody Press, 1994 (see chap. 5, "The Canon of the Old Testament," 75–88).
Bruce, F. F. *The Books and the Parchments*. Rev. ed. London: Marshall Pickering, 1991.

---

21. At the time of the Protestant Reformation, Lutherans and Anglicans (as opposed to Calvinists and Anabaptists) were more open to seeing the Apocrypha as devotionally beneficial (Norman L. Geisler and Ralph E. MacKenzie, *Roman Catholics and Evangelicals: Agreements and Differences* [Grand Rapids: Baker, 1995], 157n. 1).

_____. *The Canon of Scripture*. Leicester and Downers Grove, IL: InterVarsity Press, 1988.

Carson, D. A., and Douglas J. Moo. *An Introduction to the New Testament*. 2nd ed. Grand Rapids: Zondervan, 2005 (see chap. 26, "The New Testament Canon," 726–43).

Geisler, Norman L., and Ralph E. MacKenzie. *Roman Catholics and Evangelicals: Agreements and Differences*. Grand Rapids: Baker, 1995 (see chaps. 9–10).

Harrison, R. K. *Introduction to the Old Testament*. Grand Rapids: Eerdmans, 1969; reprint, Peabody, MA: Prince (Hendrickson), 1999 (see part 4, section 4, "The Old Testament Canon," 260–88).

Wegner, Paul D. *The Journey from Texts to Translations: The Origin and Development of the Bible*. Grand Rapids: Baker, 1999 (see pp. 101–51).

Which Is the Best English Bible Translation?

When people discover that I am a New Testament professor, they often have religious questions they would like to ask. One of the most common is this: What English version of the Bible do you recommend? During the birth of my oldest daughter, the attending physician even asked me this question in the midst of my wife's labor! Alas, I received no medical discount for my advice.

The Original Languages of the Bible

The Bible was originally written in three different languages over a period of nearly fifteen hundred years (roughly 1400 B.C.–A.D. 90). The Old Testament was written in Hebrew, with a few Aramaic portions. The New Testament was written in Greek. While sections of the Old Testament previously had been translated into a few other languages (mainly Greek), as soon as the Christian gospel began to permeate other cultures, the entire Bible was quickly translated into many other languages—Syriac, Coptic, Ethiopic, Latin, etc.

History of the English Language

Any living language is constantly changing. Modern English (as classified by linguists) is a relatively recent phenomenon—just a few hundred years old. The "grandfather language" of English is Old English, the Anglo-Saxon dialect that conquering Germanic tribes brought with them to England in the fifth century A.D. (The word *English* is derived from *Angles,* the name of one of these conquering tribes.) Later, when William the Conqueror defeated the Germanic tribes at the Battle of Hastings (1066), he and his Norman conquerors brought with them a French influence. Allegorically, we might say that the English language's Anglo-Saxon grandfather married a French lady. The intermarried Germanic-French language that evolved from the eleventh to the fifteenth centuries is known as Middle English (Modern English's metaphorical father). Latin, the language of the church for centuries, also had some influence on the development of the English language.

History of the English Bible

While Latin was the official language of the church, a few portions of the Bible were translated into Old English (Anglo-Saxon) from the seventh to the eleventh centuries. In 1382, the famous reforming church leader John Wycliffe (1330–1384) translated the entire Bible into the English of his day (Middle English). The translation was based on the Latin Vulgate and was copied by hand, as the printing press had not yet been introduced to Europe.[1] Followers of Wycliffe continued to call for reform of the church and the monarchy, based on the biblical truth they were reading. Very quickly, church officials and the king judged the availability of the Bible in English as a threat to the status quo. In 1414, reading the Bible in English became a capital offense (that is, punishable by death). In 1428, Wycliffe's body was exhumed and symbolically burned at the stake.[2]

In 1526, William Tyndale (1494–1536) published the first *printed* (with a printing press) English New Testament, translated from the Greek original. Tyndale printed the New Testaments in continental Europe and smuggled them into England. The first complete printed English Bible appeared in 1535. It was called the Coverdale Bible because it was published under the leadership of Miles Coverdale, Tyndale's assistant. Tyndale was captured by followers of King Henry VIII, and in 1536, he was strangled and burned at the stake. As he was dying, Tyndale reportedly prayed, "Lord, open the eyes of the King of England." Only one year later, Tyndale's request was granted, as the king officially licensed the distribution of an English translation of the Bible. (See figure 7 for a summary of these early English Bible translations.) During the next hundred years, a spate of English Bible translations were produced, most of them heavily dependent on Tyndale's seminal work.

The Bible in Modern English

During the last one hundred years, and especially the last fifty, many good, reliable, and readable translations have been produced in English. Modern English speakers face a choice unlike any in the history of Bible translation. Rather than ask, "Which translation is best?" It is better to recognize that all translations have strengths and weaknesses. In fact, it is advisable for a Christian to own multiple Bible translations. The only Bible translations we can label as completely bad are those done by sectarian or cultic groups, such as the New World Translation (NWT), the Jehovah's Witness translation that attempts to remove scriptural teaching on the deity of Christ.

---

1. Europeans began using the printing press in 1454. The Chinese, however, were using printing presses long before Europeans.
2. Definitely the preferred way to be burned at the stake, as a friend once noted.

FIGURE 7: EARLY ENGLISH BIBLE TRANSLATIONS		
DATE	**WORK**	**DESCRIPTION**
1382	Wycliffe Bible	First complete translation (handwritten) of the Bible into English based on the Vulgate.
1526	Tyndale Bible	First printed New Testament in English based on Greek.
1535	Coverdale Bible	First complete printed English Bible. Relies heavily on Tyndale Bible, German versions, and Vulgate.
1537	Matthew's Bible	Edited by John Rogers. Relies on Tyndale and Coverdale. First licensed English Bible.
1539	The Great Bible	Revised version of Matthew's Bible by Coverdale. Based on Tyndale, Hebrew, and Greek.
1560	Geneva Bible	The New Testament is a revision of Tyndale, and the Old Testament is revised based upon the Hebrew. First English Bible with verse divisions. Strongly Calvinistic footnotes.
1568	Bishops' Bible	A revision of the Great Bible translated by a committee of Anglican bishops.
1610	Douay-Rheims Bible	Literal rendering of the Vulgate by Roman Catholics.
1611	King James Version	Translated by a committee of scholars.

Approaches to Translation

There are two main approaches to Bible translation, and all translations fall somewhere along the spectrum between these two extremes (see figure 8). On one side is the functionally equivalent translation, sometimes called dynamically equivalency.. This is a translation that seeks to accurately convey the same meaning in a new language but is not so concerned about preserving the same number of words or equivalent grammatical constructions. The New Living Translation (NLT) is a good example of a reliable functionally equivalent translation.[3] On the other end of the spectrum is the formally equivalent translation. This type of translation is very concerned to preserve, as much

---

3. A new Bible translation, *The Voice* (New Testament released October, 2008), although billed as a dynamically equivalent translation, appears to veer into paraphrase. Moreover, *The Voice* seems unduly influenced by the theology of the emergent church movement.

as possible, the number of words and grammatical constructions from the original. Because languages are so different, a formally equivalent translation almost inevitably results in a stilted English style. The New American Standard Bible (NASB) and English Standard Version (ESV) are examples of formally equivalent translations. The New International Version (NIV) falls somewhere in the middle, being more functionally equivalent than the ESV but more formally equivalent than the NLT.

For reading larger portions of Scripture (reading through the Bible in one year, for example), a person might choose a functionally equivalent translation. For careful verse-by-verse study, one might prefer a more formally equivalent translation. In explaining a difficult passage to others in preaching or teaching, it is sometimes helpful to quote other Bible translations that clarify the meaning of the passage. Also, in personal study, reading a passage in multiple translations frequently results in increased comprehension. It is advisable to vary the Bible translation one reads to hear the text afresh.

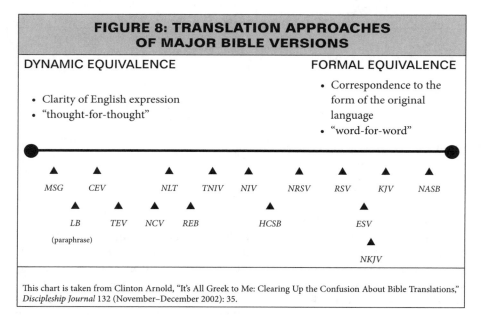

FIGURE 8: TRANSLATION APPROACHES OF MAJOR BIBLE VERSIONS

DYNAMIC EQUIVALENCE

- Clarity of English expression
- "thought-for-thought"

FORMAL EQUIVALENCE

- Correspondence to the form of the original language
- "word-for-word"

MSG   CEV   NLT   TNIV   NIV   NRSV   RSV   KJV   NASB

LB   TEV   NCV   REB   HCSB   ESV

(paraphrase)

NKJV

This chart is taken from Clinton Arnold, "It's All Greek to Me: Clearing Up the Confusion About Bible Translations," *Discipleship Journal* 132 (November–December 2002): 35.

Paraphrases

A paraphrase is not really a Bible translation but an attempt to freely word the meaning of the biblical text. A paraphrase is usually done by one person and allows for more interpretive comments than a functionally equivalent translation. Sometimes a paraphrase seeks to recast the biblical narrative in the setting of a certain subculture. *The Word on the Street*, a paraphrase by Rob Lacey, casts the Bible as "urban performance art." Clarence Jordan's famous paraphrase, *The Cotton Patch Version*, sets Jesus' ministry in the Southern United States of the 1950s, replacing Pharisees with white supremacists and Samaritans with African-Americans. *The Message*, by Eugene Peterson, seeks to clarify obscure passages and put them in the gritty language of everyday life.

The original Living Bible was a paraphrase of the American Standard Version (a formally equivalent translation completed in 1901) by Kenneth Taylor, which he composed for his children during his daily train commute.[4] (The New Living Translation, however, is not a paraphrase but a dynamically equivalent translation.) In contrast to paraphrases, Bible translations are always based on Greek and Hebrew texts and are worked on by large committees of diverse scholars, preventing a narrowness of interpretation and guaranteeing that the work remains a translation rather than veering into an idiosyncratic interpretation or paraphrase.

The King James Version
The best Bible translations are based on the most reliable ancient manuscripts of the Old and New Testaments (see question 5, "Were the ancient manuscripts of the Bible transmitted accurately?"). The King James Version (KJV) is not highly recommended because it is not based on the best manuscripts and because the seventeenth-century English is hard for most modern people to understand. Unfortunately, many hotel Bibles and other giveaway Bibles are the KJV translation. While it was an excellent work for its day, the KJV has been surpassed by many modern translations in both readability and faithfulness to the original manuscripts. Some people wrongly and often passionately claim the KJV is a superior translation of the Bible. The historical and linguistic facts do not support this claim.[5] For those who continue to insist on their preference for the KJV, the New King James Version (NKJV) is possibly a better option—being based on the same manuscript tradition of the KJV but updated somewhat in language.

Recent Translation Debates
In recent years, conservative Bible translators have clashed over how to translate generic pronouns and similar constructions. For example, in older English, as well as ancient Greek, the pronoun *he* (or *autos*, in Greek) frequently was used to refer generically to both men and women. Fifty years ago, all English teachers would have said, "If a student wants to speak to me after class, *he* should stay in the room." Recently, there has been a move in English toward an informal generic "they" or "their" ("If a student wants to

---

4. Paul D. Wegner, *The Journey from Texts to Translations: The Origin and Development of the Bible* (Grand Rapids: Baker, 1999), 372–73.
5. See James R. White, *The King James Only Controversy: Can You Trust the Modern Translations?* (Minneapolis: Bethany, 1995).

speak to me after class, *they* should stay in the room.") or the more cumbersome, "If a student wants to speak with me after class, *he or she* should stay in the room." Bible translators debate whether translating *autos* ("he") as "he or she" or *anthrōpos* ("man") as "person" faithfully conveys the meaning of the original. While the debate can be quite impassioned, the sides are closer than they appear, both acknowledging that much gender-specific language in the Bible was understood by the original recipients as applying to women too. For example, virtually all translators acknowledge that Paul's letters addressed to *adelphoi* ("brothers") in churches were in reality for all Christians, both men and women. The question remains, however, whether a Bible translation should render the expression *adelphoi* as "brothers and sisters" or "brothers." Is "brothers and sisters" an interpretation or translation? As one can see, this debate involves the distinction between formally and functionally equivalent translation theories. Scholars favoring the more gender-neutral translations are usually more inclined toward functionally equivalent translation theory. Those favoring a more strict correspondence of expressions are usually more disposed toward formally equivalent approaches to translation. Conservative, Bible-believing scholars, however, are agreed that Greek and Hebrew masculine pronouns for God should be rendered as masculine English pronouns ("he," "his" or "him") because God has revealed himself as Father.

REFLECTION QUESTIONS

1. Which version(s) of the Bible do you own? (Look in the first few pages of your Bible(s) to see.) Why do you use this Bible (or these Bibles)?

2. If your church has pew Bibles, what translation is it? Have you ever prejudged a person because of the Bible translation he or she preferred?

3. Do you prefer reading a more formally equivalent translation (word-for-word) or functionally equivalent translation (thought-for-thought)? Why?

4. If you were to obtain additional Bible translations to supplement your study, which ones would you get?

5. What translation of the Bible would you use for (a) careful, verse-by-verse study, (b) a gift to an international student, (c) reading through the Bible in one year with a group of college students?

FOR FURTHER STUDY

Brake, Donald L. *A Visual History of the English Bible: The Tumultuous Tale of the World's Bestselling Book*. Grand Rapids: Baker, 2008.

Fee, Gordon D., and Mark L. Strauss. *How to Choose a Translation for All Its Worth*. Grand Rapids: Zondervan, 2007.

Wegner, Paul D. *The Journey from Texts to Translations: The Origin and Development of the Bible*. Grand Rapids: Baker, 1999.

White, James R. *The King James Only Controversy: Can You Trust the Modern Translations?* Minneapolis: Bethany, 1995.

www.biblegateway.com (free link to various Bible translations).

www.multilanguage.com (Bibles and Christian resources in languages other than English).

PART 2

Approaching the Bible Generally

Questions Related
to Interpretation

Why Is Biblical Interpretation Important?

Appealing to the same Bible, Christians, Mormons, and Jehovah's Witnesses can reach amazingly divergent conclusions. Christians, for example, believe there is only one God, a triune Being (Father, Son, and Spirit) who has existed and will exist forever. Mormons cite verses to assert that the God of the Bible is just one among countless deities and that we ourselves, if male, can also become gods. Jehovah's Witnesses claim it is blasphemy to say that Jesus or the Spirit is a divine person. Even people who claim the name of Christian disagree vehemently as to whether the Bible condemns homosexual behavior. On another level, believing Christians can be puzzled after reading an Old Testament text regulating infectious skin diseases or land redistribution in ancient Israel (see question 19, "Do all the commands of the Bible apply today?"). How are such texts applicable today? Clearly, it is not enough to simply say, "I believe the Bible." Proper interpretation of the Bible is essential.

What Is Interpretation?

To interpret a document is to express its meaning through speaking or writing. To engage in interpretation assumes that there is, in fact, a proper and improper meaning of a text and that care must be taken to not misrepresent the meaning. When dealing with the Scriptures, to properly interpret a text is to faithfully convey the inspired human author's meaning of the text, while not neglecting divine intent (see question 3, "Who wrote the Bible—humans or God?").

The Scriptures Show the Need for Biblical Interpretation

Numerous texts in the Bible clearly demonstrate that there is both a correct and incorrect way to understand the Scriptures. A sampling of these texts with brief commentary appears below.

- *2 Timothy 2:15: "Do your best to present yourself to God as one approved, a workman who does not need to be ashamed and who correctly handles the word of truth."* In this verse, Paul exhorts Timothy to "correctly handle," or "rightly interpret" (*orthotomounta*), the word of truth, that is, the Scriptures. Such a warning implies that the Scriptures might be wrongly handled or wrongly interpreted.

- *Psalm 119:18: "Open my eyes that I may see wonderful things in your law."* Here the psalmist pleads that the Lord would allow him to understand and delight in the meaning of Scripture. This appeal shows that the experience of joyful understanding of Scripture is not universal or automatic.

- *2 Peter 3:15–16: "Bear in mind that our Lord's patience means salvation, just as our dear brother Paul also wrote you with the wisdom that God gave him. He writes the same way in all his letters, speaking in them of these matters. His letters contain some things that are hard to understand, which ignorant and unstable people distort, as they do the other Scriptures, to their own destruction."* It is clear from Peter's instructions that it is possible to distort the meaning of Scripture. And, far from countenancing such interpretive license, Peter says that perverting the meaning of Scripture is a sin of serious consequence.

- *Ephesians 4:11–13: "It was [Christ] who gave some to be apostles, some to be prophets, some to be evangelists, and some to be pastors and teachers, to prepare God's people for works of service, so that the body of Christ may be built up until we all reach unity in the faith and in the knowledge of the Son of God and become mature, attaining to the whole measure of the fullness of Christ."* If the Scriptures were automatically properly understood by all, there would be no need for divinely gifted teachers to instruct and edify the church. God's provision of a teaching office in the church demonstrates the need for people who can properly understand and explain the Bible.

- *2 Timothy 4:2–3: "Preach the Word; be prepared in season and out of season; correct, rebuke and encourage—with great patience and careful instruction. For the time will come when men will not put up with sound doctrine. Instead, to suit their own desires, they will gather around them a great number of teachers to say what their itching ears want to hear."* Paul's instructions to Timothy show that there is a correct way to preach Scriptural revelation, and there will also be distorters of that revelation.

Language and Culture Show the Need
for Biblical Interpretation

Most persons who received a document like this from Genesis 1:1:

בְּרֵאשִׁית בָּרָא אֱלֹהִים אֵת הַשָּׁמַיִם וְאֵת הָאָרֶץ׃

or this from Matthew 1:1:

Βίβλος γενέσεως Ἰησοῦ Χριστοῦ υἱοῦ Δαυὶδ υἱοῦ Ἀβραάμ.

would immediately recognize their need for a translation of the text. In some ways, translation is the most fundamental form of interpretation. The text in its original language is unintelligible to a new audience, so it must be put into a new language. Yet, the translation of a text is not like the repetition of mathematical rules simply with different symbols. All languages have cultural elements and assumed historical backgrounds that cannot be expressed with the same number of words or exactly parallel grammatical constructions. Thus there is the need for additional study, explanation, and interpretation of a text. For example, in Matthew 1:18, Mary and Joseph are described as "engaged," yet in Matthew 1:19, Joseph ponders "divorcing" Mary. Unlike modern American engagement customs, ancient Jewish customs necessitated a divorce to break a betrothal. Certainly, this concept can be explained, but it is difficult to convey succinctly in a translation. Indeed, even when communicating in one's native language, there is often need for additional clarification of ambiguous concepts.

A number of years ago, I read a report of a strange practice developing among some young Christians in China. These new believers felt that it was a sign of true faith to carry with them a small wooden cross. Apparently, on the basis of Jesus' instructions in Luke 9:23 ("If anyone would come after me, he must deny himself and take up his cross daily and follow me"), these Christians had come to think that putting a wooden cross in one's pocket was commanded by Christ. To "take up one's cross," however, is a figure of speech, meaning to deny one's own ambitions and desires in submission to the lordship of Christ.

If we are familiar with the different time periods, genres, and anticipations/fulfillments of Scripture, we are better able to confidently approach any individual part of the Bible. Assuming the unified nature of the Bible, as well as the progressive unfolding of God's plans (Heb. 1:1–3), it is clear that a person with an established understanding of God's overarching purposes will be better equipped to understand individual pieces of the story. Of course, time and study are acquired to attain such greater familiarity with the text.

It is sometimes said that Scripture is the best interpreter of Scripture. This means that the broader biblical context will help one properly understand any individual passage. Without knowing the entire book of 1 John, for example, 1 John 5:6 seems hopelessly obscure ("This is the one who came by water and blood—Jesus Christ. He did not come by water only, but by water and blood. And it is the Spirit who testifies, because the Spirit is the truth"). Knowing the broader context of the letter, assuming a unified message in the New Testament, and having some exposure to the cultural background of incipient Gnosticism, we can reasonably conclude that the verse affirms the divine-human nature of Christ, seen both in his baptism (water) and death/resurrection (blood).[1]

A proper understanding of the author's original meaning is also fundamental for proper application of the text today. For example, Proverbs 22:28 says, "Do not move an ancient boundary stone set up by your forefathers." As boundary stones were used to mark ancient property lines, this proverb forbids the dishonest acquisition of a neighbor's land. Applied more broadly, the text points to divine displeasure at any sneaky stealing—whether moving ancient stones, engaging in e-mail phishing schemes, or any other surreptitious theft. The principle ("don't steal in a sneaky way") must be distilled from a culturally conditioned command ("do not move an ancient boundary stone").

Careful interpretation is important because assumed theological presuppositions often can drive interpretations. Traditional dispensationalists, for example, sometimes insist on literal interpretation of figurative language, though they have no defensible basis for doing so.[2] Through careful biblical interpretation, the student of Scripture can become aware of others' biases, as well as coming to acknowledge and assess the student's own hermeneutical predilections.

REFLECTION QUESTIONS

1. When reading the Bible, are you conscious of the danger of misinterpreting it, that is, of misunderstanding it and distorting its meaning in explaining it to others?

2. How is interpreting the Bible different from interpreting any other piece of literature?

3. Consider other Christians whose interpretations of the Bible you have either read or heard. Whom do you consider the most reliable? Why?

---

1. See John R. W. Stott, *The Letters of John*, rev. ed., TNTC 19 (Grand Rapids: Eerdmans; Leicester: Inter-Varsity Press, 1988), 179–82.
2. See Richard D. Patterson's adept handling of figurative language in "Wonders in the Heavens and on the Earth: Apocalyptic Imagery in the Old Testament," *JETS* 43, no. 3 (2000): 385–403.

4. What would make you a more faithful biblical interpreter?

5. Are you aware of any theological or interpretive biases you have in approaching the Scriptures? Can you defend having such biases from the Bible itself?

FOR FURTHER STUDY

Brown, Jeannine K. *Scripture as Communication: Introducing Biblical Hermeneutics.* Grand Rapids: Baker, 2007.
Fee, Gordon D., and Douglas Stuart. *How to Read the Bible for All Its Worth.* 3rd ed. Grand Rapids: Zondervan, 2003.
Stein, Robert H. *A Basic Guide to Interpreting the Bible: Playing by the Rules.* Grand Rapids: Baker, 1994.

How Has the Bible Been Interpreted Throughout Church History?

Those who cannot remember the past are condemned to repeat it."[1] Or, so goes the famous historical dictum. Just as a wise child learns from the successes and mistakes of his parents and grandparents, so a wise Christian learns from his ancestors in the faith—those generations of Christians who went before him. Throughout the centuries, how have Christians interpreted the Bible? What can we learn from their approaches? Where should we beware of their missteps? We will attempt to answer these questions briefly in broad strokes. We also begin with this caveat—to survey nearly two thousand years of interpretive history in such a short space, we must employ a number of oversimplifications. For more detailed analysis, see the suggested books at the end of this section.

The Use of the Old Testament in the New Testament (A.D. 45–90)

The first place that we see Christian interpretation of the Scriptures is the citation of Old Testament texts by New Testament authors. The citations of such texts have a number of characteristics.

1. New Testament authors and characters (in narratives) cite the Old Testament Scriptures as reliable accounts of God's prior interventions and communications (e.g., Matt. 12:40–41; Rom. 4:1–25).[2] For the New Testament authors, the Scriptures were God's inspired, inerrant Word (see question 4, "Does the Bible contain error?").

2. New Testament authors respected the contexts of the passages they

---

1. George Santayana, *The Life of Reason or the Phases of Human Progress: Introduction and Reason in Common Sense* (New York: Charles Scribner's Sons, 1905), 284.
2. See John Wenham, *Christ and the Bible*, 3rd ed. (Grand Rapids: Baker, 1994).

cited. Sometimes New Testament authors are wrongly maligned for citing texts haphazardly. But a sympathetic and careful look at their usage shows that this accusation is unfounded.[3]

3. New Testament authors employed the Old Testament in a typological and messianic way (see question 24 for a more detailed explanation). This means they saw God's prior revelation as anticipatory, reaching its climactic fulfillment in the coming of Messiah Jesus. God's prior interventions pointed to the coming of Jesus and may be cited as historical anticipations of the final sacrifice, final redemption, final deliverance, final solution, etc.

4. The New Testament authors did not use the Old Testament in allegorical ways. That is, they did not assign meanings to details of the Old Testament texts that the original authors would not have countenanced. Admittedly, in one place in the New Testament (Gal. 4:24), Paul says that Hagar and Sarah may be understood "allegorically" or "figuratively" to represent the two covenants, one of slavery and one of promise. Even here, though, Paul does not claim to be interpreting the relevant Old Testament texts but freely admits that he is offering a homiletical reflection that he explicitly labels as figurative.

Some Christian scholars debate whether the New Testament authors' use of the Old Testament should be considered normative for modern interpretation. The primary issue here concerns typological use of the Old Testament, which is especially widespread in Matthew and Hebrews. It seems safe to say that any typological use of the Old Testament not explicitly sanctioned in the New Testament should be entertained with great caution. Instead, we should focus on the literal meaning of the text.[4]

Another discussion among Christian scholars concerns early Jewish interpretive methods and whether they influenced Jesus and the writers of the New Testament. Admittedly, some forms of Jewish exegesis (midrash and pesher, for example) regularly stray far from the authorial intent of Scripture and propose untenable secret meanings, sometimes based on the numerical value of words or even the shapes of letters.[5] The messianic, typological interpretation of the Old Testament found in the New Testament, while comparable to midrash or pesher, is a far cry from the fanciful interpretations of the rabbis.

---

3. See G. K. Beale and D. A. Carson, eds., *Commentary on the New Testament Use of the Old Testament* (Grand Rapids: Baker; Nottingham, England: Apollos, 2007).

4. Richard N. Longenecker, *Biblical Exegesis in the Apostolic Period* (Grand Rapids: Eerdmans, 1975), 218–19.

5. Henry A. Virkler and Karelynne Gerber Ayayo, *Hermeneutics: Principles and Processes of Biblical Interpretation*, 2nd ed. (Grand Rapids: Baker, 2007), 45.

The Rise of Allegorical Interpretation (A.D. 100–500)

Not long after the New Testament period, many early church fathers began to employ allegorical methods of interpretation. Allegory is a genre of literature that assigns symbolic significance to textual details. For example, John Bunyan's famous work, *Pilgrim's Progress*, is an allegory in which every character has a signification in relation to the Christian life. When intended by the writer and understood by the reader, allegory can be a powerful literary medium. However, if allegory is not intended by the author yet is employed as an interpretive method by the reader, then a dangerous misrepresentation of the author's meaning can result. There are several reasons why early Christians fell prey to the hermeneutical misapplication of allegory.

1. One reason early Christians were drawn to allegory was the limited presence of allegory in the Bible itself. Yes, Jesus gave an allegorical interpretation to at least one of his parables (Mark 4:1–20; also see Matt. 13:24–30, 36–43). Paul also seems to employ allegory once (Gal. 4:24, see above). Obviously, where Jesus and Paul *intended* allegorical meaning in the New Testament, faithful interpretation demands respect for this powerful genre. It is the illegitimate importation of allegory that is the problem.

2. A casual look at history or current society shows that human nature is often enamored with the secretive or conspiratorial. People love to feel that they are in the know or have access to a deeper reality than others. It seems very likely that some early Christian writers and speakers allegorized the texts in order to gain fame as purveyors of the deep, secret things of God. Likewise, the popularity of such teaching—whether ancient or modern—often is driven by an unhealthy interest in the speculative rather than holding to the clear meaning of Scripture (e.g., note the popularity of *The Bible Code* or *The Da Vinci Code*). While the Bible does claim to reveal God's mysteries, it does so through unequivocal apostolic proclamation (1 Cor. 2:1–7).

3. Perhaps most significantly, allegorical interpretive methods were commonly used in the ancient Greco-Roman world to interpret difficult religious texts.[6] The immoral and capricious actions of the Greco-Roman deities were made palatable and instructive through allegory. Possibly, such allegorical methods were rooted in a Platonic view of the world—looking for ultimate reality behind the visible world or text.[7] As the

---

6. Jean Pépin, *Mythe et Allégorie: Les origines grecques et les contestations judéo-chrétiennes*, rev. ed. (Paris: Études Augustiniennes, 1976). See especially part 2 of the volume.
7. William W. Klein, Craig L. Blomberg, and Robert L. Hubbard, *Introduction to Biblical Interpretation*, rev. ed. (Nashville: Thomas Nelson, 2004), 25–26.

Christian faith spread, former pagans applied the recognized literary conventions of their day to challenging texts in their new Scriptures. For example, unusual Old Testament laws or the strange or immoral actions of characters in Scripture were read in allegorical ways. As early Christianity faced threats from the heretic Marcion, who rejected the Old Testament, and groups espousing similar views, it became important to show that the Old Testament was inspired and relevant.[8] Not only early Christians but also early Jews immersed in Greco-Roman culture adopted the allegorical method. Philo (20 B.C.–A.D. 50), a first-century Jew living in Alexandria, regularly employed the allegorical approach to the Hebrew Scriptures. For example, in Genesis 9:20–21, we read that after the flood, Noah planted a vineyard and got drunk. Clearly, the Bible does not approve of drunkenness (Prov. 23:29–35), but in Genesis 9 there is no explicit censure of Noah's behavior. How does Philo explain how Noah, a hero of the faith, became inebriated? Rather than observing that not all behavior described in the narrative is normative, Philo writes:

> What is the meaning of the statement, "And Noah became sober after the wine?" (Genesis 9:24).

> The literal meaning is too notorious. Therefore we need only here to speak of what concerns the inner sense of the words. When the intellect is strengthened, it is able by its soberness to discern with a certain accuracy all things, both before and behind it, both present, I mean, and future; but the man who can see neither what is present nor what is future with accuracy, is afflicted by blindness; but he who sees the present, but who cannot also foresee the future, and is not at all cautious, such a man is overcome by drunkenness and intoxication; and he, lastly, who is found to be able to look all around him, and to see, and discern, and comprehend the different natures of things, both present and future, the watchfulness of sobriety is in that man.[9]

Thus, just as Philo, a Jew living in a pagan culture, came to apply the accepted literary methods to the Hebrew Scriptures, so Christian preachers and scholars living in similar settings employed allegorical methods in interpreting the Scriptures.

A striking example of this sort of early Christian allegorical exegesis appears in the Epistle of Barnabas 9.6–9. In this text, the author

---

8. David S. Dockery, *Biblical Interpretation Then and Now: Contemporary Hermeneutics in the Light of the Early Church* (Grand Rapids: Baker, 1992), 45.
9. *Questions and Answers on Genesis* 2.73 in *The Works of Philo: New Updated Edition*, trans. C. D. Yonge (Peabody, MA: Hendrickson, 1993), 838.

conflates Genesis 14:14 and Genesis 17:23, asserting that Abraham circumcised 318 members of his household. Appealing to the Greek capital letters used to abbreviate the number 318 (*IHT*), the author claims that Abraham's practice of circumcision was intended to point to Jesus (abbreviated *IH* in Greek texts) and the cross (the shape of which is similar to the Greek letter *tau* [*T*]).

Indeed, the allegorical meaning of a text came to be viewed by some as the highest meaning of the passage. The prominent early church father Origen (A.D. 185–254) cited Proverbs 22:20–21 and 1 Thessalonians 5:23 as the basis for his hermeneutical approach.[10] Just as the person is tripartite (body, soul, and spirit), Origen claimed the text also has a body (literal meaning), soul (moral meaning—teaching ethics), and spirit (spiritual or allegorical meaning). Granted, Origen employed certain caveats to his interpretive method—claiming that one could never introduce an allegorical meaning that is contrary to the "rule of faith" (early Christian doctrinal summary).[11] But even with such safeguards, it is important to note that the interpreter is giving a meaning to the text the inspired author did not intend.

While the allegorical approach to the Scriptures became dominant in the early church, it is important to note that some voices continued to clamor for a literal reading of the Bible, respecting the intent of the inspired authors. One such group was the Antiochean fathers—Lucian (A.D. 240–312), Diodore of Tarsus (d. ca. A.D. 394), John Chrysostom (A.D. 347–407), Theodore of Mopsuestia (A.D. 350–428), Theodoret (A.D. 393–457), and others. Unfortunately, the Antiocheans were a minority among early church interpreters, and the movement essentially dissolved by the eighth century.

The early church fathers' interpretations of biblical texts, while usually Christological and orthodox in conclusion, were often very distant from the authorial intent of the texts exposited. In such an environment, it became increasingly important to have some objective theological safeguards so that heretics could not claim validity for their equally ungrounded, though

---

10. Origen, *De Principiis* 4.2.4–17 (*ANF*: 4:359). Origen quotes a variant reading (not the Masoretic text) of Proverbs 22:20–21. This variant reading is also followed by the Douay-Rheims American Edition (1899): "Behold I have described it to thee *three manner of ways*, in thoughts and knowledge: That I might shew thee the certainty, and the words of truth, to answer out of these to them that sent thee" (emphasis added). The Douay-Rheims translation gives a literal rendering of the Latin Vulgate. First Thessalonians 5:23 reads, "May God himself, the God of peace, sanctify you through and through. May your whole spirit, soul and body be kept blameless at the coming of our Lord Jesus Christ" (NIV).

11. Dockery, *Biblical Interpretation Then and Now*, 89–91. Thomas Aquinas (A.D. 1225–1274) argued that all allegorical interpretation of Scripture must be grounded in the text's literal sense (*Summa theologica* 1.1.8, cited by Robert M. Grant with David Tracy, *A Short History of the Interpretation of the Bible*, 2nd ed. [Philadelphia: Fortress, 1984], 89).

unorthodox, interpretations. The "rule of faith" (the accepted and often assumed summary of orthodox Christian doctrine), along with a growing reverence for tradition and formal doctrinal summaries (that is, creeds), served this purpose.[12] The repetition of church tradition and the summarization of orthodox doctrine functionally replaced the primacy of the Bible.

The Fourfold Meaning of Scripture (A.D. 500–1500)

Moving from the patristic to the medieval period, the allegorical approach to the Bible continued, with the addition of a fourth level of meaning. As early as the writing of John Cassian (A.D. 360–435) and Augustine (A.D. 354–430), we find the assertion that every biblical text has four levels of meaning: the literal, moral, spiritual (allegorical), and heavenly (eschatological or anagogical).[13] Essentially, this fourth level of meaning was another allegorical level with heavenly or eschatological (end-times) nuances. A reference to Jerusalem, for example, would include these four dimensions.[14]

- *Literal:* plot of ground in Palestine
- *Moral:* the human soul
- *Spiritual:* the Christian church
- *Heavenly:* the heavenly city, the New Jerusalem

An oft-repeated poem summarizes this fourfold hermeneutical method in memorable rhyme.[15]

- The *letter* shows us what God and our fathers did;
- The *allegory* shows us where our faith is hid;
- The *moral* meaning gives us rules for daily life;
- The *anagogy* shows us where we end our strife.

This fourfold interpretive approach to the Bible became widespread and assumed. Indeed, much biblical scholarship in the medieval period was not true exegesis but the cataloging of church fathers' interpretations of various passages.[16] Church tradition effectively trumped the primacy of Scripture. At the same time, we should note that isolated voices continued to call for a return to the priority of the literal meaning of the text.[17]

---

12. Dockery, *Biblical Interpretation Then and Now*, 45–73.
13. Grant with Tracy, *A Short History of the Interpretation of the Bible*, 85.
14. Ibid.
15. Ibid.
16. Ibid., 83.
17. E.g., Ishodad's *Introduction to the Psalms* in the ninth century (Grant with Tracy, *A Short History of the Interpretation of the Bible*, 64–65); biblical commentaries by Andrew of St. Victor (twelfth century), abbot of an English abbey at Wigmore (Klein, Blomberg, and

The Return to a More Faithful Interpretive Method (A.D. 1500–Present)

The cry of the Reformation was *Ad fontes!* ("to the sources"). With the Protestant Reformers calling people back to the authority of the Bible (*Sola Scriptura*, "the Bible Alone"), the so-called fourfold meaning of Scripture came under increased scrutiny and criticism. The famous reformer Martin Luther (1483–1546) referred to earlier allegorical interpretations as "silly," "amazing twaddle," "absurd," and "useless."[18] Luther confessed, "When I was a young man, my own attempts at allegory met with fair success. . . . But, I ask you is this not a desecration of the sacred writings?"[19] John Calvin likewise said, "We ought to have a deeper reverence for Scripture than to reckon ourselves at liberty to disguise its natural meaning."[20] Elsewhere, Calvin wrote, "It is . . . an audacity, closely allied with sacrilege, rashly to turn Scripture in any way we please, and to indulge our fancies as in sport; which has been done by many in former times."[21]

Although heirs of the Protestant Reformation continued to fall prey to the siren song of allegory, over time biblical scholars reached an established consensus that allegory (when not intended by the authors) is a perversion of the text. Rudolf Bultmann (1884–1976), the most famous New Testament scholar of the twentieth century, set forth the following essential presupposition of sound biblical scholarship: "It belongs to the historical method, of course, that a text is interpreted in accordance with the rules of grammar and of the meaning of the words."[22] That is, to understand the Bible, we must look to the sense of the author's actual words according to the norms of language and grammar.

While the modern study of the Bible eventually eviscerated the allegorical method,[23] allegorical flights of fancy are still found in much popular Christian preaching and teaching. Charles Spurgeon (1834–1892), for example, in his

---

Hubbard, *Introduction to Biblical Interpretation*, 44); the writings of Nicolas of Lyra (1270–1340), which influenced Luther (L. Berkhof, *Principles of Biblical Interpretation*, 2nd ed. [Grand Rapids: Baker, 1952], 25); and Geiler of Keiserberg of the fifteenth century (Klein, Blomberg, and Hubbard, *Introduction to Biblical Interpretation*, 46).

18. Martin Luther, *Lectures on Genesis, Chapters 1–5*, in *Luther's Works*, ed. J. Pelikan (St. Louis: Concordia, 1958), 1:91, 98, 233.

19. Ibid., 232.

20. John Calvin, *Commentary on a Harmony of the Evangelists, Matthew, Mark, and Luke*, trans. William Pringle (Edinburgh: Calvin Translation Society, n.d.; reprint, Grand Rapids: Baker, 2003), 3:63 (vol. 17 in reprint series).

21. John Calvin, *Commentaries on the Epistle of Paul the Apostle to the Romans*, trans. and ed. John Owen (Edinburgh: Calvin Translation Society, n.d.; reprint, Grand Rapids: Baker, 2003), xxvii (vol. 19 in reprint series).

22. Rudolf Bultmann, "Is Exegesis Without Presuppositions Possible?" in *Existence and Faith: Shorter Writings of Rudolf Bultmann*, trans. Schubert M. Ogden (New York: Meridian, 1960), 291.

23. Note, for example, the death blow to allegorizing parables dealt by Adolf Jülicher in *Die Gleichnisreden Jesu* (Freiburg: Mohr, 1888).

Lectures to My Students, comments favorably on some allegorical preaching (or, as he calls it, "spiritualizing").[24]

Within the last sixty years, the body of scholars who approach the Bible self-consciously as both academics and faithful Christians has increased dramatically. The Evangelical Theological Society was founded in 1949 as a professional society of religion professors who hold to the authority and inerrancy of Scripture. The organization now boasts more than 4,600 members.[25] (Not all members are professors, but all full members must have the minimum of a Th.M. degree.) Moreover, every year, many significant commentaries and biblical reference works are produced by evangelicals. While diverse in the details of their interpretive methods, the majority of evangelicals interpret the Bible with a literal, historical, and grammatical approach to the Bible. For evangelicals, the conscious intent of the human author (whether the original author or a later biblical author in canonical reflection) is the touchstone of interpretation.

The Antisupernatural Bias and Skepticism of Modern Scholarship (A.D. 1650–Present)

Running along parallel chronological tracks with the return to a more faithful approach to Scripture, a modern hermeneutic of antisupernatural skepticism has come to flourish in the secular academy. This skeptical approach finds its roots in the Enlightenment and its optimistic elevation of human reason. The leading New Testament scholar of the twentieth century, Rudolf Bultmann, embodied this antisupernaturalism. In a pivotal article, Bultmann mentions a necessary presupposition to biblical exegesis. He writes,

> The historical method includes the presupposition that history is a unity in the sense of a closed continuum of effects in which individual events are connected by the succession of cause and effect. . . . This closedness means that the continuum of historical happenings cannot be rent by the interference of supernatural, transcendent powers, and that therefore there is not 'miracle' in the sense of the word. Such a miracle would be an event whose cause did not lie within history.[26]

In other words, Bultmann claims that a necessary presupposition to the academic study of the Bible is to maintain that supernatural events do not happen. Because the Bible contains so many descriptions of supernatural events, scholars accepting Bultmann's premise necessarily take an extremely

---

24. C. H. Spurgeon, *Lectures to My Students: Complete and Unabridged* (London: Marshall, Morgan & Scott, n.d.; reprint, Grand Rapids: Zondervan, 1954), 97–98. At the same time, Spurgeon warns, "Avoid that childish trifling and outrageous twisting of texts which will make you a wise man among fools, but a fool among wise men" (ibid., 100).
25. In an official e-mail from ETS in January, 2009, the membership was listed as 4,667.
26. Bultmann, "Is Exegesis Without Presuppositions Possible," 291–92.

skeptical view toward the historical reliability of the Bible. These scholars end up saying that the biblical authors who described miraculous events were deceived, mistaken, or attempting to convey some truth in "mythological terms." None of these three explanations, however, respects the genre of the biblical documents or the character and intelligence of their authors.[27] The writing of antisupernaturalist scholars sometimes degenerates into the sifting of supposed sources and hypothetical reconstructions of the "real events" or situations that gave rise to the texts.

Other scholars engage in sociological comparisons or the application of various philosophical lenses through which they evaluate the text (Marxism, feminism, homosexual activism, etc.). More recently, some scholars have attempted to salvage a sympathetic study of the Bible while avoiding the thorny questions of truth or historical reliability. Such "canonical" or "theological" approaches to interpreting the Scriptures insist on reading the biblical documents as a finished, interrelated whole.[28] Other scholars have proposed various forms of literary or narrative analysis, attempting to view the text as a whole.[29] Similarly, a study of reception history tries to salvage the meaning and unity of the text by considering the way it has been understood throughout church history.[30] Such interpretive methods are helpful insofar as they help the reader to listen to the text. Eventually, however, any thinking reader of the Bible must ask, "Is this true? Did God really say . . . ?" The Bible confronts the reader with ultimate claims as to the human situation (rebellion and condemnation) and the nature of God (holy and loving). In that sense, no neutral middle ground will ever be possible in biblical scholarship. Jesus said, "He who is not with me is against me, and he who does not gather with me scatters" (Matt. 12:30).

REFLECTION QUESTIONS

1. When reading the New Testament, do you pay attention to the citation of Old Testament texts? Do you ever look up the Old Testament texts cited?

---

27. Regarding the Gospel of John, for example, C. S. Lewis writes, "I have been reading poems, romances, vision-literature, legends, myths all my life. I know what they are like. I know that not one of them is like this [Gospel]" ("Fern-seed and Elephants," in *Fern-seed and Elephants and Other Essays on Christianity by C. S. Lewis*, ed. Walter Hooper [London: Fontana/Collins, 1975], 108).
28. See, for example, Brevard S. Childs, *Biblical Theology in Crisis* (Philadelphia: Westminster, 1970); idem, *The New Testament as Canon: An Introduction* (Philadelphia: Fortress, 1984); and Daniel J. Treier, *Introducing Theological Interpretation of Scripture: Recovering a Christian Practice* (Grand Rapids: Baker, 2008).
29. See, e.g., David G. Firth and Jamie A. Grant, eds., *Words and the Word: Explorations in Biblical Interpretation and Literary Theory* (Downers Grove, IL: InterVarsity Press, 2009).
30. See, e.g., the Ancient Christian Commentary on Scripture series (Downers Grove, IL: InterVarsity Press). Similarly, a study of effective history traces the effects of a text on various aspects of thought, culture, and art.

2. Have you ever heard an allegorical sermon or read an allegorical interpretation in a devotional book? At the time, did you recognize the interpretive method as allegorical? What did you think?

3. It has been said, "We can see so far only because we stand on the shoulders of giants."[31] How would this saying apply to biblical interpretation?

4. Have you noticed any of the interpretive trends mentioned above in books that you own?

5. Of what value are the allegorical expositions of the church fathers?

FOR FURTHER STUDY

Dockery, David S. *Biblical Interpretation Then and Now: Contemporary Hermeneutics in the Light of the Early Church.* Grand Rapids: Baker, 1992.

Grant, R. M., with David Tracy. *A Short History of the Interpretation of the Bible.* 2nd ed. Philadelphia: Fortress, 1984.

Hauser, Alan J., and Duane F. Watson, eds. *A History of Biblical Interpretation: The Ancient Period.* Vol. 1. Grand Rapids: Eerdmans, 2003. (Additional volumes forthcoming).

Klein, William W., Craig L. Blomberg, and Robert L. Hubbard. *Introduction to Biblical Interpretation.* Rev. ed. Nashville: Thomas Nelson, 2004. (See chap. 2, "The History of Interpretation," 23–62).

McKim, Donald K., ed. *Dictionary of Major Biblical Interpreters.* Downers Grove, IL: InterVarsity Press, 2007.

---

31. John of Salisbury, in *Metalogicon* (A.D. 1159), attributes Bernard of Chartres as originator of the oft-repeated expression. The quotation reads, "Bernard of Chartres used to say that we are like dwarfs on the shoulders of giants, so that we can see more than they, and things at a greater distance, not by virtue of any sharpness of sight on our part, or any physical distinction, but because we are carried high and raised up by their giant size" (www.wikipdia.org, "Standing on the shoulders of giants," accessed December 4, 2008).

What Are Some General Principles for Interpreting the Bible? (1)

While good biblical interpretation is better caught (that is, learned from reading and hearing those who do it well) than taught, it can be helpful to enumerate some overarching interpretive principles. Applied over time, these principles will become more second nature in your interpretation of Scripture.

Approach the Bible in Prayer

The Scriptures tell us that the human heart is desperately wicked and deceitful (Jer. 17:9). Indeed, the basic human response to God's natural revelation (through conscience or nature) is to suppress it in idolatry (Rom. 1:18–23). Even God's people, though given a new nature and the Holy Spirit as a guide, must beware of the deceitful inclinations of their remaining sinful nature. In Psalm 119, the author, traditionally assumed to be King David, serves as a good example of honest self-assessment in his approach to the Scripture. Repeatedly, he prays for insight and redirection. Below is a list of sample petitions within the psalm. Slowly praying through selected verses in Psalm 119 is an excellent way to begin a Bible study session.

- *Verse 5:* [addressing the LORD] "Oh, that my ways were steadfast in obeying your decrees!"

- *Verse 10:* "I seek you [LORD] with all my heart; do not let me stray from your commands."

- *Verse 12:* "Praise be to you, O LORD; teach me your decrees."

- *Verses 17–20:* "Do good to your servant, and I will live; I will obey your word. Open my eyes that I may see wonderful things in your law. I am a stranger on earth; do not hide your commands from me. My soul is consumed with longing for your laws at all times."

- *Verses 34–37:* "Give me understanding, and I will keep your law and obey it with all my heart. Direct me in the path of your commands, for there I find delight. Turn my heart toward your statutes and not toward selfish gain. Turn my eyes away from worthless things; preserve my life according to your word."

The great reformer Martin Luther recognized Psalm 119 as helpful instruction for studying the Bible. He noted:

> Thus you see how David keeps praying in the above-mentioned Psalm, "Teach me, Lord, instruct me, lead me, show me," and many more words like these. Although he well knew and daily heard and read the text of Moses and other books besides, still he wants to lay hold of the real teacher of the Scriptures himself, so that he may not seize upon them pell-mell with his reason and become his own teacher. For such practice gives rise to factious spirits who allow themselves to nurture the delusion that the Scriptures are subject to them and can be easily grasped with their reason, as if they were *Markolf* or Aesop's Fables, for which no Holy Spirit and no prayers are needed.[1]

As we approach the Bible, we need to realize that sin affects all of our being—our emotions, wills, and rational faculties. We can easily deceive ourselves or be deceived by others. We need the Holy Spirit to instruct and guide us. Thus, prayer is the essential starting point for any study of the Bible.[2]

Read the Bible as a Book That Points to Jesus

In a debate with the Jewish religious leaders in Jerusalem, Jesus said, "You diligently study the Scriptures because you think that by them you possess eternal life. These are the Scriptures that testify about me, yet you refuse to come to me to have life" (John 5:39–40; cf. Luke 24:25–27). If we study or teach

---

1. Martin Luther, "Preface to the Wittenberg Edition of Luther's German Writings" (1539), in *Martin Luther's Basic Theological Writings*, ed. Timothy F. Lull, 2nd ed. (Minneapolis: Fortress, 2005), 72.
2. Spurgeon advised young pastors, "Praying is the best studying. Luther said so of old— '*Bene orasse est bene studuisse,*' and the well-worn proverb will bear repeating. Pray over Scripture; it is as the treading of grapes in the wine-vat, the threshing of corn on the barn floor, the melting of gold from the ore" (C. H. Spurgeon, *Lectures to My Students: Complete and Unabridged* [London: Marshall, Morgan & Scott, n.d.; reprint, Grand Rapids: Zondervan, 1954], 86).

any part of the Bible without reference to Jesus the Savior, we are not faithful interpreters. Of course, not every text points to Jesus in the same way. The Old Testament promises, anticipates, and prepares. Jesus noted this forward-looking dimension to all of God's prior revelation, saying, "For all the Prophets and the Law prophesied until John [the Baptist]" (Matt. 11:13). The New Testament announces the fulfillment in Christ of all of Israel's law, history, prophecies, and institutions. Every passage of Scripture must be read as a chapter in a completed book. As we know how the story wraps up (in Christ's life, death, and resurrection), we must always be asking how prior chapters lead to that culmination. See question 18 ("Is the Bible really all about Jesus?") for further information on understanding the Christocentric (Christ-centered) nature of Scripture.

Let Scripture Interpret Scripture

The hermeneutical guideline of Scripture interpreting Scripture has long been espoused by Christian interpreters, going back at least to Augustine (A.D. 354–430) and Irenaeus (A.D. 130–200).[3] If we believe that all the Bible is inspired by God and thus noncontradictory, passages of Scripture that are less clear should be interpreted with reference to those that are more transparent in meaning. Cults and heretical groups often seize upon a few obscure texts, ascribe to them questionable meaning, and then interpret the remainder of the Bible through these aberrant lenses.

Another dimension of letting Scripture interpret Scripture means listening to the full panoply of texts that touch upon a subject. For example, if we were to read God's words to Abraham in Genesis 17:10–12, we might conclude that even today all male worshippers of God must be circumcised.[4] Yet, we read in 1 Corinthians 7:19, "Circumcision is nothing and uncircumcision is nothing. Keeping God's commands is what counts." By understanding the trajectory of Scripture (promise ➔ fulfillment in Christ), we see that circumcision served a preparatory role for the Jewish nation but is no longer required of God's people. As the author of Hebrews says, "The law is only a shadow of the good things that are coming—not the realities themselves" (Heb. 10:1). Paul can circumcise a coworker as a means of strategic missionary accommodation to unregenerate Jews (Acts 16:3), but when the basis of salvation is at stake, Paul is unbending (Gal. 2:3). This brief survey demonstrates how a nuanced understanding of a subject requires the consideration of multiple biblical texts that touch upon it.

---

3. Bernard Ramm, *Protestant Biblical Interpretation: A Textbook of Hermeneutics,* 3rd ed. (Grand Rapids: Baker, 1970), 36–37; and Robert M. Grant with David Tracy, *A Short History of the Interpretation of the Bible,* 2nd ed. (Philadelphia: Fortress, 1984), 49–50.

4. Genesis 17:10–12, "This is my covenant with you and your descendants after you, the covenant you are to keep: Every male among you shall be circumcised. You are to undergo circumcision, and it will be the sign of the covenant between me and you. For the generations to come every male among you who is eight days old must be circumcised."

Meditate on the Bible

The Bible is not a book for superficial reading. While it is certainly beneficial to read large portions of Scripture in one sitting, no biblical diet is complete without extended rumination on a smaller portion of text. Scripture itself is filled with instructions on such a meditative approach. Drawing from Psalm 119, Martin Luther noted this pattern.

> Secondly, [in your study of the Bible,] you should meditate, that is, not only in your heart, but also externally, by actually repeating and comparing oral speech and literal words of the book, reading and rereading them with diligent attention and reflection, so that you may see what the Holy Spirit means by them. And take care that you do not grow weary or think that you have done enough when you have read, heard, and spoken them once or twice, and that you have complete understanding. You will never be a particularly good theologian if you do that, for you will be like untimely fruit which falls to the ground before it is half ripe.
>
> Thus you see in this same Psalm [119] how David constantly boasts that he will talk, meditate, speak, sing, hear, read, by day and night and always, about nothing except God's Word and commandments. For God will not give you his Spirit without the external Word; so take your cue from that. His command to write, preach, read, hear, sing, speak, etc., outwardly was not given in vain.[5]

It is instructive that many Christians have found it best to start their prayers with quiet and sustained reflection on a small portion of Scripture. We are reminded that we come to God with empty hands. God himself provides the words for our prayers in the Bible. The Puritan Thomas Manton (1620–1677) wrote,

> Meditation is a middle sort of duty between the word and prayer, and hath respect to both. The word feedeth meditation, and meditation feedeth prayer; we must hear that we be not erroneous, and meditate that we be not barren. These duties must always go hand in hand; meditation must follow hearing and precede prayer. To hear and not to meditate is unfruitful. We may hear and hear, but it is like putting a thing into a bag with holes. . . . It is rashness to pray and not to meditate. What we take in by the word we digest by meditation and let out by prayer. These three duties must be so ordered that one may not jostle out the other. Men are barren, dry, and sapless in their prayer for want of exercising themselves in holy thoughts.[6]

---

5. Luther, "Preface," 72–73.
6. Thomas Manton, *The Complete Works of Thomas Manton*, vol. 17, *Sermons on Several Texts of Scripture* (reprint, Birmingham, AL: Solid Ground Christian Books, 2008), 272–73.

Approach the Bible in Faith and Obedience

The Bible is not a philosophy textbook to be debated; it is a revelation from God to be believed and obeyed. As we believe and obey God's Word, we will experience not only joy (Ps. 119:72) but also, more importantly, God's blessing, or approval. James writes,

> Do not merely listen to the word, and so deceive yourselves. Do what it says. Anyone who listens to the word but does not do what it says is like a man who looks at his face in a mirror and, after looking at himself, goes away and immediately forgets what he looks like. But the man who looks intently into the perfect law that gives freedom, and continues to do this, not forgetting what he has heard, but doing it—he will be blessed in what he does. (James 1:22–25)

At the same time, we must remember that obedience to God's Word can never be brought about by increased human effort. Regeneration and divine empowerment are necessary to believe and obey God's Word. Obedience is possible only through Christ. As the apostle John writes, "This is love for God: to obey his commands. And his commands are not burdensome, for everyone born of God overcomes the world. This is the victory that has overcome the world, even our faith. Who is it that overcomes the world? Only he who believes that Jesus is the Son of God" (1 John 5:3–5).

The person who reads Scripture and does not obey it is self-deceived (James 1:22). To claim to know God while consistently and consciously disobeying his Word is to demonstrate the falseness of one's claim. The apostle John writes, "The man who says, 'I know him,' but does not do what he commands is a liar, and the truth is not in him" (1 John 2:4).

Responding with faith and obedience, specifically through difficulties, seems to be one of God's chosen means of maturing his people (Rom. 5:1–11; James 1:1–12; 1 Peter 1:1–12). As we encounter trials in life and meet those difficulties trusting in God and his Word, we can expect the Lord to conform us more into the image of his Son. We can be comforted by the words of Paul in Romans 8:28–29: "And we know that in all things God works for the good of those who love him, who have been called according to his purpose. For those God foreknew he also predestined to be conformed to the likeness of his Son, that he might be the firstborn among many brothers."

Martin Luther noted that the many references to David's trials and enemies in Psalm 119 are instructive for the Christian facing similar situations. He wrote:

> Thus you see how David, in the Psalm mentioned, complains so often about all kinds of enemies, arrogant princes or tyrants, false spirits and factions, whom he must tolerate because he meditates, that is, because he is occupied

with God's Word (as has been said) in all manner of ways. For as soon as God's Word takes root and grows in you, the devil will harry you, and will make a real doctor of you, and by his assaults will teach you to seek and love God's Word. I myself (if you will permit me, mere mouse-dirt to be mingled with pepper) am deeply indebted to my papists that through the devil's raging they have beaten, oppressed, and distressed me so much. That is to say, they have made a fairly good theologian of me, which I would not have become otherwise. And I heartily grant them what they have won in return for making this of me, honor, victory, and triumph, for that's the way they wanted it.[7]

Like Luther, we can meet the troubles of life with trust in God and a reliance on him to obey his Word.

REFLECTION QUESTIONS

1. What role do prayer and meditation currently play in your study of the Bible?

2. What steps can you take to make prayer and meditation a regular part of your Bible reading?

3. Do you approach all portions of the Bible as pointing to Jesus? Which parts seem the most difficult to view in this way? Why?

4. What does it mean to let Scripture interpret Scripture?

5. Is it possible to believe and understand the Bible without obeying it? Can you back up your answer with Scripture?

FOR FURTHER STUDY

Luther, Martin. "Preface to the Wittenberg Edition of Luther's German Writings" (1539). In *Martin Luther's Basic Theological Writings*. Edited by Timothy F. Lull. 2nd ed. Minneapolis: Fortress, 2005.
Roberts, Vaughan. *God's Big Picture: Tracing the Storyline of the Bible*. Downers Grove, IL: InterVarsity Press, 2002.

---

7. Luther, "Preface," 73.

What Are Some General Principles for Interpreting the Bible? (2)

In this section, we will continue our survey of general principles for interpreting the Bible. In the prior section, we focused more on the devotional aspect of Bible study (prayer, meditation, obedience). In this section, we will focus more on technical or literary guidelines.

Take Note of the Biblical Genre You Are Reading

If your son were to come home from school and claim to have a ton of homework, you would not discipline him for lying. You would understand that he is using hyperbole to express his strong emotions. In the same way, we need to approach the Bible as sympathetic readers, respecting the various genres and authorial assumptions that accompany such genres. For example, the genre of proverbs generally assumes exceptions. Proverbs are wise advice, not fail-proof promises. For example, we read in Proverbs 10:4, "Lazy hands make a man poor, but diligent hands bring wealth." All of us can think of examples from our lives that confirm this proverb. At the same time, most of us likely know a few lazy, rich people. Such exceptions do not make the proverb false. Rather, such exceptions confirm the general rule. Proverbs 10:4 is not a promissory note. Proverbs offer wise advice for ordering our lives, but most of them assume exceptions. For more detail on interpreting proverbs, see question 28 ("How do we interpret proverbs?").

The genre of historical narrative also includes a number of authorial assumptions. For example, the biblical authors employ historical narrative to report many events of which they do not necessarily approve. The author of Judges clearly does not think sacrificing one's daughter is a good thing (Judg. 11), though he fails to comment on Jephthah's actions in the immediate context. The repeated cycle of disobedience in Judges, along with the summary statement ("In those days Israel had no king; everyone did as he saw fit"

[Judg. 21:25]), cue the reader that both God and the author are not pleased with Jephthah's actions. Similarly, many Scriptures teach that drunkenness is wrong, though the apostle John does not feel the need to note its impropriety in John 2:10, where there is a passing reference to inebriation. (A friend once appealed to John 2:10 to make a "biblical" case for excessive drinking!) The author of a historical narrative does not always give explicit sanction or condemnation for behavior reported. A careful reading of the whole work is often necessary to understand the purpose of smaller portions. One must thoughtfully determine what is simply reported and what is intended as normative. For more detail on interpreting historical narrative, see question 22 ("How do we interpret historical narrative?").

The study and application of interpretive guidelines for various genres is sometimes called the field of special hermeneutics. Much of the latter half of this book is devoted to special hermeneutics.

Be Aware of Historical or Cultural Background Issues

The sixty-six books of the Bible often assume a reader's familiarity with various cultural practices, geographic markers, or political figures. Thus, when an untrained reader opens up the book of Isaiah and starts reading about nations that no longer exist and obscure political alliances, he or she might close the Bible and say, "This is too hard to understand." As with any historical document, the reader of the Bible will need study aids to delve into the nuances of background issues. Of course, some of the books of the Bible assume little knowledge on the part of the reader and are quite accessible. The Gospel of John, for example, is often distributed as a stand-alone evangelistic tract for this reason. Depending on one's familiarity with the Scripture, some background issues may be more or less transparent. Do you know what Passover is? Then you shouldn't have trouble with John the Baptist's description of Jesus as the (Passover) lamb (John 1:29). Are you familiar with Israel's forty years of wandering the wilderness? Then Jesus' forty-day stay in the wilderness, where he was tested but did not sin, takes on added significance (Matt. 4:2; Luke 4:2).

As you study the Bible more, you will have less need to consult commentaries or study aids for the answers to basic questions. There are many introductory surveys of the Old and New Testaments, as well as books specifically on backgrounds, which provide a wealth of information to the curious student. See question 13 ("What are some helpful books or tools for interpreting the Bible?") for additional discussion on how to use outside books in studying the Bible.

In discussing Bible backgrounds, we also must note two important caveats. First, one can become so enamored with outside historical, cultural, political, or archaeological matters that he essentially ends up using the Bible as a springboard for extrabiblical trivia. The study of ancient Near Eastern culture, while fascinating in its own right, is not the purpose of Bible study. Not a few resources billed as helps for understanding the background of the Bible are little more than collations of interesting facts and speculations about tangentially related background issues. One must always ask: Did the biblical author really assume that his readers would know this fact? And, if he assumed his readers would know this fact, was it important for the meaning that he was trying to convey? If the answer to both of these questions is yes, then the background issue is indeed worthy of consideration.

Recently, a former student called to ask about Mark 3:13–19, where Jesus calls his twelve apostles. The student said, "I read that all Jewish boys were trained to be rabbis, and if they performed well enough, then they became disciples of rabbis and eventually rabbis themselves. So, in this passage, Jesus' disciples should be understood as those who had been rejected by conventional rabbinic training. I plan to preach this passage as emphasizing that Jesus chooses persons who have failed. Am I on track?" I responded, "There are passages of Scripture that speak of God choosing the lowly and rejected in this world (1 Cor. 1:26–27), but I do not think that the inspired author, Mark, is emphasizing that point here. In what book did you read this explanation of the background of Mark 3? (Student answers . . .) Have you read a similar explanation in any other reference work or commentary? (Student answers, "No.") That alone should cause you to pause and question whether there is a basis for interpreting this text in light of background information that is not found in any text in the Bible. It appears the source from which you have gathered this information has, at the very least, oversimplified and distorted its description of first-century rabbinic training. Second, and more importantly, Mark does not in any way cue his readers that he intends us to understand this passage as teaching that Jesus chose persons rejected by other rabbis. Does the passage speak of Jesus' effective call, his demand for radical discipleship, and his delegated authority? Yes! Then preach and teach the meaning of the text—not a fanciful, distorted reconstruction of a background issue."[1] Unfortunately, in attempts to provide something fresh to their congregations, too many pastors are readily taken in by far-fetched interpretations. A pastor's time would be better spent meditating prayerfully on the text to discover genuine text-driven applications.

A second error one must avoid in background issues is to neglect them. In order to understand and apply a text faithfully, one often must have some awareness of the author's historical or cultural assumptions. One cannot understand the denunciations in the Minor Prophets, for example, without knowing something of Israel's history and relations to surrounding nations. And, while much of this historical background can be garnered directly from

---

1. This report of our conversation represents the tenor and main points, not the verbatim words.

other biblical documents, an uninitiated reader will need the help of a more mature reader's summaries. A study Bible, such as *The Zondervan NIV Study Bible* or *ESV Study Bible,* provides brief but helpful comments on relevant background issues.

Pay Attention to Context

Any portion of Scripture must be read within the context of the sentence, paragraph, larger discourse unit, and entire book. The farther one moves away from the words in question, the less informative is the adduced material. Attempting to understand or apply a particular biblical phrase or verse without reference to the literary context is virtually guaranteed to result in distortion. Unfortunately, in popular Christian literature and preaching, there are many examples of such failure to respect the context of a passage. One of the most painful exhibits of such hermeneutical failure is a preacher who bullies and blusters about the authority and inerrancy of Scripture while practically denying its authority through his sloppy preaching.

If one is asked to deliver a message on 1 Corinthians 11:1 ("Follow my example, as I follow the example of Christ."), he should not simply meditate on the verse in question but begin by setting the verse in the context of Paul's argument in 1 Corinthians. Paul has been speaking of his voluntary self-denial as an apostle (1 Cor. 9:1–12) as an example for the Corinthians, whom he is calling to deny themselves of permissible food that might cause a Christian brother or sister to sin (1 Cor. 8:9–13). Paul's concern for the spread of the gospel compels him to find every way to avoid placing an obstacle in its way. No one can charge him with being motivated by greed, for he preaches without pay (1 Cor. 9:12–18). Similarly, the Corinthian Christians' concern for the spiritual well-being of others means they should be willing to forego permissible things for the spiritual benefit of others. Indeed, Christ is the supreme example of one who set aside his rights and privileges for the salvation of others (1 Cor. 11:1; cf. Mark 10:45; Phil 2:6–11). Once we understand Paul's original meaning in context, it is easier to faithfully apply the text to our current situation. What permissible things are we being called to forego so as not to lead our weaker Christian brothers and sisters into sin? How can we give priority to the spiritual well-being and salvation of others rather than our own rights and privileges? Where are we being called to self-denial out of love for others, as were Paul, the Corinthians, and ultimately Christ?

It often has been said, "A text without a context is a pretext," meaning that a preacher will be inclined to infuse a text with his own biases if he does not allow the context to direct him to the authorial intent. I have found this true in my life. When I am given the opportunity to select a text for a sermon, I sometimes already have an idea of what I want to say. But, as I go back to the text and study it within context, prayerfully meditating over it, the direction of my message often shifts. Holding tightly to the text calls me back to the inspired author's meaning. I tell my students to hold onto the biblical text like a rider in a rodeo holds onto a bull. And, I also warn them that the only persons in the rodeo ring not on bulls are clowns. When preaching the Bible, I want to be able to place my finger on specific words and phrases in the text to justify my exhortations. I want the congregation to be persuaded by the words of Scripture, not by my rhetorical ability. The power of a sermon or Bible lesson lies in its faithfulness to the inspired text.

Read the Bible in Community

We live in an individualistic age. Yet God created us to live and worship and grow spiritually together in community. The author of Hebrews writes, "Let us not give up meeting together, as some are in the habit of doing, but let us encourage one another—and all the more as you see the Day approaching" (Heb. 10:25). Only as we live out our faith in Christ together do we come to understand with depth and clarity what God has done in and through us (Philem. 6). Similarly, we see that God has structured the church as a body and that every member of that body does not have the same function (Rom. 12:4–5). Some are more gifted as teachers (Rom. 12:7). Others are more gifted in showing mercy or serving in some other way (Rom. 12:8). While all God's people are called to read and meditate on his Word (Ps. 119:9, 105), some are specially gifted in explaining that Word and exhorting others to believe and obey it (Eph. 4:11–13). If we neglect God's grace to us in the gifting of other believers, how impoverished we will be! Reading the Bible with fellow believers helps us to gain insights that we would otherwise miss. Also, our brothers and sisters can guard us from straying into false interpretations and misapplications.

A few years ago I visited a nearby church where a student pastor was preaching. Honestly, his sermon was not very good. Yet this pastor had the habit of inviting trusted persons in the church to give him honest feedback on his message every week. When I visited that church several months later, the pastor's sermon was surprisingly good. Though it can be painful, when a pastor opens himself up to constructive criticism on his teaching and preaching, the fruit of his humility can be a harvest of faithful and engaging messages. Many mediocre preachers will continue to preach the same dull and errant sermons over their whole lifetimes because they are too proud to seek constructive feedback.

If a pastor does not feel that members in his church can provide him sufficient feedback, he likely underestimates the degree to which the Holy Spirit has distributed gifts within his congregation. Regardless, one can always consult the commentaries of trusted pastors and theologians as dialogue partners in seeking the meaning and application of a biblical text.

When one is sufficiently grounded in essential Christian doctrine, it also can be beneficial to read persons who are outside the orthodox and evangelical fold. See question 13 for which commentaries to buy and how to use them.

Begin the Journey of Becoming a More Faithful Interpreter

None of us can claim to be inerrant interpreters. No matter what academic degrees or experiences one has, every person stands before the Bible as a learner. Some are farther along on the journey, but that should not intimidate those who are just beginning the trip.

One way to begin the journey toward more faithful interpretation is to start small. By choosing one particular book of the Bible and spending focused time in it over a period of several weeks or months, one will begin to see the importance and benefit of careful Bible study. Make manageable goals on reading and studying the Bible. Possibly invite a friend or friends to make the sojourn alongside you. Bible study, like athletic training, is often furthered by the camaraderie and accountability of a group.

Rome was not built in a day, and a full-orbed knowledge of the Bible is not attainable through reading one book. I am reminded of a seminary student who told me that my semester-long Greek course was much more difficult than the course he could take at an extension center over five weekends. "Yes," I replied. "That is because in my class you are actually learning the material."

Sometimes, things are worth what you pay for them. To acquire a rich knowledge of Scripture, one must be willing to spend the time and energy in study. Indeed, with the psalmist, the modern student of Scripture will come to declare, "The law from your [the LORD's] mouth is more precious to me than thousands of pieces of silver and gold" (Ps. 119:72). See question 12 for more suggestions on how to improve as an interpreter of the Bible.

REFLECTION QUESTIONS

1. When you read the Bible, do you, either consciously or unconsciously, take into account the genre of the book you are reading?

2. With whom are you reading and discussing the Bible? How have you benefited from studying the Bible with others? If you are not studying the Bible in community, do you know of an existing small-group Bible study that you can join?

3. Can you think of an instance where additional historical or cultural background information aided you in understanding a biblical text?

4. Have you ever changed your view on what a text of the Bible means by studying the context more carefully? "A text without a context is a pretext." Can you think of an example or illustration of this maxim?

5. What next step can you take on the journey to becoming a more faithful interpreter?

FOR FURTHER STUDY

Carson, D. A. *New Testament Commentary Survey.* 6th ed. Grand Rapids: Baker, 2007.

Fee, Gordon D., and Douglas Stuart. *How to Read the Bible for All Its Worth.* 3rd ed. Grand Rapids: Zondervan, 2003.

Ferguson, Everett. *Backgrounds of Early Christianity.* 2nd ed. Grand Rapids: Eerdmans, 1993.

Glynn, John. *Commentary and Reference Survey: A Comprehensive Guide to Biblical and Theological Resources.* 10th ed. Grand Rapids: Kregel, 2007.

Longenecker, Bruce W. *The Lost Letters of Pergamum.* Grand Rapids: Baker, 2003.

Longman, Tremper. *Old Testament Commentary Survey.* 4th ed. Grand Rapids: Baker, 2007.

How Can I Improve as an Interpreter of the Bible?

In the previous section, one of the interpretive guidelines I recommended was to begin the journey of becoming a more faithful interpreter. But what specific steps can you take toward becoming a more faithful interpreter?

Read the Bible

When I was thirteen years old, my mother gave me a photocopy of a hand-written guide for reading the Bible through in a year. Thus began the most important part of my theological education—immersion in Scripture.

In order to understand the Bible, one must read it. And, in order to read the individual parts of the Bible in context, one must read the whole. Thus, it is essential for any faithful interpreter of the Bible to have read the entire Bible and to continue to read through the Bible regularly. Can you imagine a teacher of Milton who admitted to having read only portions of *Paradise Lost*? How foolish it is for a minister of the gospel to seek faithfulness in expounding God's Word while remaining ignorant of the contents of that revelation.

During my freshman year in college, I attended a Bible study run by a campus ministry. The group was discussing John 3:14, "Just as Moses lifted up the snake in the desert, so the Son of Man must be lifted up." The leader of the Bible study said this verse referred to Moses picking up the serpent (which had been his rod) by the tail at the burning bush (Exod. 4:1–4). Of course, because I had already read through the Bible several times, I knew this passage referred to the bronze serpent in Numbers 21:9. I decided not to return to the campus gathering. Unfortunately, at this point in my life, my mental knowledge of the Bible far exceeded my obedience.

For reading large sections of the Bible, I recommend a modern, dynamically equivalent translation, such as the *New Living Translation* (see question 7, "Which is the best English Bible translation?"). You can start at Genesis 1 and read three or four chapters per day. By the end of the year, you will have finished the Bible. Another option is to read portions of both the Old and New Testament every day. The famous Scottish preacher Robert Murray M'Cheyne developed a reading plan that takes one through the Old Testament once and New Testament and Psalms twice over the course of a year—reading about four chapters per day. I am currently following this reading plan, which is found in an introductory section of D. A. Carson's devotional, *For the Love of God: A Daily Companion for Discovering the Riches of God's Word* (Wheaton, IL: Crossway, 1998). This book has a one-page devotional for each day of the year. At the top of each page is a list of Bible chapters to read for that day, according to M'Cheyne's reading plan. Carson, a leading evangelical New Testament scholar, provides insightful reflections on one chapter from the reading plan each day. Carson also has completed a second volume, *For the Love of God*, vol. 2, which follows the same format. I appreciate the way he faithfully interprets the passages while showing how the small pieces fit in the overall vista of Scripture, finding ultimate fulfillment in Christ. Our church leaders have talked about using Carson's devotional for training new elders. Over the course of a year or two, the bite-size chunks of biblical theology, slowly digested, could have quite a beneficial effect on the thoughtful reader.

Read and Listen to Faithful Preaching and Teaching

As I mentioned in question 10, faithful interpretation is more easily caught than taught. By reading or listening to faithful expositions of Scripture, one's heart and mind are engaged. Just as the person who regularly drinks fine coffee develops a refined taste for the beverage, a person who consumes a regular diet of faithful teaching develops a mind and heart that is able to recognize good interpretation, as well as distortions.

One of the most important questions you need to ask yourself is, "Am I hearing the Bible faithfully preached and taught at my local church?" If you are not, the second question you should ask yourself is, "Why am I a member of a church where God's Word is not being taught correctly?" If you are not experiencing the edifying and sanctifying effects of biblical teaching, you are likely withering and ineffective in your spiritual life (Col. 1:28–29; 2 Peter 1:3–8). If you are receiving a regular diet of biblical edification but only from source(s) outside your church, that is a good indication that you need to seek a new church—one where the pastors faithfully shepherd the flock, feeding them from the Word of God (Acts 20:28).

Although a local church where the Bible is faithfully taught is an absolute necessity, one can also grow spiritually from reading or listening to the sermons and Bible teaching of those outside your local church. Free audio sermons are widely available on the Web. Two Web sites I recommend are www.truthforlife.org (teaching by Alistair Begg) and www.desiringgod.org

(teaching by John Piper and others). There are, of course, many other gifted, faithful preachers to whom you can listen.

One also can learn much from reading sermons, commentaries, and devotionals by faithful exegetes. Certainly, the Bible is *The* Book, but God's gifting of his servants demands that we admit the usefulness of others' books as well. The famous British preacher, Charles Spurgeon (1834–1892), wrote:

> Some, under pretense of being taught of the Spirit of God, refuse to be instructed by books or by living men. This is no honoring of the Spirit of God; It is disrespect to Him, for if He gives to some of His servants more light than to others—and it is clear He does—then they are bound to give that light to others, and to use it for the good of the church. But if the other part of the church refuse to receive that light, to what end did the Spirit of God give it? This would imply that there is a mistake somewhere in the economy of God's gifts and graces, which is managed by the Holy Spirit.[1]

One way to discover useful books or resources is to ask a trusted fellow Christian. Maybe there is someone in your church who has demonstrated a mature knowledge of the Scriptures. Why not ask that person, "What good books have you read recently? Do you have any book recommendations?" For additional advice about books that will help with your Bible study, see question 13 ("What are some helpful books or tools for interpreting the Bible?").

Understand the Relationship Between Faith and Understanding

The early church leader Augustine (A.D. 354–430) advised, *Crede, ut intelligas* ("Believe in order that you may understand").[2] Similarly, Anselm (ca. 1033–1109) said, "For I do not seek to understand in order to believe; I believe in order to understand. For I also believe that 'Unless I believe, I shall not understand.'"[3] God demands that we approach him in faith and receive his revelation with trust. Indeed, to reject God's revelation is nothing other than calling God a liar (1 John 1:10); it is the embracing of idolatry, the exaltation of something or someone above God (Rom. 1:18–32).

This does not mean that you cannot come to God with the honesty of your emotions and questions. The lament psalms (e.g., Pss. 13, 74, 142) are prime examples of such raw honesty before God. Indeed, roughly one-third of the psalms express lament. But even in the midst of darkness, questions,

---

1. Charles Spurgeon, *Words of Counsel for Christian Workers* (Pasadena, TX: Pilgrim Publications, 1985), 112–13.
2. Augustine, *Homilia* 43.7, 9.
3. Anselm, *Proslogion* 1.1. The English translation is from Anselm, *Basic Writings*, ed. and trans. Thomas Williams (Indianapolis: Hackett, 2007), 81. At the end of this quotation, Anselm cites the Old Latin version of Isaiah 7:9.

and trials, the psalmist consistently affirms, "But as for me, I trust in you" (Ps. 55:23).

The Scriptures demand that humans approach God in a humble attitude of dependence. What other posture could finite creatures take before their infinite, holy, and all-powerful Creator? The author of Hebrews warns, "And without faith it is impossible to please God, because anyone who comes to him must believe that he exists and that he rewards those who earnestly seek him" (Heb. 11:6). Like the father who brought his demon-possessed son to Jesus for healing, we may have to cry with honesty, "I do believe; help me overcome my unbelief!" (Mark 9:24).

As we seek God's assistance to understand, believe, and obey the Scriptures, a posture of humble faith is absolutely essential. James writes:

> If any of you lacks wisdom, he should ask God, who gives generously to all without finding fault, and it will be given to him. But when he asks, he must be-lieve and not doubt, because he who doubts is like a wave of the sea, blown and tossed by the wind. That man should not think he will receive anything from the Lord; he is a double-minded man, unstable in all he does. (James 1:5–8)

Likewise, because obedience is the fruit of genuine faith (James 2:14–26), God expects his children to walk before him in a manner worthy of their calling (Eph. 4:1). Indeed, if a professed Christian does not have a lifestyle of obedience (and repentance for his failures), his relationship with the Lord will be hindered. A consistently unrepentant lifestyle of sin shows that one's profession of faith is false (1 John 1:6).

Peter warns, "Husbands, in the same way be considerate as you live with your wives, and treat them with respect as the weaker partner and as heirs with you of the gracious gift of life, so that nothing will hinder your prayers" (1 Peter 3:7). A pastor who is unloving and nonsacrificial toward his wife and children can expect little illumination from the Holy Spirit in the study or the pulpit. "Without holiness, no one will see the Lord" (Heb. 12:14), warns the au-thor of Hebrews.[4] Without lives lived in faith and obedience (though certainly full of failure and repentance too; 1 John 1:8–10), we can expect little divine assistance in understanding and explaining the Scriptures. In fact, when Paul lists the qualifications of pastors, all but one are character qualities—living in integrity before the church and the world (1 Tim. 3:1–7; Titus 1:5–9).[5] The men who explain God's Word to the gathered church must be people who live according to that Word.

---

4. Though the author of Hebrews appears to be referring to one's standing before the Lord at the final judgment, the statement is equally true in this life.
5. The only skill or non-character quality listed is having the ability to teach (1 Tim. 3:2; Titus 1:9).

After teaching his disciples a model prayer (the Lord's Prayer), Jesus warns, "For if you forgive men when they sin against you, your heavenly Father will also forgive you. But if you do not forgive men their sins, your Father will not forgive your sins" (Matt. 6:14–15). We may be able to recite a systematic theology text from memory, but if our lives are devoid of the love and faith we profess, we are nothing but clanging gongs or clattering cymbals—empty, annoying noisemakers (1 Cor. 13:1).

When Paul begins his letter to Philemon, he writes, "I always thank my God as I remember you in my prayers, because I hear about your faith in the Lord Jesus and your love for all the saints" (Philem. 4–5). Here are the essential prerequisites for biblical study that pleases God—faith in the Lord Jesus and love for others.

Do Not Just Affirm Sound Interpretive Principles; Apply Them

At the seminary where I teach, there is a large, grassy lawn in the middle of the campus. Decades ago, two parallel sidewalks ran through the middle of this lawn. Though the sidewalks have been gone for years, in the hot summer months, two brown stripes reappear in the lawn. Why does the grass continue to turn brown? Possibly it is because the dirt was packed underneath the sidewalks or perhaps it is due to the chemicals used on the sidewalks for weed control. Regardless, the memory of these sidewalks is hard to erase. Similarly, students may come to affirm sound principles of interpretation in a hermeneutics class, but in the heat of regular ministry old patterns continue to surface.

Modern ministers are not the only ones who struggle for consistency in their theoretical and practical hermeneutical methods. Historians of biblical interpretation often note that proponents of sound interpretation throughout church history have failed to consistently apply their own advice. For all his denunciations of allegorical exegesis, Martin Luther sometimes fell prey to it himself.[6] Similarly, Augustine enumerated several helpful principles of exegesis that he did not consistently employ.[7]

A student taking a course in biblical interpretation can get perfect scores on all the tests and assignments and still end up failing to faithfully interpret the Bible in his or her ministry. Once the student is out of the artificial environment of the classroom, he will discover what many ministers have before him, that it is much harder work to prepare a faithful Bible study or sermon than to talk spontaneously about what he thinks people need to hear.

One of the saddest legacies of a ministry that fails to handle God's Word correctly is a congregation that is spiritually starving and confused.

---

6. Robert H. Stein, *The Method and Message of Jesus' Teachings*, rev. ed. (Louisville, KY: Westminster John Knox, 1994), 48.
7. So judges Bernard Ramm, *Protestant Biblical Interpretation: A Textbook of Hermeneutics*, 3rd ed. (Grand Rapids: Baker, 1970), 37.

Over time, rather than learning how to understand the Bible, a congregation that sits under an unfaithful interpreter will learn how to misinterpret
the Bible. As children and grandchildren are affected, potentially hundreds,
if not thousands, of people are led into error and spiritual malaise. In considering the devastation that one bad preacher can cause, it is little wonder
that James warns us, "Not many of you should presume to be teachers, my
brothers, because you know that we who teach will be judged more strictly"
(James 3:1).

An unfaithful interpreter also can create a spiritual codependency—a
situation in which people feel they must come to the pastor to understand the
text because they are never able to see on their own the things he emphasizes
in his teaching. These poor, starving infants who should have been fed on the
pure milk of the Word (1 Peter 2:2) stare with gaunt eyes at the pulpit each
week, hoping that manna will fall from heaven.

Welcome and Receive Feedback Graciously

The main teaching pastor at my church has the habit of e-mailing his
sermon to five or six trusted friends on Saturday night. We have the responsibility of giving him correction and encouragement on his message. Often, I
have little to say, but occasionally my words have kept him from error.

When I first started preaching, I would always ask my wife to read my
sermon. Sometimes her criticisms were quite withering, and I did not want to
hear them; but after reflection, I usually came around to agree with her.

If you want to know the truth about your teaching—both at the level of
interpretation and delivery—you are going to have to ask. And it is likely you
are going to have to ask several times and make it clear that you are not going
to strike back or hold it against people if they tell you the truth. It is probably
best to decide beforehand exactly what you will say. You can rehearse the interchange in your mind. For example, here are some words you can adapt to
your setting.

> I'm a bit nervous to ask you this because I know I have room to improve,
> but I was wondering if you could e-mail me your honest feedback on my
> sermon. I want to be a more faithful interpreter and better communicator,
> and I believe you can help me. Please feel free to offer any advice at all. Do
> not be afraid to offer criticisms. That is what I want.

Also, decide beforehand not to defend yourself. Respond only with
thanksgiving—even if you feel that some of the advice was misguided or un-
justified. If you seek to defend yourself, do not expect to ever get honest feedback again from the person to whom you are responding.

If you feel sheepish about opening yourself up to criticism from someone
in your current setting, possibly you can e-mail your sermon or Bible lesson

to an old friend from college or seminary. Ideally, you should move toward asking those in your current setting. Over time, you can develop a trusted cadre of advisers and rejoice to see their interpretive skill developing along with your own. Possibly God will raise up other leaders to share the teaching ministry through these relationships.

As you seek the help of others in growing as an interpreter, here are two proverbs on which to meditate.

- *Proverbs 27:17:* "As iron sharpens iron, so one man sharpens another."

- *Proverbs 24:26:* "An honest answer is like a kiss on the lips."

Acquire and Employ Bible Study Tools

Erasmus, a church leader in the sixteenth century, said, "When I get a little money, I buy books; and if any is left, I buy food and clothes."[8] We can be thankful that we don't live in such lean days, but a diligent student of the Bible will make it a priority to purchase books to aid in his or her study of the Scriptures.

Besides acquiring several modern translations of the Bible (see question 7, "Which is the best English Bible translation?"), your first purchase probably should be a good study Bible. A study Bible will not only give you a helpful overview of each book but also provide verse notes to help you understand more obscure statements. The notes in a study Bible obviously will exhibit the doctrinal biases of the persons writing those notes. For that reason, I recommend the *Zondervan NIV Study Bible* and the *ESV Study Bible* (Crossway). Both are respected works whose notes represent the broad consensus of evangelical scholarship.

As you continue your study of the Scriptures and are seeking more in-depth study aids, consult question 13, "What are some helpful books or tools for interpreting the Bible?"

Pass on What You Are Learning

In the spiritual life, you are either a stagnant pool or a flowing fountain. If you are learning but not sharing what you are learning, you will be like an algae-covered pond. Much of the advice above has assumed that the readers of this book are engaged in or aspire to some public ministry. Possibly you don't see yourself in public ministry. Yet, when it comes to the Bible, all of

---

8. This is Erasmus' supposed quip, as it is often repeated. The closest wording I could locate in his published works reads: "The first thing I shall do, as soon as the money arrives, is to buy some Greek authors; after that, I shall buy clothes" (Letter 124, "To Jacob Batt, Paris, 12 April [1500]," in *The Correspondence of Erasmus, Letters 1 to 141, 1484 to 1500*, trans. R. A. B. Mynors and D. F. S. Thomson [Toronto: University of Toronto Press: 1974], 1:252).

God's people are to overflow with the truths they are learning. Even if your conversations about the Bible are with your children, spouse, and neighbors, you should be seeking to share the new insights you are learning about God.

REFLECTION QUESTIONS

1. Is reading the Bible your daily practice? If not, why not start today?

2. Is the Bible taught faithfully at your church? Are you and your family being edified and challenged by Scripture there?

3. If you currently teach or preach the Bible, do you have a method for receiving feedback on your teaching?

4. Do you own a study Bible? If so, who is the publisher? What is the stated aim of your study Bible notes?

5. What relationships do you have that allow you to share what you are learning from the Bible?

FOR FURTHER STUDY

ESV Study Bible. Wheaton, IL: Crossway, 2008.
Zondervan NIV Study Bible. Rev. ed. Edited by Kenneth L. Barker, et al. Grand
  Rapids: Zondervan, 2008.

What Are Some Helpful Books or Tools for Interpreting the Bible?

As a New Testament professor, I am often asked for advice on word study tools and commentaries. Certainly, I am an advocate of having excellent tools to aid in Bible study, but in order to orient ourselves properly before delving into this question, let us begin with two quotes from the Puritan pastor Richard Baxter (1615–1691).

> Make careful choice of the books which you read. *Let the holy Scriptures ever have the pre-eminence*; and, next [to] them, the solid, lively, heavenly treatises, which best expound and apply the Scriptures; and next [to] those, the credible histories, especially of the church . . . but take heed of the poison of the writings of false teachers, which would corrupt your understandings.[1]

> *It is not the reading of many books which is necessary to make a man wise or good; but the well reading of a few*, could he be sure to have the best. And it is not possible to read over very many on the same subjects, without a great deal of loss of precious time.[2]

Two things stand out in these quotes: the preeminence of Scripture and the necessity of having discernment in which books to consult. In this question, we will assume the priority of Scripture and move on to give advice on which particular books to acquire in various categories.

---

1. Richard Baxter, "A Christian Directory," part I ("Christian Ethics"), chapter II, Direct XVI, in *The Practical Works of Richard Baxter* (London: George Virtue, 1846; reprint, Morgan, PA: Soli Deo Gloria, 2000), 1:56 (my emphasis).
2. Richard Baxter, "A Christian Directory," part III ("Christian Ecclesiastics"), "Ecclesiastical Cases of Conscience," Question 174, in *The Practical Works of Richard Baxter* (London: George Virtue, 1846; reprint, Morgan, PA: Soli Deo Gloria, 2000), 1:731 (my emphasis).

Study Bibles

A study Bible provides extensive notes on the text of Scripture. Such Bibles often advocate a certain theological perspective (e.g., *The Reformation Study Bible, The Spirit-Filled Life Study Bible*), or a concern for the questions of a particular demographic subgroup (e.g., *Woman's Study Bible, Military Study Bible*), or the investigation of questions from the vantage point of a certain theological discipline (*The Apologetics Study Bible, The Archaeological Study Bible*), or the influence of a certain prominent Christian teacher (*The MacArthur Study Bible* [John MacArthur], *The New Inductive Study Bible* [Kay Arthur]). For a young Christian, a study Bible can be very helpful by providing brief summaries and historical backgrounds for each book of the Bible, supplying discussion of difficult and debated texts, and offering cross-references and indices. Wrongly used, a study Bible can provide a crutch that discourages Christians from thinking about and wrestling with texts for themselves. Also, if a person purchases a study Bible from an avowed theological perspective, one faces the danger of letting theological predilections take priority over the text of Scripture.

If you are seeking a study Bible that represents the broad consensus of evangelical scholarship, it is difficult to do much better than *The Zondervan NIV Study Bible* or *The ESV Study Bible*.

Concordances

A concordance is an index for the Bible. An exhaustive concordance lists every occurrence of every word in the Bible. (Yes, even the words *the* and *and*!) Many people who grew up using the King James Version (KJV) are familiar with *Strong's Concordance*, an exhaustive concordance of the KJV compiled by James Strong (1822–1894) and first published in 1890. Concordances are available for all major English Bible translations, and if you purchase a concordance, you should get one for the translation you regularly use. Because of their attempt to consistently translate the underlying Greek or Hebrew words, formally equivalent (word-for-word) translations (for example, the New American Standard Bible or the English Standard Version) are easier to use with a concordance. Properly employed, a concordance allows one not only to find the repetition of the same word in the English translation but also to determine the underlying Greek or Hebrew word. (Greek and Hebrew words are assigned numbers so that those who do not know these languages can trace the repetition of the words throughout Scripture.)

In using a concordance, those with a limited knowledge of linguistics can make wrong assumptions about how to apply their recognition of repeated words. For example, a basic principle of linguistics is that words have a range of meaning and that the immediate context is the most important determiner of meaning. With a concordance, a beginning interpreter could illegitimately force the contextual nuances of a word in one occurrence onto other passages. With appropriate caveats, however, a concordance can be a helpful tool. Any decent

Bible software program also will have a search feature that functions like an exhaustive concordance (see below on software programs).

Word Study Tools

Never before in the history of Christianity has there been less need for word studies. With the multiplicity of many excellent modern English Bible translations, readers of the Bible have the fruit of scholars' painstaking research. At the same time, it is a healthy desire for Christians to want to suck the marrow from every word of Scripture. However, as noted above, an uninformed linguistic euphoria can result in distortions of the text, rather than greater understanding. The following represents two common dangers regarding word studies.

1. *Illegitimate Totality Transfer.* All words have a range of meaning, and the nuances of each particular use cannot be read into all other uses of the word. That is, if the reader takes the totality of what a word *can* mean and reads that potentiality as a reality in every word occurrence, he has illegitimately transferred the totality of what the word means onto each instance (thus, the label "illegitimate totality transfer"). People tolerate erroneous linguistic approaches to the Bible that they would never accept in ordinary speech. For example, imagine the howls one would encounter if he said, "You just used the word *cell* to describe your phone. By that, I take it that your phone is a small room of incarceration, that your phone is a wireless device, and that your phone is a microscopic blob of protoplasm." Obviously, only one of the potential meanings of "cell" is intended. Yet, how many times have we heard a similar litany of potential meanings from a preacher presented as "the real meaning" of a word in the Bible? One can see the danger of tools like *The Amplified Bible,* which provides several possible meanings of most words. Without further instruction, such tools lead one down the path of illegitimate totality transfer.

2. *Etymological Fallacy.* Etymology is the study of the ancestry of words. Thus, the etymological fallacy is to wrongly believe that knowing the history of a word gives us deeper insight into its current meaning. There have been periods in biblical scholarship when even well-trained scholars were taken in by the siren song of etymology. More commonly, in popular preaching, one hears the etymology of a word sometimes given as "what this word really means." To illustrate the foolishness of the etymological fallacy to my classes, I give examples from the English language. For example:

   - When you hear the word *tuxedo,* undoubtedly, you think of the Algonquian Indian word for "wolf," from which the word *tuxedo* was derived. Unconsciously, you almost hear yourself saying, "There goes that dapper wolf!"

- When your neighbor speaks of spraying herbicide on dandelions in his yard, you think about the underlying French words *dent de lion* ("tooth of the lion"). You might ask, "Those roaring weeds are sinking their sharp incisors into your lawn again, eh?"

- Your wife says that she is cooking lasagna for supper. You can't help recalling that the word *lasagna* ultimately derives from the Greek term for "chamber potty" (*lasonon*). "Going to dish us up another one from the toilet?" you innocently ask.

The reality is that words mean what the writers intended for them to mean in the historical context in which they were written. The ordinary use of language (a word's potential range of meaning) constrains the possible meanings unless the author clearly points out that he is using a word differently from the way it would normally be understood. Thus, in the early twenty-first century, to say that someone is wearing "gay clothing" (without further qualification) means something quite different from what it meant when the translators of the KJV chose that expression when translating James 2:3 in the early seventeenth century.

In spite of all these warnings against the misuse of word studies, they can be helpful in clarifying the nuances of important words. In the case of a very rare word where we have few or no other instances of the word in the same time period, it can be legitimate to appeal to etymology to help us determine its meaning. Also, proper names (the names of people or places) often are presented in Scripture as informed by their etymology.[3] The most reliable and accessible word study tool for those lacking knowledge of Greek and Hebrew may be *Mounce's Complete Expository Dictionary of Old and New Testament Words*. For more detail, see *The New International Dictionary of Old Testament Theology and Exegesis* and *The New International Dictionary of New Testament Theology*.

Commentaries

Commentaries are books that explain the text of Scripture, usually in a verse-by-verse or paragraph-by-paragraph method. There are one-volume commentaries on the whole Bible,[4] but the most extensive and thoughtful

---

3. See Robert H. Stein, *A Basic Guide to Interpreting the Bible: Playing by the Rules* (Grand Rapids: Baker, 1994), 173.
4. One of the best one-volume Bible commentaries is *The New Bible Commentary: 21st Century Edition*, ed. G. J. Wenham, J. A. Motyer, D. A. Carson, and R. T. France (Downers Grove, IL: InterVarsity Press, 1994).

reflections on Scripture can be found in monographs devoted to individual books of the Bible. Individual commentaries also sometimes focus on a few related books, such as the Johannine Epistles (1, 2, and 3 John) or the Pastoral Epistles (1 and 2 Timothy, Titus).

If one were to teach through Romans, the careful teacher should obtain several good commentaries on Romans to read in his weekly preparation. At their best, commentaries function as a virtual community of other believers dialoguing with the teacher about the text. A Christian teacher was not meant to function in isolation or to refuse the beneficial input of other Spirit-gifted teachers in the church. At the most fundamental level, a commentary guards a teacher from idiosyncratic interpretations. Indeed, if you are the only person to understand a biblical passage in a certain way, you are almost certainly wrong.

A number of caveats about commentaries should be noted.

1. Pastors or diligent laypersons are sometimes eager to obtain a complete commentary series, that is, a set produced under the same series title by one publisher. While such a commentary set looks nice with the matching dust jackets on one's shelf (and gives the air of erudition to the owner), it is better to purchase individual volumes based on the quality of the scholarship. Commentaries within the same series can vary greatly in quality. Money spent to acquire mediocre or poor work is money wasted. I own several complete commentary series, but they were all acquired at a great discount.

2. Studious Christians often are attracted to software programs that promise hundreds of commentaries and/or the ability to acquire other commentaries electronically. Nevertheless, if one does not currently prefer to read books on the computer, he should be forewarned of spending money to buy a digital library. Moreover, many of the titles that come as standard on some Bible software programs are volumes already in the public domain (likely available as free downloads on Web sites) or works of limited scholarly value. To truly get the best commentaries, one will usually have to pay—whether for a digital copy or bound book. I do have one complete Bible commentary series loaded onto the hard drive of my laptop computer, *The Expositor's Bible Commentary* (Zondervan). This set also comes in hard copy as twelve volumes. I like having this series in digital format for two reasons. First, when I am traveling with my computer, I am sure to have access to at least one generally helpful commentary on any book of the Bible. Second, in giving quick replies to e-mails about particular passages of the Bible, I sometimes save time by pasting in a portion of the commentary (with adequate citation, of course).

3. Christians are advised to build their libraries slowly and thoughtfully. Every time you begin the detailed study of a new book in the Bible, you should consult one of two guidebooks to determine which individual commentaries to purchase: Tremper Longman's *Old Testament Commentary Survey* or D. A. Carson's *New Testament Commentary Survey*.[5] These texts are filled with excellent advice and are also worth skimming in their entirety for their more general suggestions on acquiring and using commentaries.

4. Many pastors and professors have bookshelves full of tomes they have never read and never will read. Money to acquire books you will never read is better spent on more productive things. There are many ways to acquire needed books in an affordable fashion. Be creative and diligent. You will prize the fruit of your frugality.

Software Programs

Software programs are helpful for studying the Bible in two areas:

1. *Navigating the text of the Bible.* If you have some training in Greek or Hebrew, software programs have some incredible, time-saving features—linking lexicons, diagramming the texts, allowing morphological searches, etc. In my opinion, the best programs are Bibleworks (my personal favorite), Accordance (for Mac users), Logos/Libronix, and Gramcord. If you cannot use Greek or Hebrew but want software to search the English text, possibly a free program like E-sword would suffice (see www.e-sword.net).

2. *Providing helpful secondary texts.* Personally, I prefer bound volumes, but if you are a reader of digital books, the best software for a digital library is Logos/Libronix. Of the major theological publishers, only Zondervan does not make its titles available through Libronix.

Web Sites

Without endorsing all their content, a few Web sites I have found helpful for biblical and theological research are:

- www.biblegateway.com: to look up verses and compare Bible translations.

---

5. Tremper Longman, *Old Testament Commentary Survey*, 4th ed. (Grand Rapids: Baker, 2007); and D. A. Carson, *New Testament Commentary Survey*, 6th ed. (Grand Rapids: Baker, 2007). Also see John Glynn, *Commentary and Reference Survey: A Comprehensive Guide to Biblical and Theological Resources*, 10th ed. (Grand Rapids: Kregel, 2007).

- www.bible.org: for a variety of biblical and theological resources.

- www.desiringgod.org: John Piper's ministry Web site, with a variety of resources available.

- www.fpcjackson.org: for accessing hundreds of Ligon Duncan's sermon manuscripts.

- www.monergism.com: for resources from a Calvinistic perspective.

- www.theopedia.com: Wikipedia (online encyclopedia) for theology.

- www.equip.org: apologetics Web site run by "The Bible Answer Man," Hank Hanegraaff.

- www.watchman.org: an anticults Web site.

- www.4truth.net: apologetics Web site run by the North American Mission Board of the Southern Baptist Convention.

- www.ntgateway.com: a "scholarly index" for Web sites related to the New Testament.

- www.greekbible.com: for accessing the Greek New Testament with vocabulary and parsing helps.

- www.biblicalfoundations.org: helpful biblical reflections by New Testament scholar Andreas Köstenberger.

The amount of material available at the click of a mouse is nearly intoxicating. The wisdom of digested truth, however, is harder to find. The neophyte theologian must beware the dangers of plagiarism, superficial reading, and repeating the mistakes and misunderstandings of others.

Advanced Study

As one grows in skill as an interpreter of the Bible, he will also desire to study in other areas, such as systematic theology, practical ministry, church history, missiology, etc. Christian classics (works of a previous generation) should not be neglected; there is a reason such works have survived. Reading a modern summary of a classic text never compares with ruminating on the original. One springboard to more advanced study is to listen to one of the many high-quality audio lectures by leading evangelical scholars at the following two Web sites: www.biblicaltraining.org and www.worldwide-classroom.com.

REFLECTION QUESTIONS

1. What tools, besides a Bible, do you currently use in your study of Scripture?

2. Do you own any useful Bible study tools that you are failing to use? Why?

3. Of the resources discussed above, what are the top ones on your wish list of future acquisitions?

4. Have you ever engaged in any of the word study fallacies discussed above? Do you feel that you sufficiently understand the fallacies to avoid them in the future?

5. If someone were to ask you, "What book can you recommend to help me understand Ecclesiastes?" where would you go for trustworthy advice on relevant resources?

FOR FURTHER STUDY

BibleWorks Version 8.0: Software for Biblical Exegesis and Research. Bible-Works, LLC. 2009. See www.bibleworks.com.

Brown, Colin., ed. *New International Dictionary of New Testament Theology.* 4 vols. Grand Rapids: Zondervan, 1975, 1986.

Carson, D. A. *Exegetical Fallacies.* Grand Rapids: Baker, 198.4 (See "Word-Study Fallacies," 25–66).

_____. *New Testament Commentary Survey.* 6th ed. Grand Rapids: Baker, 2007.

The Expositor's Bible Commentary 5.0 (computer software). Edited by Frank E. Gæbelein, J. D. Douglas, and Richard P. Polcyn. Grand Rapids: Zondervan, 2003.

Glynn, John. *Commentary and Reference Survey: A Comprehensive Guide to Biblical and Theological Resources.* 10th ed. Grand Rapids: Kregel, 2007.

Longman, Tremper. *Old Testament Commentary Survey.* 4th ed. Grand Rapids: Baker, 2007.

Mounce, William D., ed. *Mounce's Complete Expository Dictionary of Old and New Testament Words.* Grand Rapids: Zondervan, 2006.

VanGemeren, Willem A., ed. *New International Dictionary of Old Testament Theology and Exegesis.* 5 vols. Grand Rapids: Zondervan, 1997.

Questions Related to Meaning

Who Determines the Meaning of a Text?

In any act of communication (a speech, conversation, handwritten letter, or e-mail), there are three elements: a writer or speaker, a text or spoken words, and a reader or listener.[1] In what way do these different parts of the communication process affect or determine meaning? Who or what is the final arbiter of meaning, assuming there is such an arbiter? Scholars reach highly divergent conclusions to these questions. We will survey the main approaches below, arguing for the author as the ultimate determiner of meaning.

The Reader as Determiner of Meaning

The dominant approach in the secular academy to interpreting literature highlights the reader as the ultimate determiner of meaning. According to this approach, even if the author were to stand up and say, "That's not what I meant," the reader would respond, "Who cares what you meant? This is the meaning *for me*." Such a reader-determined meaning is sometimes also called a reader-response approach to literature. (That is, each reader responds to the literature in the creation of meaning.) These reader-created meanings are at times self-consciously driven by various philosophical or social concerns (e.g., the Marxist reading, the feminist reading, the homosexual reading, the environmentalist reading, the liberationist reading). Other times, the reader may simply appeal to his or her idiosyncratic view without any reference to a broader social agenda. We should note that the reader-response approach to literature is *not* the reader discovering the author's meaning or the application

---

1. Of course, this is the main paradigm of communication, but there are related permutations—for example, with two deaf persons there would be a signer, the signs used, and the viewer of the signs. Or, with spies, there might be an encoder, the code used, and the decoder.

of the authorial meaning in the reader's life. The reader is the actual determiner or creator of meaning, with the exclusion of any external judge.[2]

Such an interpretive approach, of course, inevitably results in readers
proposing a variety of contradictory meanings. Adherents of the reader-response approach to literature would rather affirm various irreconcilable interpretations than suggest that one interpretation is more valid than another. A
rejection of absolutist statements underlies the reader-response approach. An
unwelcome sentence begins: "*The* meaning of this text is . . ." Permissible is:
"*To me*, this text means . . ." In a pluralistic and multicultural society, it is seen
as arrogant to claim final legitimacy for only one interpretation or opinion.

Another issue often underlying the reader-response approach to literature
is the assumption that language is an instrument of oppression or liberation.[3]
That is, texts are primarily used to assert power rather than to convey and
receive information. While it is true that texts, including the Bible, do bring
about action and change, one must be quite cynical to reduce the reading and
writing of texts to underhanded power plays.

As modern America is imbued by the reader-response approach to literature and the assumptions that underlie it, it is difficult not to be influenced
by it. In fact, many self-proclaimed Christian writers and scholars have adopted the reader-response approach in much the same way the early church
adopted the allegorical approach of the surrounding Greco-Roman culture
(see question 9, "How has the Bible been interpreted throughout church history?"). I will offer two examples of the reader-response approach to the Bible
from my everyday experiences.

1. In a children's Bible that was given to my daughter, the story of Joseph
   is followed by these questions: "Has anyone ever given you something
   like a new coat or sweater? How did it make you feel to put on the
   new clothes?"[4] It is clear that the author of this children's Bible values
   self-esteem and affirmation. Even though the writer of the biblical text
   obviously is not relating the story of Joseph to cause sentimental reflection on how others have affirmed us, the modern author of the chil-

---

2. Robin Parry offers this helpful caveat: "Reader-response theory is not a single theory but a
   family of diverse hermeneutical theories that share a focus on the *active role* of the reader
   (or communities of readers) in interpretation. The various theorists disagree on a range of
   issues: how much control texts exercise in interpretation, the role of communities within
   which readers live, the role of the interpretative histories of texts, whether the readers
   they speak of are experts or ordinary readers, and so on" ("Reader-Response Criticism,"
   in *Dictionary for Theological Interpretation of the Bible*, ed. Kevin J. Vanhoozer [Grand
   Rapids: Baker; London: SPCK, 2005], 658–59).
3. Technically, this assumption belongs more to deconstructionism, but the approaches
   overlap.
4. These are the questions as I recall them. We did not keep the Bible.

dren's Bible has used the story for this purpose. He or she has created meaning alien to the biblical author's intent. The issue is not whether the interpreter's point is valid (that is, encouraging sentimental reflections to build self-esteem). The issue is: what was the purpose, intent, or meaning of the inspired biblical author?

2. A while back, my wife and I met with a lady who had recently come to saving faith through a parachurch ministry but was still attending a largely unregenerate mainline church. She was puzzled because her pastor preached from Matthew 13:24–30 (the parable of the wheat and the weeds), encouraging parishioners to remove the weeds from their lives and tend the wheat. "But," the lady said in consternation, "when I look in my Bible, Jesus himself explains the parable and says the weeds are wicked people who are cast into hell!" (Matt. 13:37–43). The pastor at this lady's church likely found the doctrine of hell offensive, so he reinterpreted the parable to offer a more palatable message.

The Text as Determiner of Meaning

Another approach to communication that was popular in literary circles from the 1930s to the 1960s is to look to the text as the determiner of meaning.[5] Unlike the reader-response approach, the text-determined approach does accept an objective arbiter of meaning, but it is not the author. After the author finishes his work, the text is viewed as taking on a life of its own— containing meanings beyond the intent, and possibly contrary to the desire of, the original composer. Thus, knowing the historical setting and original addressees of a document is of no importance, according to this approach.

It is necessary to point out a few potential misunderstandings of the text-determined approach to meaning. First, most people who state, "The Bible says" are not advocating the text-determined approach to meaning. In saying, "The Bible says," the speaker usually means the same thing as, "The inspired biblical author says." Second, the text-determined view should not be confused with the normal interpretive process of proposing implications that go beyond the conscious thought of the author. For example, in Proverbs 23:10, the inspired author forbids stealing of a neighbor's property through moving

---

5. This interpretive approach is called the new criticism or Formalism. Michael E. Travers notes, "Philosophically, modern versions of formalism developed out of Immanuel Kant and aesthetically from the Romantic poets of the early nineteenth century. . . . In the United States, formalism received its classic expression in the New Criticism of the mid-twentieth century, in the works of such writers as Cleanth Brooks, John Crowe Ransom, Robert Penn Warren, and William Wimsatt. The term 'New Criticism' is to be understood in the context of their wish to move past the historical and biographical study of literature in American university classrooms of the day to a literary criticism that is more text-based" ("Formalism," in *Dictionary for Theological Interpretation of the Bible*, 230).

boundary stones. By implication, any other underhanded method to defraud your neighbor of his property is also forbidden. Though the ancient author of Proverbs was not thinking about the falsification of a land survey using a computer scanner, surely such behavior is also forbidden by implication. Such implications flow within the channel of meaning intended by the author at the time of his original composition.

A major criticism of text-determined meaning is that texts are inanimate objects—ink on paper, or scratches on stone.[6] Meaning, on the other hand, is a construction of intelligent thought. Texts can convey meaning, but texts cannot construct meaning. Constructing meaning is the role of the author. Meaning, ultimately then, lies in the purview of the author.

The Author as Determiner of Meaning

The final theory of communication (and the one I am advocating) is that the author of a text is the ultimate arbiter of its meaning.[7] Thus, as much as possible, it is important to study the historical setting and original addressee(s) of a document to understand better the author's intent and purpose in writing. At times, it may be difficult to determine the author's meaning, but that is the goal that all valid interpretation seeks. The role of the reader of a text, then, is to discover the author's consciously-intended meaning.

One of the main arguments for the author-determined approach to meaning is that this method is the commonsense approach to all communication. If your friend says, "I would like a hamburger for lunch," and you respond, "Why is it that you hate Caucasians?" the person would rightly respond, "Are you crazy? Did you not hear what I said?" Any act of communication can progress only on the assumption that someone is trying to convey meaning to us and we then respond to that meaning intended by the speaker or writer.

Objections to the Author as Determiner of Meaning

Below is a list of objections to the author as determiner of meaning, with responses following.

1. *We can never access the author's thoughts, so the authorial meaning of the text is inaccessible to us.*[8] It is true that we can never access the

---

6. Robert H. Stein, "The Benefits of an Author-Oriented Approach to Hermeneutics," *JETS* 44, no. 3 (2001): 53.

7. E. D. Hirsch, *Validity in Interpretation* (New Haven, CT: Yale University Press, 1967).

8. William K. Wimsatt Jr. and Monroe C. Beardsley, "The Intentional Fallacy," *Sewanee Review* 54 (1946): 468–88. Hirsch writes, "The argument that an interpreter's understanding is necessarily different because he is different assumes a psychologistic conception of meaning which mistakingly identifies meaning with mental processes rather than with an object of those processes" (*Validity in Interpretation*, 32).

private thoughts of an author. Right now, as I am typing on my computer keyboard, am I ambivalent or engaged in writing this book? Am I motivated by duty, devotion, or a desire for money or fame? You will never know. But, unless I am an incompetent writer, you are able to understand the meaning and intent of my writing. The multitude of thoughts and feelings I have while writing this book are of no import to the actual intent of my communication.[9] To seek the author's meaning is not to seek his private thoughts or feelings.

2. *An author's worldview might be so distant from our own that we can never claim to understand his meaning.*[10] This criticism might especially be offered for the Bible, where the most recent of its works is nearly two thousand years old. What this criticism fails to recognize, however, is the common nature shared by all human persons. As creatures in the image of God, humans are never so culturally different from each other that understanding is impossible. Cultures and times vary, but the rational human intellect is able to perceive and explain those differences.

3. *To seek the author's intended meaning makes the document irrelevant for modern readers.* This criticism fails to understand the relationship between meaning and implications (see question 15, "Can a text have more than one meaning?"). The meaning is the original, author-intended purpose of the document. The implications are those modern-day applications of the authorial principle in changing times and cultures. Defining clearly the authorial meaning creates a channel in which the interpreter's implications can safely flow.

4. *To delimit meaning to the conscious intent of the human author is to deny the divine authorship of Scripture.* Two responses can be offered to this criticism. First, for the vast majority of Scripture, the conscious human author's meaning and the divinely intended meaning are indistinguishable. When Paul said, "Do everything without complaining or arguing" (Phil. 2:14), one cannot imagine a difference between divine and human authorial intent.

---

9. A point made well by C. S. Lewis in his essay, "Fern-seed and Elephants," in *Fern-seed and Elephants and Other Essays on Christianity by C. S. Lewis*, ed. Walter Hooper (London: Fontana/Collins, 1975), 104–25.
10. Hirsch writes, "Only the absolute form of radical historicism threatens the enterprise of re-cognitive interpretation by holding that the meanings of the past are intrinsically alien to us, that we have no 'authentic' access to those meanings and therefore can never 'truly' understand them" (*Validity in Interpretation*, 40).

Second, the problem of distinguishing human and divine intent arises only in prophecy texts, especially those few texts that seem to be used in ways that vary from the human author's explicitly distinguishable original intent. For example, Matthew 2:15 cites Hosea 11:1 with reference to Jesus' return from Egypt. In Hosea, however, the context seems to be referring only to Israel's exodus out of Egypt (as a paradigm applied to the Assyrian exile in Hosea's day). Such quotations of the Old Testament by New Testament authors provide the greatest challenge for maintaining the original human composer as the ultimate determiner of a text's meaning. I would argue, however, that divine intent can and should be subsumed under an author-oriented approach to interpreting the Bible. The human authors of Scripture shared an understanding that they were on a salvation-historical trajectory that would climax in the coming of Messiah. God intervened savingly in history in repeated and progressively climactic ways. Old Testament writers who picked up earlier divine interventions to understand their own day (for example, Hosea's allusion to the Egyptian exodus [Hos. 11:1]) implicitly allows for later authors to propose a future divine intervention as the climactic counterpart to their own day. Biblical authors were conscious of being part of a larger divine story and expected later chapters to build upon and escalate what they had already related. See question 24 ("How do we interpret prophecy? [Typology]") for more discussion of this type of biblical prophecy.

REFLECTION QUESTIONS

1. Can you recall hearing someone who interpreted the Bible according to a reader-response approach?

2. In your opinion, why is the reader-response approach to literature so popular at the current time?

3. Do you see any positive qualities to the reader-response or text-determined approaches to meaning?

4. Can the divine inspiration of Scripture (and thus the dual authorship of Scripture) genuinely be subsumed under the author-oriented approach to meaning?

5. Of the four objections to the author as determiner of meaning presented above, which seems to have the most validity to you? Why?

FOR FURTHER STUDY

Hirsch, E. D. *Validity in Interpretation*. New Haven, CT: Yale University Press, 1967.

Stein, Robert H. *A Basic Guide to Interpreting the Bible: Playing by the Rules*. Grand Rapids: Baker, 1994. (See chap. 1, "Who Makes Up the Rules? An Introduction to Hermeneutics," 17–36).

Can a Text Have More Than One Meaning?

This question relates directly to the previous question ("Who determines the meaning of a text?"). If we are correct that the conscious intent of the divinely inspired human author is the ultimate determiner of meaning, then the obvious answer to this question is, "Yes, a text can have more than one meaning, *if* the human author consciously intended multiple meanings of his work."

Confusion in discussing "meaning" can be caused by those who use the same word in different ways. For example, someone might speak of the "meanings" of the text, but in reality, he is referring to modern-day implications. As we think in more detail about whether a text can have multiple meanings, it is important to begin by clarifying our terms.

A Vocabulary for Interpretation

In teaching biblical interpretation to seminary students, I begin by defining basic terms that we use repeatedly over the course of the semester. Below are some important terms for interpretation with definitions drawn from Robert Stein.

- *Meaning:* "The paradigm or principle that the author consciously willed to convey by the shareable symbols [i.e., writing] he or she used."[1]

- *Implication:* "Those submeanings of a text that legitimately fall within the paradigm or principle willed by the author, whether he or she was aware of them or not."[2]

---

1. Robert H. Stein, "The Benefits of an Author-Oriented Approach to Hermeneutics," *JETS* 44, no. 3 (2001): 457.
2. Ibid., 458

- *Significance:* "How the reader responds to the willed meaning of the author."[3] Upon being confronted with these implications, the modern-day reader/hearer will then respond with acceptance (obedience) or rejection (disobedience).

- *Subject Matter:* "The content or 'stuff' talked about in the text" (that is, the textual details in and of themselves without reference to their use in conveying the author's meaning).[4]

We can illustrate these terms by looking at a sample text. Let us consider Proverbs 11:1: "The LORD abhors dishonest scales, but accurate weights are his delight." What is the meaning of this text? The author intends to teach his readers that God is pleased when one uses honestly weighted scales in business transactions, and thus the readers should use such scales. Likewise, God is displeased when one uses skewed scales to cheat others. The readers of this proverb are implicitly warned not to engage in such trickery. The author's original meaning, likely made with reference to the measuring of precious metals or agricultural produce, is clear.

What are the implications? Depending on the setting of the modern-day reader, a variety of implications are possible. The implications must flow within the channel of meaning determined by the conscious intent of the author; they must be "submeanings" of the original paradigm. For example, an hourly worker who punches in and out on a time clock can say, by implication, that God is pleased when he honestly clocks in and out as he comes and goes from work. Likewise, God is displeased with the worker who has his friends clock him out ten minutes after he has already left (so that he is paid for additional time for which he did not work). When hearing these implications declared, the hourly worker will then respond with obedience or disobedience (–significance). The writer of Proverbs clearly was not thinking of a time clock, but the paradigm of honest and dishonest business practices has many modern-day implications of which the author was not consciously aware. If the original author were consulted (obviously only a hypothetical possibility), he should agree that the modern-day implications flow legitimately from his meaning. The original author is the determiner of meaning, which in turn, limits implications. Sometimes, it can be helpful to imagine a dialogue with the original author over proposed implications in an attempt to make sure they flow directly from the author's consciously intended purpose.

What about the "subject matter" in Proverbs 11:1? The "scales" and "weights" (the "stuff" mentioned in the text) are examples of subject matter. In and of themselves, scales and weights are not the purpose of the author's

---

3. Ibid., 460.
4. Ibid., 461.

instruction. One can imagine a misguided preacher going into great detail on the composition of ancient weights and the construction of ancient scales. Neither issue, however, is of real import to the author's meaning (that is, honesty in business transactions). Scales and weights in and of themselves are not the meaning of the text, but the author of Proverbs mentions them to convey a teaching about honesty with reference to the original readers' regular activities. The subject matter is essential for conveying meaning but does not contain meaning in and of itself without regard to the author's purpose.

Challenging Texts and Multiple Meanings

The text chosen above (Prov. 11:1) is relatively straightforward, but what about more difficult texts—texts that later biblical authors seem to infuse with additional meaning beyond the conscious intent of the original authors? Let's consider such a text and various ways of interpreting it.

In Isaiah 7:14, we read, "Therefore the Lord himself will give you a sign: The virgin will be with child and will give birth to a son, and will call him Immanuel." In the original context, this text refers to a child who would be born to "the prophetess" as a sign to King Ahaz of Judah, who reigned from 732 to 716 B.C. Isaiah says that before the promised child is a few years old, Ahaz's adversaries (the kings of Aram and Israel) will be defeated by Assyria (Isa. 7:11–17; 8:1–4).

More than seven hundred years later, Matthew quotes Isaiah 7:14 as fulfilled in the birth of Jesus (Matt. 1:23). How can Isaiah's text legitimately apply to both his own day (722 B.C.) and Matthew's day (ca. 4 B.C.)? Below are several possible approaches.

1. One approach to this challenging text is to assert that Matthew has misunderstood and/or illegitimately used Isaiah 7:14. That is, Matthew haphazardly quoted the text without reference to Isaiah's original intent. While some non-Christian scholars take this view, Christians should not consider this a valid option, as Matthew was divinely inspired and would not illegitimately quote the Old Testament (2 Tim. 3:16). Moreover, how likely is it that the author of one of the most beautiful and influential works ever written was incompetent or deceptive? As a Jew writing to Jews who knew the Hebrew Scriptures, Matthew could not afford to be sloppy in his quotations from the Old Testament.

2. Another approach to Isaiah 7:14 claims that the Holy Spirit had an additional hidden meaning for Isaiah's prophecy. Isaiah was not cognizant of a later fulfillment, but the Spirit-inspired author, Matthew, applied the text to Jesus in his day—showing that God had a fuller, deeper sense to the original prophecy, which he revealed at a later time. This later meaning is called the *sensus plenior* (Latin: "fuller sense"). The *sensus plenior* interpretive approach appeals to secret, divine intent as the

trump card explanation, seeing no need to justify later usage from the original context. Yet, if an Old Testament text is to be legitimately applied to Jesus, it seems only natural to expect the original human author to have consciously intended that usage on some level.

3. Robert Stein has proposed that we understand difficult texts such as Matthew 1:23 as implications of the original text. That is, Matthew's use is not the original meaning of Isaiah 7:14 but a submeaning of the text that legitimately falls within the principle willed by the author. To my knowledge, Stein has not commented on this specific text in writing, yet he would likely argue like this: "In the original setting, Ahaz faced certain destruction at the hands of his enemies. God gave the sign of an impending birth to signify the coming divine deliverance. In Matthew's day, with the even greater enemies of death and sin facing God's people (as they had for so long), God does not leave them without ultimate deliverance but signifies his coming climactic intervention in a supernaturally born child." In the end, however, because of the historical particularity of the original prophecy in Isaiah, it seems difficult to explain Matthew's usage as an implication. How can there be an implication for a singularly promised event that has long ago been fulfilled?

4. Another approach for difficult texts like this is to understand that Matthew is employing Isaiah 7:14 typologically. The Old Testament authors shared the understanding that God intervened progressively and repeatedly, working toward a final climactic intervention. Old Testament authors saw deliverance in their day as foreshadowed in God's earlier deliverances. By their reference to earlier divine interventions to explain God's work in their own day and their anticipation of greater deliverance in the future, the Old Testament authors implicitly agree to the future typological use of their own writings.[5] So, if we could go back in time to just after Isaiah penned chapter 7, verse 14 (reporting the prophet's earlier interchange with Ahaz), the dialogue might go like this:

Plummer: "Pardon me, Isaiah. I'm from the distant future, and I've come back to chat with you. I was peeking over your shoulder, and I just noticed that you wrote that prophecy down about the promised child. Is that about Jesus?"

---

5. Jared M. Compton advocates a similar approach ("Shared Intentions? Reflections on Inspiration and Interpretation in Light of Scripture's Dual Authorship," *Themelios* 33, no. 3 [2008]: 23–33).

Isaiah: "Who is Jesus?"

Plummer: "Jesus is the coming Messiah who conquers sin and death forever."

Isaiah: "Hallelujah! I didn't know his name, but I knew he was coming. What do you mean by asking, 'Is this text about Jesus?'"

Plummer: "Well, in the future, before the Messiah is born, God promises through his angel that a virgin will give birth, similar to the events in your day. Matthew, one of God's messengers in Jesus' day, says that this text of yours was pointing to the Messiah."

Isaiah: "Yes, I see. Just as God signified his coming intervention with the supernatural birth of a child in my day, so in the final deliverance, again he promises the supernatural birth of a child. The historical parallels show God's consistent intentions! Of course, not knowing exactly how God would repeat his deliverance, I was not fully conscious of the final typological correspondence until you told me. But, I knew later deliverances were coming. I wrote this text, consciously knowing it might be reiterated in a later, parallel, heightened saving event. Yes, yes, of course that is a valid use. That's what is called biblical typology, with a correspondence between earlier events (the type[s]) and later events (the antitype[s])."

Plummer: "Thanks for talking with us, Isaiah."

Isaiah: "Shalom."

See question 24 ("How Do We Interpret Prophecy? [Typology]") for more discussion of typology in the Bible.

While I think the typological approach is likely the best way to explain Matthew's usage of Isaiah 7:14, this text in particular has some additional characteristics that are worth noting. One could argue that Isaiah intended multiple references in his original prophecy. That is, Isaiah consciously intended the "virgin prophecy" of Isaiah 7:14 to be applied to the setting in his own day, as well as to some other promised child in the distant future.

What details might indicate that Isaiah has in mind another child beyond the one who will be a sign to King Ahaz in his day? There are, in fact, several descriptions of the child in the immediate context that seem to point beyond anything that was fulfilled by the child in Ahaz's day. For example, soon after our debated text, in Isaiah 9:6–7, we read:

> For to us a child is born, to us a son is given, and the government will be on his shoulders. And he will be called Wonderful Counselor, Mighty God, Everlasting Father, Prince of Peace. Of the increase of his government and peace there will be no end. He will reign on David's throne and over his kingdom, establishing and upholding it with justice and righteousness from that time on and forever. The zeal of the LORD Almighty will accomplish this.

Such an exalted description certainly would be odd for Maher-Shalal-Hash-Baz (Isaiah's son?), the child in Ahaz's day who makes no additional appearances in the biblical text (Isa. 8:1–4). Furthermore, in Isaiah 8:18, the prophet writes, "Here I am, and the *children* the LORD has given me. We are *signs* and *symbols* in Israel from the LORD Almighty, who dwells on Mount Zion" (my emphasis). It is interesting that the original child-sign (singular) has been broadened out here to refer to "children," "signs," and "symbols"—all plural.

It is possible that Isaiah had a prophetic vision of two children in much the same way that we see two mountains from a distance. Viewed from far away, the two mountains appear side by side as one monolithic structure. One cannot tell how far apart they are or even if they are distinct formations. Only as we draw closer to the initial mountain do we see that the other mountain is actually separated from it by some distance. Similarly, it has been argued, some ancient prophets had visions of multiple forthcoming events in such a way that they could not distinguish the chronological distance between them. The technical term for a variety of future events being viewed together (without strict chronological sequencing) is *prophetic foreshortening*. It has been pointed out that the first and second comings of Jesus are described in the Old Testament with prophetic foreshortening. That is, only with the completion of the first coming of Jesus are we able to see clearly that the Messiah's visible and universal reign (the consummated kingdom) will come after a gap of time.

REFLECTION QUESTIONS

1. Is the distinction between meaning and implications clear to you? Explain the difference in your own words.

2. With reference to Ephesians 5:18, discuss meaning, implications, significance, and subject matter.

3. It is not uncommon to hear someone speak of applying a biblical text to his or her life (or the application of a text). Using the interpretive vocabulary introduced above, explain what people mean by application.

4. Which of the four approaches to Isaiah 7:14 seems the most convincing to you?

5. Consider Matthew 2:15. Look up the text that Matthew quotes (Hos. 11:1), noting the original context. Of the four approaches to difficult texts surveyed above, which one best fits Matthew's use of Hosea? See question 24 ("How Do We Interpret Prophecy? [Typology]") for more discussion of this text.

FOR FURTHER STUDY

Stein, Robert H. *A Basic Guide to Interpreting the Bible: Playing by the Rules*. Grand Rapids: Baker, 1994. (See chap. 2, "Defining the Rules: A Vocabulary for Interpretation," 37–60).
Virkler, Henry A., and Karelynne Gerber Ayayo. *Hermeneutics: Principles and Processes of Biblical Interpretation*. 2nd ed. Grand Rapids: Baker, 2007.

What Is the Role of the Holy Spirit in Determining Meaning?

As Christians study and talk about the Bible, it is not uncommon for some to appeal to the Holy Spirit's supernatural guidance in determining the meaning or application of a text. Does the Bible, in fact, present the Holy Spirit as working in this way? That is, does the Spirit guide believers to a true meaning or application of the biblical text?

The Person and Work of the Holy Spirit

Before we look at the role of the Holy Spirit in interpretation, we must be clear about the identity of the Spirit. Who is the Holy Spirit? The Holy Spirit is the third person of the triune God. According to Scripture, God is Father, Son, and Spirit (Matt. 28:19)—three distinct "persons" in one Being.[1] The Father is God. The Son is God. The Spirit is God. But there is only one God. And the Father is not the Son, nor is the Spirit the Son, nor is the Father the Spirit. Yet with regard to their divine nature, the Father, Son, and Spirit share the same goodness, wisdom, holiness, knowledge, power, etc.[2]

The Holy Spirit is sent by the Father and the Son into the world (John 14:26; 15:26). He indwells all true followers of Jesus (Rom. 8:9; 1 John 2:20) and enables them to live in repentance and faith (Rom. 8:1–17). The Holy Spirit empowers God's people with spiritual gifts for the building up of

---

1. Although *person* is the word that Christian theologians have traditionally used to refer to the Father, Son, and Spirit, we must note that divine personhood and human personhood differ. A human person has a distinct intellect, background, perspective, etc. The divine persons of the Trinity, however, share exactly the same divine attributes (wisdom, holiness, etc.).

2. For further reflection on the Trinity, see Wayne Grudem, *Systematic Theology: An Introduction to Biblical Doctrine* (Grand Rapids: Zondervan; Leicester: Inter-Varsity Press, 1994), 226–61.

Christ's body, the church (Eph. 4:11–16; 1 Cor. 12:4–11). Furthermore, the Spirit intercedes on behalf of God's people (Rom. 8:26) and reminds us of our filial status (Rom. 8:15; Gal. 4:6).

The Holy Spirit inspired the authors of Scripture so that every word they wrote, while inscribed by a thinking, human author, was also divinely inspired and free from all error. As Peter notes, "No prophecy of Scripture came about by the prophet's own interpretation. For prophecy never had its origin in the will of man, but men spoke from God as they were carried along by the Holy Spirit" (2 Peter 1:20–21). Paul likewise writes, "All Scripture is God-breathed and is useful for teaching, rebuking, correcting and training in righteousness" (2 Tim. 3:16). After Jesus' ascension, the Spirit reminded the apostles of the Lord's teaching and taught them further things, which, when written, resulted in our New Testament (John 14:25–26; 16:13–15).

There can be little doubt that the Bible presents itself as the product of the Spirit's inspiration, but does the Bible also present the Spirit as giving believers special aid in understanding its contents?

The Illumination of the Holy Spirit

Most Protestant theologians affirm that the Holy Spirit illumines the believer. That is, the Spirit brings to the Christian greater cognitive understanding of the biblical text.[3] Theologians also affirm the Spirit's related work of bringing conviction, that is, impressing upon the believer's conscience that the teachings of Scripture are in fact true, applicable, and incumbent upon the reader.

It is also important to note what illumination is not. Grant Osborne offers this helpful caveat:

> "The Spirit does not whisper to us special reasons which are not otherwise available; rather, he opens our eyes to acknowledge those reasons which *are* available" (1986:234). In other words, the Spirit makes it possible for the reader to use every faculty to discern the Word and apply it. How does this explain the fact that equally spiritual scholars interpret the same passage

---

3. In his Ph.D. thesis on illumination, Kevin D. Zuber writes, "The results of illumination are seen as primarily cognitive. From this primary result, illumination may also yield an appreciation of and application of the information cognitively gained. Divine illumination enables one to gain a deeper grasp and comprehension of the content of a divine disclosure. One illumined is actually enabled to 'see,' mentally grasp, more of the content than one who is not illumined. The conceptual insight provided by illumination is like the insight one comes to when a line drawing in which one 'sees' an object is suddenly 'seen as' another object. The onlooker simply experiences a conceptual gestalt that enables more of the content to be seen" ("What is Illumination? A Study in Evangelical Theology Seeking a Biblically Grounded Definition of the Illuminating Work of the Holy Spirit" [Ph.D. thesis, Trinity Evangelical Divinity School, 1996], abstract).

quite differently? The Spirit makes it possible to overcome our preunderstanding in order to discern the Word, but he does not guarantee that we will do so. On difficult passages we must use every tool we can muster and still will often read a text the way our experience and theological proclivities dictate. . . . Some passages are so ambiguous that more than one interpretation is possible. We must make our hermeneutical choice but remain open to further leading from the Spirit and challenge from our peers. The Spirit enables us to free our minds to the text but does not whisper to us the correct answer.[4]

I will now offer an analogy to help explain how the Holy Spirit helps Christians in reading the Bible. Let's compare studying the Bible to treasure hunting. Imagine two boats, one with a green-shirted treasure hunter (Christian with the Holy Spirit) and another boat with a brown-shirted treasure hunter (non-Christian without the Holy Spirit). Both adventurers stare through the same murky waters. Both see something shimmering at the bottom of the sea. The green-shirted adventurer says, "I see something shiny, and it looks like gold to me. I am going to dive." The brown-shirted adventurer says, "I only see light reflecting on the sand at the bottom of the ocean. I am not going to dive." All other things being equal, the believer is enabled to weigh the evidence before him more accurately and, consequently, experiences the inner compulsion to act that comes along with recognizing the true state of things. This is not to say, however, that believers always see things rightly because of the Spirit's illuminating work. Many other factors affect interpretation, such as the believer's innate intelligence, skills, predispositions, and, not least, his intimacy with and obedience to God.

Biblically speaking, cognition (mental understanding) and volition (choices of the human will) are two sides of the same coin. The biblical authors do not envision a situation in which someone can affirm the correct meaning of the Bible and at the same time refuse to obey it. Analogously, we cannot imagine a normal person sitting in a smoke-filled room, stating, "I affirm cognitively that the fire alarm is going off, but volitionally I am neither capable nor desirous of acting on this fact."

The human mind and will are conjoined in sinful interdependence. The human heart is prone to self-deception, distortion, wickedness, deceit, and self-justification (Jer. 17:9). The person who will not submit to God inevitably distorts the Bible's teaching and/or his perception of reality to rationalize his

---

4. Grant R. Osborne, *The Hermeneutical Spiral: A Comprehensive Introduction to Biblical Interpretation*, rev. ed. (Downers Grove, IL: InterVarsity Press, 2006), 436–37. Osborne's quotation is from John Frame, "The Spirit in the Scriptures," in *Hermeneutics, Authority and Canon*, ed. D. A. Carson and John D. Woodbridge (Grand Rapids: Zondervan, 1986), 234.

ungodly behavior. As the writer of Proverbs warns, "The sluggard says, 'There is a lion outside!' or, 'I will be murdered in the streets!' " (Prov. 22:13). Note, the sluggard does not say, "I am lazy, so I don't want to go out and work."[5] The sinful human heart manufactures evidence to justify its distorted perspective. Moreover, when we reject the truth, God sends greater blindness and the removal of his gracious divine restraint as punishment. As Paul explains to the Christians in Rome, "Since [some] did not think it worthwhile to retain the knowledge of God, he gave them over to a depraved mind, to do what ought not to be done" (Rom. 1:28). In this verse the interdependence between darkened thinking and wicked deeds is made clear. Similarly, in 2 Thessalonians 2:10–12, Paul affirms, "[Nonbelievers] perish because they refused to love the truth and so be saved. For this reason God sends them a powerful delusion so that they will believe the lie and so that all will be condemned who have not believed the truth but have delighted in wickedness." The punishment for embracing the darkness of sin is a further darkened mind and the wicked life that flows from such inner darkness.

A few conservative Christian scholars have attempted to deny or redefine the illuminating work of the Spirit, claiming the Bible teaches only that the Spirit affects the will, bringing conviction, but does not aid in cognition.[6] Unfortunately, this newly proposed view does not take seriously the noetic effects of the fall (that is, how sin distorts the human thought processes) or biblical indications that the Spirit will counteract the sinful inclinations of our minds. As noted above, the Spirit does *not* whisper some secret meaning inaccessible to others,[7] but the Spirit does enable us to perceive facts and judge the plausibility of arguments with greater clarity. If we believe that God will give a doctor wisdom in diagnosing a disease (as Christians prayers would indicate), or a college student increased mental concentration on a calculus test, why would God not also give assistance to our weak minds in studying the Bible? Indeed, as the Bible says that God gives teachers to the church (Eph. 4:11–16), would that not indicate, at the least, that *some* in the church are illumined by the Holy Spirit?

---

5. See John Piper's helpful exposition of Proverbs 22:13 in his "Taste and See" article, www.desiringgod.org (September 16, 1998).
6. E.g., Daniel P. Fuller, "The Holy Spirit's Role in Biblical Interpretation," in *Scripture, Tradition, and Interpretation*, ed. W. Ward Gasque and William Sanford LaSor (Grand Rapids: Eerdmans, 1978), 189–98; Robert H. Stein, *A Basic Guide to Interpreting the Bible: Playing by the Rules* (Grand Rapids: Baker, 1994), 61–71.
7. We can easily dismiss the assertion of Alan F. Johnson, who writes, "Since the Holy Spirit, not the human authors, is the ultimate Author of Scripture, meanings of the text unknown and unintended by the human authors are possible to discover through the continuing direct revelatory work of the Holy Spirit to believers, both in their reading of the Bible and apart from Scripture" (foreword to *Beyond the Obvious: Discover the Deeper Meaning of Scripture*, by James DeYoung and Sarah Hurty, [Gresham, OR: Vision House, 1995], 13).

The fact that nonbelievers can understand portions of the Scripture does not deny the illuminating work of the Spirit but points to God's common grace in giving all humans (regenerate and nonregenerate) rational minds. (Similarly, nonbelievers made in the image of God can act lovingly without having come to truly love God or love others.) Moreover, nonbelievers' intermittent correct readings of the Bible testify to the clarity of God's revelation. Even hearts in willful rebellion against God sometimes cannot miss his point. Finally, the fact that sincere, godly, Jesus-loving, Bible-believing scholars continue to disagree about the interpretation of some texts does not deny the illuminating work of the Spirit. The amount of disagreement among Bible-believing scholars is easily overstated, and in those cases where disagreement continues (on the proper meaning of baptism, for example), the ongoing disagreement only demonstrates the biases that remain among God's people in spite of his Spirit's work. The Scriptures themselves indicate that, until Jesus returns, believers will continue to disagree on secondary matters. Paul writes:

> One man considers one day more sacred than another; another man considers every day alike. *Each one should be fully convinced in his own mind.* He who regards one day as special, does so to the Lord. He who eats meat, eats to the Lord, for he gives thanks to God; and he who abstains, does so to the Lord and gives thanks to God. For none of us lives to himself alone and none of us dies to himself alone. If we live, we live to the Lord; and if we die, we die to the Lord. So, whether we live or die, we belong to the Lord. (Rom. 14:5–8, my emphasis)

Only God knows how many of our theological viewpoints are truly motivated by self-interest, bias, and denominational or ecclesiastical chauvinism rather than a genuine Spirit-led conviction. We must pray with the psalmist,

> Who can discern his errors? Forgive my hidden faults. Keep your servant also from willful sins; may they not rule over me. Then will I be blameless, innocent of great transgression. May the words of my mouth and the meditation of my heart be pleasing in your sight, O LORD, my Rock and my Redeemer. (Ps. 19:12–14)

Biblical Texts Supporting Illumination

Listed below is a sampling of biblical texts that support the doctrine of illumination.

- *Psalm 119:17–20:* [*The psalmist, praying to God*] *"Do good to your servant, and I will live; I will obey your word. Open my eyes that I may see wonderful things in your law. I am a stranger on earth; do not hide your commands from me. My soul is consumed with longing for your laws at all times."* The authors of the psalms pray repeatedly for divine assistance in understanding and applying God's Word (see, for example, the many petitions in Ps. 119).

- *Matthew 13:11–16: "[Jesus] replied, 'The knowledge of the secrets of the kingdom of heaven has been given to you [i.e., the disciples], but not to them [i.e., nonbelieving outsiders]. Whoever has will be given more, and he will have an abundance. Whoever does not have, even what he has will be taken from him. This is why I speak to them in parables: "Though seeing, they do not see; though hearing, they do not hear or understand." In them is fulfilled the prophecy of Isaiah: "You will be ever hearing but never understanding; you will be ever seeing but never perceiving. For this people's heart has become calloused; they hardly hear with their ears, and they have closed their eyes. Otherwise they might see with their eyes, hear with their ears, understand with their hearts and turn, and I would heal them." But blessed are your eyes because they see, and your ears because they hear.'"* In this passage, Jesus differentiates his followers from those outside. His followers are able to truly see, hear, and understand Jesus' teaching because it has been "given" to them by God (i.e., they have received divine assistance).

- *1 Corinthians 2:14: "The man without the Spirit does not accept the things that come from the Spirit of God, for they are foolishness to him, and he cannot understand them, because they are spiritually discerned."* In this passage, "the things that come from the Spirit of God" are the verbal and written proclamations of the gospel from Paul. The volitional rejection of God's message by nonbelievers is integrally related to their sinfully distorted cognition.

- *2 Corinthians 3:13–16: "We are not like Moses, who would put a veil over his face to keep the Israelites from gazing at it while the radiance was fading away. But their minds were made dull, for to this day the same veil remains when the old covenant is read. It has not been removed, because only in Christ is it taken away. Even to this day when Moses is read, a veil covers their hearts. But whenever anyone turns to the Lord, the veil is taken away."* Here Paul speaks of nonbelieving Jews as having dull minds and veiled hearts—metaphorical language to describe the blindness and hardness they demonstrate in failing to acknowledge how the Scriptures point to Messiah Jesus (see also Rom. 11:7–8).

- *Luke 24:44–45: "He said to them, 'This is what I told you while I was still with you: Everything must be fulfilled that is written about me in the*

Law of Moses, the Prophets and the Psalms.' Then he opened their minds so they could understand the Scriptures." John 20:22: "And with that he breathed on them and said, 'Receive the Holy Spirit.'" These parallel passages describe the same resurrection appearance of Jesus from different vantage points. It is striking that what Luke describes as the opening of the disciples' minds to understand the Scriptures, John describes as the reception of the Holy Spirit. Only by the Spirit's aid can we rightly perceive Christ as the ultimate meaning of the Bible.

Practical Implications of Illumination

If the Bible teaches that the Holy Spirit helps believers in understanding, applying, and obeying Scripture (as argued above), then there are clear implications for the way we should approach the Bible. While showing due diligence in reading, studying, researching, and thinking, the Christian ultimately must bow before the divine author of Scripture to confess his sinfulness and seek supernatural aid. Studying the Bible must begin with prayer and worship. See question 10 ("What are some general principles for interpreting the Bible? [1]") for further practical advice on approaching the Bible with reverence.

REFLECTION QUESTIONS

1. Have you ever heard someone appeal to the Holy Spirit to support a meaning of Scripture that seemed to you an illegitimate interpretation? How did you handle the situation?

2. Of the two views about the Spirit's role in biblical interpretation presented above (traditional illumination view versus the Spirit only aids in volition), which do you think is correct? Why? (Or, is there some other view of the Spirit's work you espouse?)

3. If the view on illumination presented above is correct, how should that affect the way you personally study the Bible?

4. If the view on illumination presented above is correct, how should that affect the way you talk about the Bible with others?

5. Pray this prayer slowly and thoughtfully prior to reading your Bible:

A Prayer of Illumination

Living God,
help us to hear your holy Word with open hearts

so that we may truly understand;
and, understanding,
that we may believe;
and, believing,
that we may follow in all faithfulness and obedience,
Seeking your honor and glory in all that we do.
Through Christ, our Lord. Amen.[8]

FOR FURTHER STUDY

Ferguson, Sinclair B. *The Holy Spirit.* Contours of Christian Theology. Downers Grove, IL: InterVarsity Press, 1997.

Thompson, Mark D. *A Clear and Present Word: The Clarity of Scripture.* New Studies in Biblical Theology. Vol. 21. Downers Grove, IL: InterVarsity Press, 2006.

---

8. Huldrych Zwingli (1484–1531), altered, as collected in *The Worship Sourcebook*, ed. Emily R. Brink and John D. Witvliet (Grand Rapids: Baker; Calvin Institute of Worship; Faith Alive Christian Resources, 2004), 142.

What Is the Overarching Message of the Bible?

Consisting of sixty-six distinct works written over more than a millennium and a half, the Bible can be an intimidating book. Is there an overarching message to the Bible? How do the seemingly disparate parts fit together? What is the big picture we should keep in mind as we look at smaller portions of Scripture?

The Person and Saving Work of Jesus Christ

Whatever portion of the Bible one is studying, it is important to remember that the person and saving work of Jesus Christ is the ultimate focus of God's revelation. To his contemporaries, Jesus said, "You diligently study the Scriptures because you think that by them you possess eternal life. These are the Scriptures that testify about me" (John 5:39). Likewise, the Gospel of Luke tells us that when Jesus spoke with two disciples on the road to Emmaus, "Beginning with Moses and all the Prophets, he explained to them what was said in all the Scriptures concerning himself" (Luke 24:27). The author of Hebrews writes,

> In the past God spoke to our forefathers through the prophets at many times and in various ways, but in these last days he has spoken to us by his Son, whom he appointed heir of all things, and through whom he made the universe. The Son is the radiance of God's glory and the exact representation of his being, sustaining all things by his powerful word. After he had provided purification for sins, he sat down at the right hand of the Majesty in heaven. So he became as much superior to the angels as the name he has inherited is superior to theirs. (Heb. 1:1–4)

From the outset, the Bible establishes that though God created a perfect world, humans destroyed that perfection through their rebellion (Gen. 1–3). Only through the promised Messiah (Christ) would the creation be restored to perfect communion with its Creator (Gen. 3:15). The story line of the Bible reveals the need for Jesus, the promise of Jesus, the anticipation of Jesus, the incarnation/arrival of Jesus, the teachings of Jesus, the crucifixion of Jesus, the resurrection of Jesus, the ascension of Jesus, and the promised return of Jesus. The Bible is a book about Jesus. For more on the Christocentric (Christ-centered) nature of Scripture, see question 18 ("Is the Bible really all about Jesus?").

With this assumed Christocentric foundation, we will now suggest a few additional organizing categories that can be helpful in seeing the big picture of the Bible's message.

Promise-Fulfillment

In the Sermon on the Mount, Jesus said, "Do not think that I have come to abolish the Law or the Prophets; I have not come to abolish them but to fulfill them" (Matt. 5:17). Thus, in speaking of the Bible, Jesus uses the categories of anticipation/promise (for the Old Testament) and fulfillment (for his life, death, and resurrection). We see a similar framework in Matthew 11:12–13, where Jesus makes clear the preparatory nature of the Old Testament and the inauguration of long-awaited promises through the preaching of the messianic forerunner, John the Baptist. Jesus says, "From the days of John the Baptist until now, the kingdom of heaven has been forcefully advancing, and forceful men lay hold of it. For all the Prophets and the Law prophesied until John."

Again, though the words *promise* and *fulfillment* are not explicitly used in 1 Peter 1:9–12, the passage contains these same ideas. The apostle Peter writes to believers in Rome:

> You are receiving the goal of your faith, the salvation of your souls. Concerning this salvation, the prophets, who spoke of the grace that was to come to you, searched intently and with the greatest care, trying to find out the time and circumstances to which the Spirit of Christ in them was pointing when he predicted the sufferings of Christ and the glories that would follow. It was revealed to them that they were not serving themselves but you, when they spoke of the things that have now been told you by those who have preached the gospel to you by the Holy Spirit sent from heaven. Even angels long to look into these things. (1 Peter 1:9–12)

Thus, in reading the Bible, one can ask this basic question: Am I reading the promise or fulfillment part of Scripture? In what way is Christ anticipated in this text, or in what way is his arrival heralded?

Kingdom Anticipated—Kingdom Inaugurated—Kingdom Consummated

When Jesus began his itinerant teaching ministry, he announced the arrival of the kingdom of God (Mark 1:15).[1] Jesus was not announcing that there was a kingdom but that the expected kingdom was inaugurated in his life and ministry.[2] Throughout the Old Testament, God is repeatedly referred to as king over all of creation, especially over Israel (1 Chron. 29:11; Dan. 4:32; Obad. 21; Pss. 22:27–28; 103:19; 145:11–13). God's divine kingship is mediated to Israel through the prophets, judges, and human kings (1 Sam. 8:4–9; Ps. 2:6–7), but a day is anticipated when God's kingship will be universally acknowledged (Ps. 67). Jesus declares that in him, the inbreaking of God's final, decisive eschatological reign is taking place (Matt. 12:28). Yet, Jesus also speaks of the consummation of God's kingdom in the future, when God's people will rest in the presence of God and God's enemies will be subdued (Matt. 8:11). Sometimes scholars speak of the "already" and "not yet" dimensions of God's kingdom in the New Testament. The kingdom already has arrived in Jesus' life, death, and resurrection, but the kingdom is not yet fully present.[3] While forcefully advancing and amazingly productive, the kingdom is not fully and universally instituted (Matt. 11:12–13; Mark 4:26–32).

Several biblical scholars have offered detailed frameworks based around the kingdom motif in the Bible.[4] Also, an influential children's Bible that tries to teach the big picture of the Bible using "kingdom" as a significant organizing principle was recently published. Fittingly, this children's Bible is titled *The Big Picture Story Bible.* While I see much that is good in approaching the Bible through the grid of kingdom (see figure 9), I offer three caveats. (1) There is a danger of losing the Christ-centered nature of Scripture by focusing on the kingdom. Ultimately, Christ is the king and the kingdom is present in him. "The kingdom advances here on earth *where faith and obedience to Christ are found.*"[5] (2) Some attempts to explain portions of Scripture with kingdom language, while quite clever, go beyond any explicit references to kingdom in the actual biblical text. (3) In an attempt to systematize the Bible under the theme of kingdom, some poignant details of the text can be over-

---

1. The terms "kingdom of heaven," "kingdom of God," and "kingdom," though having slightly different nuances, are used interchangeably in the New Testament.
2. Leonhard Goppelt, *Theology of the New Testament,* ed. Jürgen Roloff, trans. John E. Alsup (Grand Rapids: Eerdmans, 1981), 1:45.
3. George E. Ladd, *A Theology of the New Testament,* ed. Donald A. Hagner, rev. ed. (Grand Rapids: Eerdmans, 1974), 61–67; and idem, *Jesus and the Kingdom: The Eschatology of Biblical Realism* (New York: Harper & Row, 1964).
4. E.g., Graeme Goldsworthy, *Gospel and Kingdom: A Christian Interpretation of the Old Testament,* 2nd ed. (Carlisle, UK: Paternoster, 1994).
5. Mark Seifrid, "Introduction to the New Testament: Historical Background and Gospels, Course Number NT 22200" (unpublished notes, Southern Baptist Theological Seminary, fall 1998), 54.

looked. For example, after I read the account of the conquering of Jericho to my four-year-old daughter from *The Big Picture Story Bible*, her response was, "Where is the lady? Why did they leave out the lady?" The author of the children's Bible had left Rahab and her heroic faith out of the story.

FIGURE 9: THE KINGDOM OF GOD IN THE BIBLE	
KINGDOM STAGES	**BIBLICAL/HISTORICAL PERIOD**
The Pattern of the Kingdom	Genesis 1–2
The Perished Kingdom	Genesis 3
The Promised Kingdom	Genesis 12:1–3
The Partial Kingdom	Genesis 12–2 Chronicles (Patriarchs, Exodus, Law, Conquest, Monarchy)
The Prophesied Kingdom	Ezra–Malachi
The Present Kingdom	The Gospels (the birth, life, death and resurrection of Christ)
The Proclaimed Kingdom	Acts–Revelation
The Perfected Kingdom	Inaugurated at Jesus' Second Coming

Source: Vaughan Roberts, *God's Big Picture: Tracing the Storyline of the Bible* (Downers Grove, IL: InterVarsity Press, 2002), 157.

Old Covenant—New Covenant

Another way of thinking about the Bible as a whole is to employ the idea of covenant. A covenant establishes the basis of a relationship and the expectations of the parties involved, as well as consequences for not meeting those expectations. Biblically, the relationship between God and human beings is founded upon a covenant (Gen. 17:1–14; Exod. 2:23–25; 20:1–24:18; Jer. 31:31–34; Luke 22:20; 1 Cor. 11:25). As humans are in active rebellion against God and undeserving of a relationship with him, covenants between God and humans are always based on God's undeserved kindness and self-disclosure.

The underlying covenantal basis of biblical revelation is made clear in Jeremiah 31:31–34. The text reads:

> "Behold, days are coming," declares the LORD, "when I will make a new covenant with the house of Israel and with the house of Judah, not like the covenant which I made with their fathers in the day I took them by the hand to bring them out of the land of Egypt, My covenant which they broke, although I was a husband to them," declares the LORD. "But this is the covenant which I will make with the house of Israel after those days," declares the LORD, "I will put My law within them and on their heart I will write it; and I will be their God, and they shall be My people. They will not teach again, each man his

neighbor and each man his brother, saying, 'Know the LORD,' for they will all know Me, from the least of them to the greatest of them," declares the LORD, "for I will forgive their iniquity, and their sin I will remember no more." (NASB)

God describes the relationship between himself and Israel as based on a covenant made at Sinai (cf. Exod. 20–24). But according to the text above, the covenant was broken by Israel's repeated sin. A coming new covenant is promised that will be radically different from the old. The new covenant results in a forgiven people who know the Lord and have his requirements written on their hearts. Jesus declared that his atoning death instituted this promised new covenant (Luke 22:20; Heb. 8:6–13; 12:24).

Covenantal theology, a common Reformed approach to the Scriptures, attempts to view all post-fall relationship between God and his people under the canopy of a covenant of grace. Nevertheless, the old covenant-new covenant distinction present in Scripture would lead us to eschew the term "covenant of grace" in favor of more explicit biblical categories.

Conceptually parallel to the distinction between old and new covenants, the apostle John writes, "For the law was given through Moses; grace and truth came through Jesus Christ" (John 1:17). One should not understand the old covenant stipulations as intending to save or transform (and thus not subsumed under a covenant of grace) but primarily as intending to prophesy and prepare for the necessity of the new covenant instituted by Messiah Jesus. The theological system that attempts to systematize the Bible through the lens of old and new covenant, especially focusing on the "newness" brought in Jesus, is called "new covenant theology."[6]

Noting the biblical basis for covenantal distinctions (e.g., Jer. 31:31–34), a key question to ask in reading the Scriptures is whether the passage reflects the old or new covenant. During the administration of the old covenant, there were many institutions and laws that were preparatory in nature. As the author of Hebrews says, "The law is only a shadow of the good things that are coming—not the realities themselves. For this reason it can never, by the same sacrifices repeated endlessly year after year, make perfect those who draw near to worship" (Heb. 10:1). Under the old covenant, God's people discovered experientially that they were unable to keep his laws and in need of a more radical solution—a spiritual rebirth and a righteousness that comes from outside, a righteousness from God himself (John 1:9–13; Rom. 3:19–26).

Law-Gospel

Similar to the old and new covenant distinctions, one also can view the Bible through the grid of law and gospel. Paul certainly seems to make a

---

6. See Tom Wells and Fred Zaspel, *New Covenant Theology: Description, Definition, Defense* (Frederick, MD: New Covenant Media, 2002).

distinction between the law and gospel in his writings. In Galatians 3:23–25, the apostle writes:

> Before the way of faith in Christ was available to us, we were placed under guard by the law. We were kept in protective custody, so to speak, until the way of faith was revealed. Let me put it another way. The law was our guardian until Christ came; it protected us until we could be made right with God through faith. And now that the way of faith has come, we no longer need the law as our guardian. (NLT)

It would seem, then, that a *sine qua non* (an essential prerequisite) of biblical theology is the distinction between the preparatory law and the promised gospel.

One of the most outspoken advocates of the law-gospel distinction was the reformer Martin Luther (1483–1546). With reference to his conversion, Luther declared,

> I learned to distinguish between the righteousness of the law and the righteousness of the gospel. I lacked nothing before this except that I made no distinction between the law and the gospel. I regarded both as the same thing and held that there was no difference between Christ and Moses except the times in which they lived and their degrees of perfection. But when I discovered the proper distinction—namely, that the law is one thing and the gospel is another—I made myself free.[7]

The difference between law and gospel is explained briefly in these two sentences:

> The law says, "Do this, and you will live."
> The gospel says, "It is done. Now, live."[8]

Any portion of Scripture can be divided into "demand" (law) or "grace-gift" (gospel). The demands of Scripture are incumbent upon us, but because of our sin-stained hearts, minds, and wills, even our most righteous acts are like filthy rags in God's sight (Isa. 64:6). As Paul writes, "For no one can ever be made right with God by doing what the law commands. The law simply shows us how sinful we are" (Rom. 3:20 NLT). God's demands reveal our incurable

---

7. Martin Luther, *Table Talk,* in *Luther's Works,* ed. J. Pelikan, H. Oswald, and H. Lehmann (Philadelphia: Fortress, 1967), 54:442.
8. Luther writes, "I must hearken to the Gospel, which teacheth me, not what I ought to do (for that is the proper office of the Law), but what Jesus Christ the Son of God hath done for me: to wit, that he suffered and died to deliver me from sin and death" (Martin Luther, *A Commentary on St. Paul's Epistle to the Galatians* [London: James Clarke, 1953], 101).

moral sickness and drive us to his gracious promises in the gospel. We then can cling to Jesus' words in John 6:37: "All that the Father gives me will come to me, and whoever comes to me I will never drive away." Similarly, Paul writes:

> But now God has shown us a way to be made right with him without keeping the requirements of the law, as was promised in the writings of Moses and the prophets long ago. We are made right with God by placing our faith in Jesus Christ. And this is true for everyone who believes, no matter who we are. For everyone has sinned; we all fall short of God's glorious standard. Yet God, with undeserved kindness, declares that we are righteous. He did this through Christ Jesus when he freed us from the penalty for our sins. (Rom. 3:21–24 NLT)

All biblical Christians would agree that at least one of the functions of the Old Testament laws was to point out human moral bankruptcy and lead the sinner to Christ (Gal. 3:23–25). But what of the moral demands in the New Testament? While it is clear that the New Testament writers expected Jesus' followers to have truly changed behavior because of the indwelling Spirit (1 Cor. 6:9–11; 1 John 2:4), it is also true that Jesus' followers remain people who "stumble in many ways" (James 3:2). A Christian who says that he is without sin is a liar (1 John 1:8–10). Undoubtedly, in the new covenant period, there is new empowerment to enable the Lord's people to reflect his character. Yet we are imperfectly transformed, which makes us rely on Christ's righteousness and long for his return and the promised transformation of our bodies (1 John 3:2). Only in the final state, as we stand eternally changed in Jesus' presence, will we be completely free from sin.

Salvation History

"Salvation history" is the usual English translation of the German term *Heilsgeschichte* (literally, in German, "holy history"), a term coined by Oscar Cullmann (1902–1999). *Salvation history* is an expression used to summarize all of biblical revelation, culminating in the central saving event of Christ's life, death, and resurrection. That is, the Bible is a story of God intervening in history to save a people for himself. While this assertion is obviously true, the categorization of the entire Bible as "salvation history" (or "redemptive history") is so broad that it is questionable how helpful it is in explaining how the pieces of the Bible fit together. Still, it can be beneficial to ask, "In what ways does this passage reveal God's progressive, saving revelation of himself to wayward humans?" Or, "Where does this passage fit into God's saving plan—is it anticipatory, climactic, or looking backward to God's culminating intervention in Christ" (see Heb. 1:1–3)?

Dispensationalism

While not advocated in this book, dispensationalism is another method for explaining the unity of the Bible. Dispensationalism is an approach to the Bible that is characterized by a sharp distinction between God's plans for ethnic Israel and God's plan for the church. Also, dispensationalists have an admitted bias toward reading the Bible, especially prophecies, as literal whenever possible. Figurative or symbolic approaches to Old Testament prophecy, especially those that concern Israel, are viewed with great suspicion.[9]

There is great diversity among dispensationalists, but the traditional dispensationalism—made popular by notes in the Scofield Reference Bible—divides biblical history into seven God-human arrangements, or dispensations. Most dispensations consist of a divine self-disclosure, human failure, and resulting judgment. The seven dispensations classically taught are:

1. Dispensation of Innocence (Gen. 1:3–3:6, Creation to the Fall).

2. Dispensation of Conscience (Gen. 3:7–8:14, The Fall to the Flood).

3. Dispensation of Civil Government (Gen. 8:15–11:9, Rainbow Covenant with Noah to the Tower of Babel).

4. Dispensation of Patriarchal Rule (Gen 11:10–Exod. 18:27, Abraham to the Exodus).

5. Dispensation of Mosaic Law (Exod. 19:1–Acts 1:26, Moses to the death of Christ).

6. Dispensation of Grace (Acts 2:1–Rev. 19:21, Pentecost to the second coming of Christ. The tribulation period is the judgment of persons who rejected Christ in this dispensation.).

7. Dispensation of the Millennium (Rev. 20:1–15, Post-Advent thousand-year reign of Christ, ending in the Great White Throne judgment).[10]

Dispensationalists are also well known for teaching the "secret rapture" of the church, a view first promulgated in the 1830s by the father of dispensationalism, J. N. Darby (see question 36, "What does the Bible tell us about the future?"). Many members of evangelical churches in America have unwittingly adopted dispensationalist views—especially on end-times issues.

---

9. Charles C. Ryrie, a prominent dispensationalist scholar, writes, "The essence of dispensationalism is (1) the recognition of a consistent distinction between Israel and the church, (2) a consistent and regular use of a literal principle of interpretation, and (3) a basic and primary conception of the purpose of God as His own glory rather than the salvation of mankind" (*Dispensationalism*, rev. ed. [Chicago: Moody Press, 1995], 45).

10. This list is derived from Ryrie, *Dispensationalism*, 51–57.

This influence has come through books such as *The Late Great Planet Earth* and the *Left Behind* books and movies.

Recognizing weaknesses in traditional dispensationalism, a new and influential movement called progressive dispensationalism has emerged within evangelicalism. Like traditional dispensationalists, progressives maintain a distinction between Israel and the church and the expectation of a literal millennial kingdom. Yet, there are significant differences. Progressive dispensationalist scholars generally contend for fewer dispensations or salvation-historical periods—allowing the explicit covenants of Scripture (Abrahamic, Davidic, New) to have greater hermeneutical influence. Sometimes progressives are charged with having created a mediating position between traditional dispensationalism and covenant theology. With the disapproval of most traditional dispensationalists, progressives are also readier to acknowledge nonliteral fulfillments of some Old Testament prophecies in the New Testament, as well as the emerging presence of Jesus' Davidic reign in the current age.[11]

REFLECTION QUESTIONS

1. What is the overarching message of the Bible?

2. While reading through the above sections, did you recognize a theological system or framework that has been presented to you in the past?

3. Did any of the organizing structures presented above help you see more clearly the big picture of the Bible?

4. Which of the interpretive grids seems most faithful to the explicit language of Scripture?

5. Read aloud this hymn by Isaac Watts ("The Law Commands and Makes Us Know"). Ask yourself, "Have I personally experienced the freedom of the gospel spoken of here?"

> The Law commands and makes us know
> What duties to our God we owe;
> But 'tis the Gospel must reveal
> Where lies our strength to do His will.
> The Law discovers guilt and sin,

---

11. See Craig A. Blaising and Darrell L. Bock, *Progressive Dispensationalism* (Wheaton, IL: BridgePoint, 1993).

And shows how vile our hearts have been;
Only the Gospel can express
Forgiving love and cleansing grace.
What curses doth the Law denounce
Against the man that fails but once!
But in the Gospel Christ appears
Pard'ning the guilt of num'rous years.
My soul, no more attempt to draw
Thy life and comfort from the Law;
Fly to the hope the Gospel gives;
The man that trusts the promise lives.

FOR FURTHER STUDY

Goldsworthy, Graeme. *According to Plan: The Unfolding Revelation of God in the Bible*. Downers Grove, IL: InterVarsity Press, 1991.

_____. *Gospel and Kingdom: A Christian Interpretation of the Old Testament*. 2nd ed. Carlisle, UK: Paternoster, 1994.

_____. *Gospel-Centered Hermeneutics: Foundations and Principles of Evangelical Biblical Interpretation*. Downers Grove, IL: InterVarsity Press, 2006.

Helm, David. *The Big Picture Story Bible*. Illustrated by Gail Schoonmaker. Wheaton, IL: Crossway, 2004. (A children's Bible but beneficial for adults to see the Christological theme of Scripture.)

Lloyd-Jones, Sally. *The Jesus Storybook Bible*. Illustrated by Jago. Grand Rapids: ZonderKidz, 2007. (Another children's Bible but beneficial for adults to see the Christological theme of Scripture.)

Roberts, Vaughan. *God's Big Picture: Tracing the Storyline of the Bible*. Downers Grove, IL: InterVarsity Press, 2002.

Seifrid, Mark A. "Rightly Dividing the Word of Truth: An Introduction to the Distinction Between Law and Gospel." *SBJT* 10, no. 2 (2006): 56–68.

Is the Bible Really All About Jesus?

Christians know that Jesus is the Son of God and the climax of God's rev-elation of himself (Heb. 1:1–3). Indeed, Jesus discounted any study of the Scriptures that does not ultimately point to him (John 5:39). Yet, if one randomly opens a page of the Bible, especially parts of the Old Testament, it can sometimes be difficult to discern the Christ-centered nature of certain events or stipulations. In what way is the Bible all about Jesus? What do we mean when we say that our interpretation of the Bible should be Christ-centered, or Christocentric?

The New Testament

The New Testament is so named because it is a witness to the fulfillment of God's promise of a new covenant (Latin: *testamentum*), instituted and centered on the person of Jesus (Jer. 31:31–34; Luke 22:20). Compared with the Old Testament, the New Testament's Christ-centered nature is readily apparent.

1. *Jesus as the Subject of Revelation.* The New Testament begins with four Gospels, or theological biographies about the life of Jesus. Nearly every sentence in the Gospels records something Jesus said or did, or something other persons said or did to Jesus. The fifth book in the New Testament, Acts, reports the Holy Spirit's propelling the early church outward in witness to Jesus. Wherever the apostles and their converts go, they proclaim the new life and forgiveness available in Jesus. Acts is the continuing story of Jesus, now exalted but living and reigning through his Spirit and revealed Word in the ongoing advance of the church (Acts 1:1–8).

2. *Jesus as the Source of Revelation.* While he was present bodily with his disciples, Jesus explicitly said that he would send his Spirit, who would bring to their memory his teaching and instruct them in further things (John 14:25–26; 16:13–25). Thus, in the New Testament we have both the

Spirit-enabled recollection of Jesus' words and deeds (primarily in the Gospels) and the ongoing instruction of his church through specially designated eyewitnesses (primarily in the epistolary literature). We should not read the epistles as disconnected ethical and moral reflections "tacked on to the story of Jesus. Rather, all the materials in the New Testament are integrally and organically related to the person and work of Christ. Sometimes this connection is more on the surface of the text, when, for example, the apostle Paul prefaces his comments Christologically or pneumatologically (for example, "I speak the truth in Christ—I am not lying, my conscience confirms it in the Holy Spirit" [Rom. 9:1]).

3. *Jesus as the Supporting Substructure of Revelation.* How then, should we understand the various ethical exhortations in the New Testament as being Christ-centered? Cannot such paranesis (moral encouragement) be read as simply the eternal moral demands of a holy God without specific reference to the life and work of Jesus? No, they cannot. Jesus, in his person and work, provides the undergirding (the theological substructure) for the expected response of God's people. Note how Paul begins the section of moral exhortation in his letter to the Ephesians: "I urge you to live a life worthy of the calling you have received" (Eph. 4:1). The Ephesians were "called," or chosen, by God's gracious saving intervention in Christ.[1] They had been forgiven a debt they could never pay, and now the inspired apostle is charging them to live transformed lives in conscious dependence on their Savior (cf. Matt. 6:14–15; 18:23–35). That is, the Christians in Ephesus are to live worthily of their calling. Where there is a departure from pure faith in the sufficiency of Jesus' atoning death, the inevitable result is community strife and immoral behavior. (See Paul's letter to the Galatians, where both doctrinal and moral problems must be understood as interconnected.)[2] Too many Christian authors and preachers fall into the error of moralism ("Do this! Don't do that!") when they fail to connect the ethical instructions in Scripture with the finished work of Christ and his subsequent empowerment of his people. A defining element of our fallen condition is

---

1. L. Coenen writes, "Paul understands calling as the process by which God calls those, whom he has already elected and appointed, out of their bondage to this world, so that he may justify and sanctify them (Rom. 8:29f.), and bring them into his service. This means that the call is part of God's work of reconciliation and peace (1 Cor. 7:15)" ("Call," "καλέω," in *NIDNTT*, 1:275). K. L. Schmidt writes, "If God or Christ calls a man, this calling or naming is a *verbum efficax*" ("καλέω," in *TDNT*, 3:489). Note meaning number 4 of καλέω in BDAG: "choose for receipt of a special benefit or experience" (503). Cf. Jost Eckert, "καλέω," in *EDNT*, 2:242–43.

2. John M. G. Barclay shows this interconnectedness in his careful study, *Obeying the Truth: Paul's Ethics in Galatians* (Minneapolis: Fortress, 1988).

that we are sinfully prone to justify ourselves before God (Rom. 10:3–4). We like to keep score, being especially conscious of those whom we have surpassed in our façade of righteousness (Gal. 1:14).

4. *Jesus as Solution and Sufficient Savior of Revelation.* Persons who claim to have a relationship with God in Christ but do not demonstrate conviction of sin or righteous behavior belie their empty affirmation (Matt. 7:15–27, James 2:14–26; 1 John 2:4). At the same time, the Bible consistently teaches that all persons, both Christian and non-Christian, regularly fail to keep God's commands (Ps. 130:3–4; Rom. 3:9–20; James 3:2; 1 John 1:8–10). When confronted with God's ultimate standard of holiness, whether in the Old or New Testament, we are always reminded of our inherent unworthiness and are pointed to the sufficiency of Christ. Our sin is the problem. Jesus is the solution. In this sense, Martin Luther was right to speak of dividing all of Scripture into the categories of "law" and "gospel."[3] Every passage of the Bible is a two-sided coin, one side showing us our need (law) and the other showing us the provision of God in Christ (gospel). When confronted with a sin nature we cannot remove, we cry out with the apostle Paul, "What a wretched man I am! Who will rescue me from this body of death? Thanks be to God—through Jesus Christ our Lord!" (Rom. 7:24–25).

The dialogue between the Foul Fiend and Christian in *Pilgrim's Progress* illustrates this ongoing tension in the Christian life.[4]

> *Apollyon*: "You have already been unfaithful in your service to him. How do you think you will receive wages from him?"
>
> *Christian*: "Where, O Apollyon, have I been unfaithful to him?"
>
> *Apollyon*: "You lost courage when you first set out and you fell into the Swamp of Despond; then you tried to get rid of your burden in the wrong ways instead of waiting till your Prince had taken it off; you sinfully slept and lost your scroll; you were almost persuaded to go back at the sight of the lions; and when you talk about your journey and what you have heard and seen, inwardly you are seeking your own glory in all that you say and do."

---

3. See Mark A. Seifrid, "Rightly Dividing the Word of Truth: An Introduction to the Distinction between Law and Gospel," *SBJT* 10, no. 2 (2006): 56–68.
4. *Pilgrim's Progress* is a book-length allegory filled with symbolic characters to illustrate the Christian life.

Christian: "All this is true, and much more that you have left out; but the Prince whom I serve and honor is merciful and ready to forgive. And besides, these failings possessed me in your country, and I have groaned under them, been sorry for them, and have obtained pardon from my Prince."[5]

The Old Testament

Most Christians are aware of a few messianic promises from the Old Testament that point to Jesus. At the least, churches recite such verses every Christmas season. But, what about the many other Old Testament texts that on the surface seem to deal with matters unrelated to Jesus and his saving work—things such as Old Testament cleanliness regulations or reports of obscure battles and forgotten kings? How can we legitimately say that all these texts point to Jesus?

5. *Jesus as Propositionally Promised Messiah.* A number of texts in the Old Testament explicitly promise the coming of Jesus in such a way that the passages apply only to him. In Isaiah 53:3–6, for example, we read:

> He was despised and rejected by men, a man of sorrows, and familiar with suffering. Like one from whom men hide their faces he was despised, and we esteemed him not. Surely he took up our infirmities and carried our sorrows, yet we considered him stricken by God, smitten by him, and afflicted. But he was pierced for our transgressions, he was crushed for our iniquities; the punishment that brought us peace was upon him, and by his wounds we are healed. We all, like sheep, have gone astray, each of us has turned to his own way; and the LORD has laid on him the iniquity of us all.[6]

Most Christians assume that any messianic Old Testament citation in the New Testament is in this category. In reality, most New Testament messianic citations of the Old Testament are not propositional predictions. Much more common is the following category.

6. *Jesus as Typologically Anticipated Savior.* Many New Testament authors cite Old Testament texts as applying to Jesus that originally had different but related references. The authors of the Bible share a common view of redemptive history. That is, they see God as the providential Lord of history who intervenes in consistent and increasingly climactic

---

5. John Bunyan, *The New Pilgrim's Progress,* rev. Judith E. Markham, notes by Warren W. Wiersbe (Grand Rapids: Discovery House Publishers, 1989), 85–86.
6. Other examples include: Psalm 22; 110:1; Isaiah 11:1; Jeremiah 23:5; Micah 5:2.

ways. The climax of God's intervention is the life, death, and resurrection of Messiah Jesus. For example, the biblical authors' understanding of redemptive history works out in this way: God's deliverance of the Israelites out of Egypt (Exod. 1–15) foreshadowed his bringing them back from Assyrian exile (Hos. 11:1–12). Moreover, if, on the basis of God's unwavering promise, he did not allow Israel, his chosen "Son," to perish in slavery or exile (Exod. 4:22–23), how much more, when the unique Son (Jesus) faces the danger of death and exile, God the Father preserves him and brings him back into the Promised Land (Matt. 2:13–15). Otherwise, how can the Son fulfill his mission to the lost sheep of Israel (Matt. 10:6; 15:24)? Seeing such divine intentionality in God's increasingly climactic historical interventions is called typological interpretation (see question 24, "How do we interpret prophecy? [Typology]").

While we must allow the biblical authors' explicit typological reflections to guide us, nearly any Old Testament texts can be legitimately viewed in this way. The Old Testament sacrifices reminded the Israelites of sin, but Jesus' once-for-all sacrifice does away with sin (Heb. 10:1–10). The Old Testament food laws pointed to the need for a people set apart and pure to God, but Jesus brings the fulfillment of purity rules by purifying the heart (Mark 7:14–23). David was a great king and deliverer of Israel, but Jesus, as David's Son, is the true eternal King and great Deliverer from sin and death (Luke 20:41–44; Acts 2:22–36). The humble Moses led God's people as a prophet, but now a prophet like never before speaks of what he has seen and heard directly from the Father (John 6:46; 8:38 ; Acts 3:22; 7:37). Virtually any of God's interventions and revelations prior to Jesus can be followed with the words "how much more then in Jesus. . . ." This is biblical typology.[7]

---

7. Pascal writes, "Every author has a meaning in which all the contradictory passages agree, or he has no meaning at all. We cannot affirm the latter of Scripture and the prophets; they undoubtedly are full of good sense. We must, then, seek for a meaning which reconciles all discrepancies. The true meaning, then, is not that of the Jews; but in Jesus Christ all the contradictions are reconciled. The Jews could not reconcile the cessation of the royalty and principality, foretold by Hosea, with the prophecy of Jacob. If we take the law, the sacrifices, and the kingdom as realities, we cannot reconcile all the passages. They must then necessarily be only types. We cannot even reconcile the passage of the same author, nor of the same book, nor sometimes of the same chapter, which indicates copiously what was the meaning of the author. As when Ezekiel, chap. 20, says that man will not live by the commandments of God and will live by them" (*Pensées*, fragment 684, in *Great Books of the Western World: Pascal*, ed. Mortimer J. Adler, 2nd ed. [Chicago: Encyclopedia Britannica, 1990], 30:299). Within the volume, *Pensées* was translated by W. F. Trotter.

7. *Jesus as Solution and Savior.* As noted above, one should see all the demands of Scripture as ultimately impossible of being fulfilled by fallen human beings. Our constant failure in light of God's holiness points us to our need for a savior. Paul reflects repeatedly on this issue in his letters. For example, in Romans 3:20, the apostle writes, "Therefore no one will be declared righteous in [God's] sight by observing the law; rather, through the law we become conscious of sin." Similarly, in Galatians 3:23–24, Paul writes, "Before this faith came, we were held prisoners by the law, locked up until faith should be revealed. So the law was put in charge to lead us to Christ that we might be justified by faith."

REFLECTION QUESTIONS

1. Do you have a Christ-centered approach to reading Scripture? That is, when you read the Bible, do you expect every text to cause you to savor more deeply the saving work of Christ on the cross?

2. If you are a preacher, have your messages tended to be more moralistic ("Do this!" "Don't do that!") or more Christocentric ("Christ did it all!")?

3. What steps can one take to avoid a moralistic reading of the Scriptures?

4. How would you convince a naysayer that the person of Christ really is the central, unifying theme of Scripture?

5. Has the discussion above aided you in seeing Christ as the unifying hub around which the wheel of the Bible turns? If so, how?

FOR FURTHER STUDY

Goldsworthy, Graeme. *According to Plan: The Unfolding Revelation of God in the Bible.* Downers Grove, IL: InterVarsity Press, 1991.

_____. *Gospel and Kingdom: A Christian Interpretation of the Old Testament.* 2nd ed. Carlisle, UK: Paternoster, 1994.

_____. *Gospel-Centered Hermeneutics: Foundations and Principles of Evangelical Biblical Interpretation.* Downers Grove, IL: InterVarsity Press, 2006.

Seifrid, Mark A. "Rightly Dividing the Word of Truth: An Introduction to the Distinction Between Law and Gospel." *SBJT* 10, no. 2 (2006): 56–68.

Do All the Commands of the Bible Apply Today?

Why do you insist that homosexual behavior is wrong when the Bible also commands people not to wear clothes woven from two different kinds of materials (Lev. 19:19)? You just pick and choose your morality from the Bible." Such accusations against Christians are not uncommon today. How can we, in fact, determine what biblical commands are timeless in application? Do we have a biblical basis for obeying some commands in Scripture while neglecting others?

Covenant-Bound Commands

In looking at this important question, we first need to distinguish between commands linked to the old covenant that have been superseded in Christ and commands that are still to be lived out on a daily basis by God's people. Though a bit of an oversimplification, it can be helpful to think of God's commands in the Old Testament as divided into civil (social), ceremonial (religious), and moral (ethical) categories. Those laws that relate to the civil and ceremonial (for example, food laws, sacrifices, circumcision, cities of refuge, etc.) find their fulfillment in Christ and no longer apply. The idea that Christians are not expected to obey the Old Testament's civil and ceremonial commands is found throughout the New Testament. For example, in Mark 7, we read:

> Again Jesus called the crowd to him and said, "Listen to me, everyone, and understand this. Nothing outside a man can make him 'unclean' by going into him. Rather, it is what comes out of a man that makes him 'unclean.'" After he had left the crowd and entered the house, his disciples asked him about this parable. "Are you so dull?" he asked. "Don't you see that nothing that enters a man from the outside can make him 'unclean'? For it doesn't

go into his heart but into his stomach, and then out of his body." (*In saying this, Jesus declared all foods "clean."*) He went on: "What comes out of a man is what makes him 'unclean.' For from within, out of men's hearts, come evil thoughts, sexual immorality, theft, murder, adultery, greed, malice, deceit, lewdness, envy, slander, arrogance and folly. All these evils come from inside and make a man 'unclean.'" (Mark 7:14–23, my emphasis)

Similarly, in the book of Acts, we read:

The apostles and elders met to consider [the question of whether Gentiles needed to be circumcised to be saved]. After much discussion, Peter got up and addressed them: "Brothers, you know that some time ago God made a choice among you that the Gentiles might hear from my lips the message of the gospel and believe. God, who knows the heart, showed that he accepted them by giving the Holy Spirit to them, just as he did to us. He made no distinction between us and them, for he purified their hearts by faith. Now then, *why do you try to test God by putting on the necks of the disciples a yoke that neither we nor our fathers have been able to bear?* No! We believe it is through the grace of our Lord Jesus that we are saved, just as they are." (Acts 15:6–11, my emphasis)[1]

Not only the civil and ceremonial laws but also the timeless moral demands of God find their fulfillment in Christ. Yet, these moral commands continue to find their expression through the Spirit-empowered lives of Christ's body, the church (Rom. 3:31).

Some speculate as to the reasons for some of the more unusual commands in the Old Testament. Why does touching someone's dead body make one unclean for seven days (Num. 19:11–13)? Why was eating catfish forbidden (Lev. 11:9–10)? Sometimes, pseudoscientific reasons are offered, such as in books that encourage people to eat like the ancient Israelites.[2] Elsewhere, pastors or commentators wax eloquent on the symbolic meaning of various commands. Admittedly, there are some symbol-laden divine instructions; yeast, for example, seems to have repeated negative connotations in the Bible (Exod. 12:8–20; 23:18; Lev. 10:12; Luke 12:1; 1 Cor. 5:6–8; Gal. 5:9).[3] Moving beyond the few explicit indications, however, the suggested symbolic significance for Old Testament regulations quickly becomes quite fanciful. Whatever the reason for the various commands (frankly, some of which *are* puzzling), it is

---

1. As a missionary accommodation (so as not to offend Jews), the early Christians did forego some permitted foods (Acts 15:20; 1 Cor. 8–10).
2. E.g., Jordan Rubin, *The Maker's Diet: The 40 Day Health Experience That Will Change Your Life Forever* (Lake Mary, FL: Siloam, 2004).
3. Yeast can refer to pride, hypocrisy, false teaching, etc. But note how it symbolizes a positive pervasive influence in Luke 13:21.

clear that one of their main functions was to keep God's people as a separate, distinct group, untainted by the pagan cultures around them (Exod. 19:6; Ezra 9:1; 10:11). Also, some of the biblical commands imply that the surrounding nations engaged in the exact practices God forbade, apparently with pagan religious connotations (Lev. 19:26–28). God preserved the Jews as his chosen people, through whom he revealed his saving plan and finally brought the Savior at the fullness of time (Gal. 4:4).

Many supposed inconsistencies of Christian morality (for example, the charge that Christians pick and choose their morality from the Bible) are explained by understanding the provisional and preparatory nature of the civil and ceremonial laws of the old covenant period. The parallel is not exact, but imagine how foolish it would be for someone to raise the accusation, "Millions of people in every state of the Union are flaunting the Constitution! You don't really believe or obey your Constitution, which clearly states in the Eighteenth Amendment:

> The manufacture, sale, or transportation of intoxicating liquors within, the importation thereof into, or the exportation thereof from the United States and all territory subject to the jurisdiction thereof for beverage purposes is hereby prohibited.[4]

To which we would reply, "Yes, that amendment once was the law of the land, but it was superceded by the Twenty-first Amendment, which begins, 'The eighteenth article of the amendment to the Constitution of the United States is hereby repealed.'"[5]

The Bible is not a policy book, with each page giving equally timeless instruction. Yes, "Every word of God is flawless" (Prov. 30:5). Nevertheless, the Bible is more like a multivolume narrative, in which the later chapters clarify the ultimate meaning and sometimes the temporary, accommodating nature of earlier regulations and events (e.g., Matt. 19:8). Old Testament commands that are repeated in the New Testament (for example, moral commands, such as the prohibition of homosexuality [Lev. 18:22; 1 Cor. 6:9]) or not explicitly repealed (as are the civil and ceremonial laws [Mark 7:19; Heb. 10:1–10]) have abiding significance in the expression of God's Spirit-led people.

Prescriptive Versus Descriptive

If we reflect on what biblical texts are applicable today, it is also important to consider whether a text is prescriptive or descriptive. That is, does a text prescribe (command) a certain action, or does it describe that behavior? This question can be complex, as some behaviors are described in praiseworthy

---

4. The Eighteenth Amendment was ratified January 16, 1919.
5. The Twenty-First Amendment was ratified December 5, 1933.

ways so that they essentially have a secondary prescriptive function. Luke, for example, repeatedly reports Jesus' praying (e.g., Luke 3:21; 5:15–16; 6:12; 9:18–22, 29; 10:17–21; 11:1; 22:39–46; 23:34, 46). Such descriptive passages complement more explicit exhortations to pray in Luke's Gospel (Luke 11:2–13; 18:1–8; 22:40, 46). So, a good general rule is that a behavior reported in the text may be considered prescriptive only when there is subsequent explicit teaching to support it.

Another situation where we must consider the prescriptive and descriptive nature of texts is Christian baptism in the New Testament. Some Christians claim that baptism must be performed immediately upon a convert's initial profession of faith. In support, they cite a number of narrative texts in the New Testament, which describe baptism as coming immediately or very soon after a person believes (e.g., Acts 2:41; 8:12, 38; 9:18; 10:48; 16:15, 33; 18:8). However, nowhere in the New Testament do we find an explicit prescription such as this: "Baptize persons immediately after they believe." It is clear that all believers are to be baptized (Matt. 28:19; Rom. 6:3–4; 1 Cor. 1:13–16), but the exact timing of that baptism in relation to conversion is not explicitly stated.

In further thinking about the timing of baptism, we should note that many early conversions reported in Acts came within families or groups that were steeped in the Old Testament Scriptures. Yes, the early church was quick to obey Jesus' command for disciples to be baptized, but the background and setting of these early believers differs considerably from those of many converts today. Also, the evidence of conversion that accompanied the apostolic preaching in Acts was often dramatic and/or miraculous. Since we lack an explicit command on the timing of baptism, wisdom must be applied in discerning the reality of our converts' faith. Thus we conclude: immediate baptism could be advisable or further times of instruction and observation may be necessary.

Culture, Time, and Biblical Commands

In relation to culture and time, the *moral* commands of Scripture can be divided into two categories.

1. Commands that transfer from culture to culture with little or no alteration.

2. Commands that embody timeless principles that find varying expressions in different cultures.

Many commands in Scripture are immediately applicable in other cultures with little or no alteration. For example, in Leviticus 19:11 we read, "Do not steal." While cultures may have varying understandings of private property and the public commons, all humans are equally bound by this clear supracultural command. It is wrong to pilfer the private property of others.

Other commands of Scripture, while immediately applicable across various cultures, have wider implications depending on the culture in which they find expression. For example, in Ephesians 5:18, we read, "Do not get drunk on wine." This command applies in a timeless way across all cultures. It is always wrong to get drunk with wine at any time in any culture. In more detailed application, however, the student of Scripture also should ask what other substances a culture may offer that have a similar effect to wine (for example, being drunk with vodka, getting high on marijuana, etc.). In seeking such implications within new cultures, the initial command, while immediately understandable, is given broader application. One way to develop applications is to distill the *principle* of the original command—for example, "Do not take a foreign substance into your body to the degree that you lose control of your normal bodily functions or moral inhibitions." Then, one can go on to discuss what substances in different cultures would present this danger and thus should be forbidden from human intake to the degree that they cause the deleterious effect.[6]

The close similarity between drunkenness from beer, vodka, or wine is relatively transparent to most readers. But what about a command with more cultural veneer? In 1 Corinthians 11:5, for example, Paul writes, "And every woman who prays or prophesies with her head uncovered dishonors her head—it is just as though her head were shaved." Should women today, then, always cover their heads when they pray in public? Again, it is important to ask the *purpose* behind Paul's original command. Was it specifically the physical placing of a piece cloth on a woman's head that concerned him? Was it not, rather, the woman's submission to her husband that this head covering expressed in the culture to which Paul wrote (see 1 Cor. 11:1–16)?[7] If so, we ask, "Does a woman covering her head in our culture express submission to her husband?" Transparently, it does not. What behaviors, then, communicate a woman's submission to her husband? Two examples from the Southeastern United States are a woman's wearing of a wedding ring on her left ring finger and the taking of her husband's last name (without hyphenation). While a woman keeping her maiden name may not express an unbiblical independence in some cultures (China, for example), within the circles where I grew up, a woman keeping her last name after marriage was an implicit rejection of biblically defined gender roles.

---

6. Stein uses Ephesians 5:18 to illustrate implications (Robert H. Stein, *A Basic Guide to Interpreting the Bible: Playing by the Rules* [Grand Rapids: Baker, 1994], 39).

7. See Benjamin L. Merkle, "Paul's Argument from Creation in 1 Corinthians 11:8–9 and 1 Timothy 2:13–14: An Apparent Inconsistency Answered," *JETS* 49, no. 3 (2006): 527–48.

Finally, we should note that there are some nonmoral commands that are not applicable outside of their original setting. These are commands the author intended to be fulfilled only once by the intended recipient(s) and did not see as paradigmatic in any way. The list of such commands is very small. One example would be 2 Timothy 4:13, where Paul asks Timothy, "When you come, bring the cloak that I left with Carpus at Troas, and my scrolls, especially the parchments." Such a command was obeyed by Timothy, we presume, and has no further application in any other culture or time.

Below is a list of guidelines to help determine in what way a biblical command may find varying expressions in other settings.

1. Rephrase the biblical command in more abstract, theological terms. Is the injunction a culturally specific application of an underlying theological principle? Or are the command and cultural application inseparable?

2. Would a modern-day *literal* application of the command accomplish the intended objective of the biblical author's original statement (assuming you can determine the objective of the biblical author's command)?

3. Are there details in the text that would cause one to conclude that the instructions are only for a specific place or time?

4. Are there details in the text that would cause one to conclude that the instructions have a supracultural application (that is, the command applies unchanged in different cultures)?

5. Do your conclusions about the debated passage cohere with the author's other statements and the broader canonical context?

6. Is there a salvation historical shift (old covenant→new covenant) that would explain an apparent contradiction with other biblical instructions?

7. Beware of a deceitful human heart that would use hermeneutical principles to rationalize disobedience to Scripture. Interpretive principles, like a sharp knife, can be used for both good and ill.

REFLECTION QUESTIONS

1. Has anyone ever accused you of picking and choosing your morality from the Bible? How did you respond?

2. Do you feel confident explaining why Christians are not to obey food laws or sacrificial laws in the Old Testament? Try giving a brief explanation. Be sure to cite Scriptures to support your assertions.

3. Read Judges 11. Is the behavior of Jephthah prescriptive or descriptive? How do you know?

4. In Romans 16:16, Paul writes, "Greet one another with a holy kiss." In what way is this command applicable today? Explain.

5. Are there any commands in Scripture about which you have interpretive questions or doubts?

FOR FURTHER STUDY

Schreiner, Thomas R. *Interpreting the Pauline Epistles*. Grand Rapids: Baker, 1990. (See chap. 9, "Delineating the Significance of Paul's Letters," 151–59).
Virkler, Henry A., and Karelynne Gerber Ayayo. *Hermeneutics: Principles and Processes of Biblical Interpretation*. 2nd ed. Grand Rapids: Baker, 2007. (See chap. 8, "Applying the Biblical Message: A Proposal for the Transcultural Problem," 193–216).

Why Can't People Agree on What the Bible Means?

The diversity of biblical interpretations can tempt a Christian to cynical resignation: "If all these Bible scholars can't even agree on (*fill in the blank*), then what makes me think I can figure it out?!" Faithful Christians disagree on what the Bible teaches on issues such as baptism, divorce, and predestination, but such lack of unanimity should not lead to hermeneutical despair. The Bible itself provides us with insights in dealing with the interpretive disagreements we will inevitably encounter.

Non-Christians Can Be Expected to Misunderstand and Distort the Bible

Many times the so-called Bible scholars who appear on television or are quoted in the media are actually non-Christians antagonistic toward Christian orthodoxy. The apostle Paul warns us that such people have been given over to depraved and deceived minds as punishment for their continuing rejection of the truth (Rom. 1:18–32; 2 Thess. 2:11–12). Thus, we should not be surprised by non-believers' misinterpretations of the Bible and misrepresentations of Christ. Neither should we be surprised that the world applauds opinions that confirm it in its rebellion (1 John 4:5).

Non-Christian scholars often start with the assumption that God does not intervene miraculously in the world. It is no surprise, then, that they end up denying supernatural events such as the virgin birth. It is dishonest, however, not to admit that one's starting presupposition ("miracles do not happen") is essentially the same as one's conclusion ("this miracle did not happen"). A revealing question to ask the skeptic is, "What evidence would convince you that the Bible is reporting a factual event here?"

Describing the period between his first and second comings, Jesus warned, "Many false prophets will appear and deceive many people" (Matt.

24:11). Such false prophets often come dressed in the clothes of religiosity. Jesus cautioned, "Watch out for false prophets. They come to you in sheep's clothing, but inwardly they are ferocious wolves" (Matt. 7:15). In similar language, Paul warned the Ephesian elders:

> Keep watch over yourselves and all the flock of which the Holy Spirit has made you overseers. Be shepherds of the church of God, which he bought with his own blood. I know that after I leave, savage wolves will come in among you and will not spare the flock. Even from your own number men will arise and distort the truth in order to draw away disciples after them. So be on your guard! Remember that for three years I never stopped warning each of you night and day with tears. (Acts 20:28–31)

Do non-Christians ever have accurate insights into the meaning of the Bible? Of course they do. In his common grace, God has given rational minds to both redeemed and unredeemed persons. At a fundamental level, however, the unbelieving mind remains veiled to the gospel and is unable to perceive or overcome its distorted judgments on spiritual matters (2 Cor. 4:3).

The Amount of Disagreement Among Genuine Believers Is Overstated

In considering debated biblical interpretations, we must be certain that we are considering real cases of disagreement and not vague notions of incongruity. On what interpretive issue are Christians disagreeing? What are the various positions? Who supports each position, and what are their arguments?

If you are troubled by a particular text or topic, it can be helpful to write out the answers to the questions above. You will likely discover that there is actually a great deal of agreement among persons who submit to the authority of Scripture. This is an important point. If you find someone arguing, "Yes, the Bible says that, but . . . [followed by some reason suggesting that you should disregard the Bible's teaching]," then recognize this interpretive opinion as what it really is—disobedience to and distortion of God's Word. At the same time, we should not accuse other Christians of denying the faith or undermining biblical authority for disagreement on secondary issues. In fact, we should always remain open to being persuaded by the Scriptures to change our views. Otherwise, God's revealed Word, the Bible, is no longer our authority.

Let us consider briefly how one might approach the debated topic of divorce. A partial list of notations might include:

Christians agree: Divorce is bad. God does not like divorce (Mal. 2:16; Mark 10:2–9).

Christians disagree: Are there ever valid reasons for divorce (e.g., abandonment, adultery, etc.)? Consider Matthew 5:32; 19:9; and
1 Corinthians 7:15.

Christians agree: God forgives repentant divorced persons (1 John 1:9).

Christians disagree: May divorced persons be church leaders? May divorced
persons remarry and, if so, under what circumstances?
Consider Deuteronomy 24:1–4; Matthew 1:19; 19:3–9;
and 1 Timothy 3:2, etc.

Obviously, a thorough study of divorce goes beyond the scope of this
book, but in such a study numerous relevant texts need to be considered
carefully.[1]

It is also important to recognize that none of us has arrived. We are all on
a hermeneutical journey (see question 12, "How can I improve as an interpreter of the Bible?"). If you submit to the authority of Scripture, however, you
will find yourself changing your views and behaviors as you discover what
God has revealed on various matters.[2]

God Did Not Reveal All Issues with the Same Clarity

A traditionally accepted doctrine in Protestant Christian theology is the
perspicuity (clarity) of Scripture. To simply assert that the Bible is clear, however, is to be less than clear. In fact, as noted above, the Bible is not clear to
non-believers, who are blinded by their sin. Also, the supernatural work of
the Holy Spirit is necessary to bring greater clarity to God's people as they
study his Word (see question 16, "What is the role of the Holy Spirit in determining meaning?"). Wayne Grudem is right to qualify the doctrine of perspicuity accordingly: "The clarity of Scripture means that the Bible is written in
such a way that its teachings are able to be understood by all who will read it
seeking God's help and being willing to follow it."[3]

Still, it seems that further definitional qualifications may be necessary. In
fact, some texts in the Bible indicate that God did not intend for all things to be
made clear. For example, in Romans 14:5, Paul allows for continued Christian
disagreement on whether some days have special significance for Christian

---

1. See, for example, Craig S. Keener, *And Marries Another: Divorce and Remarriage in the
Teaching of the New Testament* (Peabody, MA: Hendrickson, 1991).
2. For example, see William A. Heth, "Jesus on Divorce: How My Mind Has Changed," *SBJT*
6, no. 1 (2002): 4–29.
3. Wayne Grudem, *Systematic Theology: An Introduction to Biblical Doctrine* (Grand Rapids:
Zondervan; Leicester: Inter-Varsity Press, 1994), 108. See also Mark D. Thompson, *A Clear
and Present Word: The Clarity of Scripture*, New Studies in Biblical Theology 21 (Downers
Grove, IL: InterVarsity Press, 2006).

worship. Paul does not say, "Don't you know? The Scriptures are clear on that. Everyone should . . ." Rather, Paul says, "Each one should be fully convinced in his own mind" (Rom. 14:5). Thus, it appears that continuing disagreement *on some secondary issues* is not a matter of failing to submit to Scripture or evidence of a lack of interpretive skill. For whatever reason, God did not intend to make all things clear.

Neither did God intend to make all matters easy. The apostle Peter writes:

> Bear in mind that our Lord's patience means salvation, just as our dear brother Paul also wrote you with the wisdom that God gave him. He writes the same way in all his letters, speaking in them of these matters. His letters contain some things that are hard to understand, which ignorant and unstable people distort, as they do the other Scriptures, to their own destruction. (2 Peter 3:15–16)

We note that Paul's letters, as well as other portions of Scripture, contain some things that are "hard to understand," though not impossible to understand. Some texts are challenging and when wrongly handled (by false teachers) lead persons to heresy and damnation. It is noteworthy that one can never blame God for misunderstanding the Bible. Just as all are without excuse when they view God's glory revealed in creation (Rom. 1:20), so interpreters are without excuse for distorting God's special revelation of himself in Scripture (Matt. 22:29). In *The Bondage of the Will*, Luther excoriated Erasmus for implying that the Scriptures were unclear, when in actuality it was Erasmus's sinful and vacillating mind that was to blame.[4] The Bible promises that true believers have God's assurance that, whatever their innate weaknesses or interpretive challenges, the Holy Spirit will ultimately guard them from denying the faith (Phil. 1:6; 1 Peter 1:5; 1 John 2:20–27). Such promises should lead not to hubris but to humility.

While God's revelation is sufficient for us (giving us all we need), it is not exhaustive. Moses says, "*The secret things belong to the* LORD *our God, but the things revealed belong to us and to our children forever, that we may follow all the words of this law*" (Deut. 29:29, my emphasis). Similarly, speaking in the third person, Paul describes a revelatory experience he had: "This man . . . was

---

4. Luther writes, "Come forward then, you, and all the Sophists with you, and cite a single mystery which is still obscure in Scripture. I know that to many people a great deal remains obscure; but that is due, not to any lack of clarity in Scripture, but to their own blindness and dullness, in that they make no effort to see truth which, in itself could not be plainer. . . . They are like men who cover their eyes, or go from daylight into darkness, and hide there, and then blame the sun, or the darkness of the day, for their inability to see. So let wretched men abjure that blasphemous perversity which would blame the darkness of their own hearts on the plain Scriptures of God!" (Martin Luther, *The Bondage of the Will*, trans. J. I. Packer and O. R. Johnston [Westwood, NJ: Fleming H. Revell, 1957], 72).

caught up to paradise. He heard inexpressible things, things that man is not permitted to tell" (2 Cor. 12:3–4). Clearly, God did not speak to every issue in the Scriptures. In divine wisdom, the Bible provides sufficiently clear paradigms for whatever ethical or theological implications we need in our day. We are not promised insight into the mysteries of all God's work. "Now we see but a poor reflection as in a mirror," but one day we will see Christ face to face (1 Cor. 13:12).

A few final caveats on hard-to-understand biblical texts are in order. (1) It is sometimes advisable to reserve judgment on debated issues or texts. I am reminded of a prominent pastor who told me that he suspended his expositional series of Revelation at chapter 11 until he had more confidence in his understanding of the rest of the book. (2) It is also acceptable to have a provisional opinion on debated matters. An honest interpreter might say, "I'm 70 percent convinced of this view." Depending on the setting, it also can be appropriate to educate your hearers about the strengths and weaknesses of proposed alternatives. In a traditional sermon, however, it is generally best to deliver the fruit of your study rather than enlisting laborers to glean behind you in the fields of exegesis. (3) If you are the only advocate of an interpretation, it is almost certainly wrong. Strange and idiosyncratic interpretations should be recognized for what they are.

Interpreters Have Varying Levels of Knowledge and Skill

While it is true that some technical arguments related to the Greek and Hebrew texts of our Bible can be engaged in only by linguistic experts, it is striking that the Bible discounts or ignores characteristics that one might normally list as prerequisites for skilled interpretation. The apostles are described as theologically untrained by the cultural standards of their day (Acts 4:13). One would not normally choose a fisherman as the leader of a new religious movement (Matt. 16:18). In fact, the exaltation of human intelligence is seen as a barrier to understanding God's revelation. The apostle Paul writes,

> Do not deceive yourselves. If any one of you thinks he is wise by the standards of this age, he should become a "fool" so that he may become wise. For the wisdom of this world is foolishness in God's sight. As it is written: "He catches the wise in their craftiness"; and again, "The Lord knows that the thoughts of the wise are futile." (1 Cor. 3:18–20)

Similarly, Jesus prays, "I praise you, Father, Lord of heaven and earth, because you have hidden these things from the wise and learned, and revealed them to little children. Yes, Father, for this was your good pleasure" (Matt. 11:25–26).

What, then, makes a person truly wise in God's eyes? In Psalm 119, David tells us that the wise person has a thorough knowledge of and obedient response to God's Word. Addressing God, the psalmist writes,

> Your commands make me wiser than my enemies, for they are ever with me. I have more insight than all my teachers, for I meditate on your statutes. I have more understanding than the elders, for I obey your precepts. (Ps. 119:98–100)

We also should note that it is possible to have immense knowledge but lack the obedient response the psalmist describes. In such cases, the knowledge is empty and dead, like a body without a spirit (Matt. 7:15–20; James 2:14–26; 1 John 2:4). Without love and good deeds, a knowledgeable teacher might as well be a noisy gong or a clanging cymbal (1 Cor. 13:1–3).

Although some people in the church are gifted with timely messages from God or the ability to teach his Word (1 Cor. 12:8; Rom. 12:7), Christianity has no high priestly intelligentsia. God made his Word accessible to his people so that they might, by the power of his Spirit, believe it, obey it, and teach it to others (Deut. 6:6–7; Matt. 28:20).

Interpreters Have Varying Levels of Spiritual Illumination and Diligence

Regardless of their natural gifting, all Christians are assured of the supernatural presence of the Holy Spirit, who will teach them and protect them from error (1 John 2:20–27; cf. John 16:13). At the same time, believers are called to responsibility, being exhorted to diligence. Paul writes to Timothy: "Do your best to present yourself to God as one approved, a workman who does not need to be ashamed and who correctly handles the word of truth" (2 Tim. 2:15).

God calls us to approach his Word with prayer, meditation, repentance, faith, and obedience (Ps. 119). The Holy Spirit works to correct our sinful biases and give us clarity of observation and judgment (see question 16, "What is the role of the Holy Spirit in determining meaning?"). If, however, we approach the Scriptures haphazardly or in disobedience, we should not expect the Holy Spirit to aid us. If we are living in unrepentant sin, we are grieving the Holy Spirit rather than opening our ears to listen to and follow him (Eph. 4:30; 1 Peter 3:7).

Martin Luther spoke of the need to approach the Scriptures reverently and meditatively.

> And take care that you do not grow weary or think that you have done enough when you have read, heard, and spoken [the words of Scripture] once or twice, and that you have complete understanding. You will not be a particularly good theologian if you do that, for you will be like untimely fruit which falls to the ground before it is half ripe.[5]

---

5. Martin Luther, "Preface to the Wittenberg Edition of Luther's German Writings" (1539), in *Martin Luther's Basic Theological Writings*, ed. Timothy F. Lull, 2nd ed. (Minneapolis: Fortress, 2005), 66.

When discussing a biblical text, however, one can never appeal to one's spiritual preparation as the basis for the correctness of one's interpretation (for example, "I prayed over this text for three hours, so I know I am right!"). Neither can one accuse his opponents of error because of perceived spiritual maladies. Arguments and appeals must always be made with a finger on the text, pointing to evidence that is available to all. Apollos can serve as a model, "For he vigorously refuted the Jews in public debate, *proving from the Scriptures* that Jesus was the Christ" (Acts 18:28, my emphasis).

Interpreters Have Various Biases

All interpreters come to the text with biases, both perceived and unperceived. The families we were reared in, our church upbringing (or lack of it), our education, our jobs, our life experiences—all of these influence our thinking. We can pray with the psalmist, "Who can discern his errors? Forgive my hidden faults" (Ps. 19:12). But until we stand in Christ's presence, we will have to contend with indwelling sin and its concomitant mental and spiritual distortions (Gal. 5:17).

I was born to Baptist parents, raised in a Baptist church, attended a Baptist seminary, and now teach at a Baptist school. I am firmly convinced that the Bible teaches believer's baptism by immersion, but I am not so simpleminded as to think that my upbringing and employment have not influenced my judgment. Hypothetically speaking, what would it take to convince me of the paedobaptist (infant baptism) view? The cost of moving to such a position (resignation from the school where I teach and the church where I pastor) likely have a strong unconscious influence on me. The same could be said for paedobaptist pastors and professors who would have to resign from their positions for moving to a credobaptist view (that is, believer's baptism).

REFLECTION QUESTIONS

1. Have you been struggling to reach an opinion on a particular biblical text or theological issue? What is the next step you should take in dealing with this matter?

2. Who is the most recent religious expert you have heard quoted in the news? Could you tell if he or she was a Christian?

3. Can you think of an interpretive issue on which you have changed your mind? What convinced you to change?

4. As noted above, Wayne Grudem defines the perspicuity of Scripture accordingly: "The clarity of Scripture means that the Bible is written in such

a way that its teachings are able to be understood by all who will read it seeking God's help and being willing to follow it."[6] Based on the discussion above and your own reflections, would you add any further qualifications?

5. Is there some topic on which you wish the Lord had provided additional comment in Scripture?

FOR FURTHER STUDY

Grudem, Wayne. *Systematic Theology: An Introduction to Biblical Doctrine.* Grand Rapids: Zondervan; Leicester: Inter-Varsity Press, 1994.
Thompson, Mark D. *A Clear and Present Word: The Clarity of Scripture.* New Studies in Biblical Theology 21. Downers Grove, IL: InterVarsity Press, 2006.

---

6. Grudem, *Systematic Theology,* 108.

PART 3

Approaching Specific Texts

Shared Genres (Questions Apply Equally to Old and New Testament)

How Do We Identify Literary Genre—And Why Does It Matter?

Upon picking up a new text, a reader will usually quickly identify the genre. That is, the reader will decide (consciously or unconsciously, rightly or wrongly) whether the text is to be understood as fiction or nonfiction, scientific writing or poetry, etc. The accurate determination of the genre of a work is essential to its proper interpretation.

Defining "Genre"

According to the Merriam-Webster dictionary, genre is "a category of artistic, musical, or literary composition characterized by a particular style, form, or content."[1] In this book, of course, we are concerned primarily with *literary* genres and, more specifically, the literary genres of the Bible.

In choosing to express his or her ideas through a particular literary genre, the author submits to a number of shared assumptions associated with that genre. For example, if I were to begin a story, "Once upon a time," I immediately cue my readers that I am going to tell a fairy tale. Such a story likely will have fantastical creatures (e.g., dragons, unicorns), a challenge to be overcome, and a happy ending. Readers will expect the story to be directed at young children, primarily for the sake of entertainment, but possibly also for moral instruction.

Many times every day, we make decisions about how to understand a literary composition based on our unconscious assessment of its genre. For example, if I receive an envelope in the mail that reads, "MR. PLUMER (note misspelling), YOU MIGHT HAVE JUST WON TEN MILLION DOLLARS!" I realize I am holding some sort of advertisement that has no interest in giving me ten million dollars but rather wants me to buy something. Likewise, if I

---

1. Online version (accessed August 29, 2008).

receive an official-looking letter from the "Louisville Water Company" that is stamped with red letters, "Final Late Payment Notice," I understand that important, factual information related to an outstanding debt is in my hand. And when I drive home, I realize that the sign that says, "Speed Limit 35" is not simply to decorate the roadside or to offer a suggestion but is, in fact, a legally binding notice.

Identifying the Genre of Biblical Writings

In everyday life we become familiar with the genres we encounter. Initially, the advertisement letter described above might have excited us to the possibility of winning ten million dollars, but after several years of failed entries, we come to recognize the true genre of such materials. Similarly, young children may have trouble distinguishing between the genre of the evening news, a science-fiction movie, and a documentary. An educated adult, however, should be able not only to recognize a movie as a documentary but also to identify some of the biases and aims of its producers.

Certain books in the Bible are written in genres that are familiar to us, but others are foreign to the modern reader. And even familiar genres sometimes include assumptions that the modern reader might not expect. One way to identify the genre of a biblical book is to read it and note significant literary details and authorial comments that cue the reader as to how it should be understood. For example, the most common genre in the Bible is historical narrative, which makes up roughly 60 percent of its contents.[2] The biblical genre of historical narrative is similar to factual historical reporting that we read today in a newspaper or history book. Still, there are a few differences. (1) Biblical historical narratives often are peppered with unfamiliar subgenres, such as genealogies (Matt. 1:1–17), songs (Exod. 15:1–18), proverbs (Matt. 26:52), prophecies (Mark 13:3–37), or covenants (Josh. 24:1–28). (2) Biblical historical narratives generally are not concerned with some of the same details that modern readers might wish addressed (for example, strict chronological identification or sequencing, biographical details from the entire span of a person's life, etc.). (3) Biblical historical narratives, while accurate, never claim to be objective. The biblical authors have a purpose in writing—to convince the readers of God's revelatory message and the necessity of responding to God in repentance, faith, and obedience (e.g., John 20:30–31). See question 22 ("How do we interpret historical narrative?") for further guidance in interpreting biblical historical narrative.

One way to identify and learn about the genres of books in the Bible is to consult a study Bible, commentary, or other theological reference work (see question 13, "What are some helpful books or tools for interpreting the

---

2. Robert H. Stein, *A Basic Guide to Interpreting the Bible: Playing by the Rules* (Grand Rapids: Baker, 1994), 151.

Bible?"). The latter half of this book also will prove helpful, as it provides a brief introduction to various biblical genres and the specific assumptions and caveats we should keep in mind as we approach them.

See figure 10 for a list of literary genres found frequently in the Bible and a sampling of books or passages so classified.

FIGURE 10: LITERARY GENRES IN THE BIBLE	
GENRE	**SAMPLE TEXTS**
Historical Narrative	Genesis, Mark
Genealogy	1 Chronicles 1–9; Matthew 1:1–17
Exaggeration/Hyperbole	Matthew 5:29–30; 23:24
Prophecy	Isaiah; Malachi
Poetry	Joel; Amos (also prophecy)
Covenant	Genesis 17:1–4; Joshua 24:1–28
Proverbs/Wisdom Literature	Proverbs, Job
Psalms and Songs	Exodus 15:1–18; Psalms
Letters	1 Corinthians, 2 Peter
Apocalypse	Daniel, Revelation

Interpretive Missteps

Several interpretive dangers lurk in the genre minefield. Three important ones to note are as follows.

1. *Misunderstanding the genre of a work can result in skewed interpretation.* Judges 11:39 reports that Jephthah kept the oath he made to the Lord by sacrificing his daughter. The genre of historical narrative, to which Judges belongs, does not *in and of itself* tell us whether the actions reported are good or bad. Additional authorial indications are necessary to let the reader know how the inspired writer assessed the event or person reported. As is clear from the repeated downward spirals of sin in Judges (3:7–16:31), along with the author's despairing summary statements (17:6; 18:1; 19:1; 21:25), the action of Jephthah is not to be praised or imitated.[3] The assumption that the behaviors

---

3. Note the six main cycles connected with the judges: Othniel, Ehud, Deborah, Gideon, Jephthah, and Samson. A note in *The New Oxford Annotated Bible* observes, "With each major judge, the cycle unravels. In turn, this unraveling enhances the communication of the moral deterioration taking place throughout the period of the judges. In fact, by the time of Samson, the cycle has almost disappeared. The Samson cycle serves as both the literary climax and moral nadir of the 'cycles' section" (*The New Oxford Annotated Bible*,

of major figures in historical narrative should always be copied could result in a horrific application in this case.

2. *Mislabeling a biblical genre can be an underhanded way of denying the text's truthfulness.* It is not uncommon to encounter prominent religious experts in the media who assure us that large portions of the Bible should be understood as myth rather than historical narrative.[4] That is, the texts should not be understood as reporting factual historical information but as painting mythological pictures to inspire or challenge us. Such a claim, however, denies clear authorial indications to the contrary (e.g., Luke 1:1–4), as well as extrabiblical evidence that confirms the historicity of the Bible's contents.[5] Concerning those who labeled the Gospels as myths in his day, renowned author and literary critic C. S. Lewis remarked,

> Whatever these men may be as Biblical critics, I distrust them as critics. They seem to me to lack literary judgement, to be imperceptive about the very quality of the texts they are reading. It sounds a strange charge to bring against men who have been steeping in those books all their lives. But that might be just the trouble. A man who has spent his youth and manhood in the minute study of the New Testament texts and of other people's studies of them, whose literary experience of those texts lack any standard of comparison such as can only grow from a wide and deep and genial experience of literature in general, is, I should think, very likely to miss the obvious things about them. If he tells me that something in a Gospel is legend or romance, I want to know how many legends or romances he has read, how well his palate is trained in detecting them by the flavour; not how many years he has spent on that Gospel.[6]

Similarly, it is not uncommon to find scholars who claim that Jonah is a fictitious story. In fact, an elderly colleague of mine (now retired) once confided in me that he mentioned to his class that he

---

ed. Michael D. Coogan, 3rd ed. [New York: Oxford University Press, 2001], 354 [Hebrew Bible section]).

4. E.g., John Dominic Crossan, *The Historical Jesus: The Life of a Mediterranean Jewish Peasant* (San Francisco: HarperSanFrancisco, 1991).

5. See Walter C. Kaiser Jr., *The Old Testament Documents: Are They Reliable and Relevant?* (Downers Grove, IL: InterVarsity Press, 2001); and F. F. Bruce, *The New Testament Documents: Are They Reliable*, 6th ed. (Downers Grove, IL: InterVarsity Press; Grand Rapids: Eerdmans, 1981).

6. C. S. Lewis, "Fern-Seed and Elephants," in *Fern-Seed and Elephants and Other Essays on Christianity*, ed. Walter Hooper (London: Fontana/Collins, 1975), 106–7.

thought Jonah was fictional. "Afterwards," the professor told me, "a student came up to me and said, 'Dr. _____, you probably shouldn't say that publicly. We like you and want you to keep teaching here.'"[7]

The student's intuition was correct, for not only does the book of Jonah report persons and places without any fictional artifice, but also Jesus refers to Jonah as a historical figure who was literally and historically inside the belly of a large fish (Matt. 12:40–41).

3. *Principles for interpreting genres can be misused to excuse oneself from the demands of Scripture.* Kierkegaard wryly remarked, "Christian scholarship is the human race's prodigious invention to defend itself against the New Testament, to ensure that one can continue to be a Christian without letting the New Testament come too close."[8] This cynically delivered truth can prove especially true with the academic application of various interpretive principles related to genre. For example, in considering Matthew 5:42 ("Give to the one who asks you, and do not turn away from the one who wants to borrow from you"), the interpreter may rightly note that Jesus' teaching here is classified as exaggeration. He may go on, then, to note correctly that one is not obligated to give a suicidal person a gun. In understanding the implicit qualifications of exaggeration, however, we go astray if we do not hear the radical call in Matthew 5:42 to let go of worldly goods. One may qualify and explain the text away until consciences are dulled into happy disobedience. As Pascal remarked, "Men never do evil so completely and cheerfully as when they do it from religious conviction."[9] Modern-day interpreters need to fear God's judgment if they seek to explain the text away as did Jesus' opponents (Mark 7:13).

REFLECTION QUESTIONS

1. Make a list of the different literary genres you encounter in a normal day. What are some of the assumptions you unconsciously make about such genres?

---

7. The school had recently gone through a major turnover, and most students were more conservative than the older faculty.
8. Søren Kierkegaard, *Søren Kierkegaard's Journals and Papers*, ed. and trans. Howard V. Hong and Edna H. Hong (Bloomington, IN: Indiana University Press, 1975), 3:270.
9. Pascal, *Pensées*, fragment 895 in *Great Books of the Western World: Pascal*, ed. Mortimer J. Adler, 2nd ed. (Chicago: Encyclopedia Britannica, 1990), 30:347. Within the volume, *Pensées* was translated by W. F. Trotter.

2. Look through a table of contents in the front of the Bible. Can you identify the literary genres that are contained in the various books?

3. Of the different literary genres included in the Bible (see chart above, if necessary), which, in your opinion, is most unfamiliar to modern readers?

4. Have you ever heard a sermon or Bible lesson that was in error because the interpreter misunderstood the genre of a biblical passage?

5. Can you think of an instance where interpretive principles were appealed to as an excuse for disregarding the clear teaching of Scripture?

FOR FURTHER STUDY

Osborne, Grant R. *The Hermeneutical Spiral: A Comprehensive Introduction to Biblical Interpretation*. Rev. ed. Downers Grove, IL: InterVarsity Press, 2006. (See part 2, "Genre Analysis").

How Do We Interpret Historical Narratives?

Historical narratives recount factual events in story format. A modern example would be the book *Flyboys* (2003), in which James Bradley reports the story of nine American airmen who were shot down in the Pacific during World War II. Historical narratives can be told for the storyteller's sake alone (for instance, to record memories) or for the audience—to teach, entertain, convince, etc. In reality, all historical narratives include some mixture of motives on the part of the narrator.

A large portion of the Old and New Testaments is historical narrative—about 60 percent.[1] In the Old Testament, for example, we find extensive historical narratives in Genesis, Exodus, Numbers, Joshua, Judges, Ruth, 1 and 2 Samuel, 1 and 2 Kings, 1 and 2 Chronicles, Ezra, Nehemiah, and Esther. In the New Testament, we have the Gospels (Matthew, Mark, Luke, and John) and Acts. The two-volume work Luke-Acts alone makes up one-fourth of the New Testament. It is worth noting that historical narrative is rarely a pure genre, in that it is often found mixed with other genres, such as genealogies (Matt. 1:1–17), songs (Exod. 15:1–18), proverbs (Matt. 26:52), prophecies (Mark 13:3–37), letters (Acts 23:25–30), or covenants (Josh. 24:1–28).

The Nature, Purpose, and Effectiveness of Biblical Narratives

Sometimes the truth value of biblical narrative is dismissed by labeling it as "mythological" or "tendentious." For a more general discussion of the trustworthiness of Scripture, see question 4 ("Does the Bible contain error?"), but a few comments are also in order here. Just as modern writers give clues to

---

1. Robert H. Stein, *A Basic Guide to Interpreting the Bible: Playing by the Rules* (Grand Rapids: Baker, 1994), 151.

their readers as to their own attitudes toward the truthfulness of their information, ancient writers did the same. It is clear from the mention of specific dates and persons, as well as general writing style, that the biblical authors believed themselves to be presenting factually accurate historical information. As with any narrative, we would not want to press the authors to be more specific than they intended. So, for instance, when Mark uses chronological introductions to his stories, they are quite indistinct (e.g., "One Sabbath Jesus was going through the grainfields" [Mark 2:23]). A survey of his work quickly shows that Mark is not intending to give a strict chronological account of Jesus' ministry.[2]

While the biblical narrative records many facts (the locations where the Israelites wandered in the wilderness or the names of Jesus' disciples, for example), the purpose of the narrative is to bring the reader to submit to God in Christ. The writers of biblical narratives want readers to side with the God-honoring and truth-loving characters in the story. The purpose of all Scripture, historical narratives included, is to make people wise, leading to a saving knowledge of Christ, as Paul noted was the case in Timothy's life (2 Tim. 3:15).

Historical narratives can be an especially effective form of communication. Some of the most successful speakers regularly punctuate their talks with stories. Stories are more memorable than other genres (compared with epistolary exhortation, for example). Readers or listeners are drawn into the accounts and even wish to enter the narratives for themselves. There is a strong affective (emotion-producing) dimension to narrative that makes it remarkably effectual in persuasion. Moreover, in the current state of American culture, the indirect nature of a narrative is sometimes more palatable to spiritually jaded listeners. Also, as a father of young children, I can testify that children are more open to hearing a story that illustrates God's grace than an abstract discussion of propositions or terms.

Guidelines for Interpreting Historical Narratives

Historical narratives also present some unique interpretive challenges. The biblical writer's purposes are usually undercurrents of the text rather than floating unmistakably on the surface. Because of this, unskilled interpreters

---

2. This fact is confirmed by the early church's understanding of Mark's intent. Papias (ca. A.D. 130) writes, "And the elder [the apostle John?] used to say this: 'Mark, having become Peter's interpreter, wrote down accurately everything he remembered, though not in order, of the things either said or done by Christ. For he neither heard the Lord nor followed him, but afterward, as I said, followed Peter, who adapted his teachings as needed but had no intention of giving an ordered account of the Lord's sayings. Consequently Mark did nothing wrong in writing down some things as he remembered them, for he made it his one concern not to omit anything that he heard or to make any false statement in them'" (*Fragments of Papias* 3.15 in *The Apostolic Fathers: Greek Texts and English Translations*, ed. and trans. Michael W. Holmes, 3rd ed. [Grand Rapids: Baker, 2007], 739–41).

are prone to missteps, leading both themselves and their listeners astray from the real meaning of the text. For example, many details in stories are not presented as normative. That is, the author is not intending to present all persons or actions as moral lessons. For example, my wife and I were once listening to some audio messages for new parents. The speaker exhorted parents to put their babies in cribs (as opposed to having them in the parents' bed) because Mary put Jesus in the manger (Luke 2:7). The key interpretive question of course is: why does Luke tell us that Jesus was placed in a manger? Was it to teach us how to put our children to bed, or was it to emphasize the Savior's humble origins? I've always wanted to point out to the speaker advocating cribs that Jesus told a parable in which a man's children are described as being in bed with him (Luke 11:7), probably the more normal sleeping convention of that day, yet still only a colorful detail in a memorable story—not a normative principle.

It is important to understand that interpretation of narratives should not simply be a reiteration of the facts in the narrative. Facts are included, grouped, and commented on by the writer for the purpose of convincing the reader of some truth. So, the interpreter's quest should be directed to the question of "why?" Robert Stein recommends the following type of exercise to get at the "why" of the narrative: "I, *Mark*, have told you this story about *the Gerasene demoniac* (Mark 5:1–20) because . . ." The italicized portions of this statement, of course, should be replaced with whatever author and account the interpreter is considering. The intent of this exercise is to prevent the interpreter from simply rehashing the story and to focus on the *intent* of the account. In the case of the demoniac, the story occurs in a litany of accounts that demonstrates Jesus' authority over different elements: nature (4:35–41); the demonic (5:1–20); disease (5:25–34); and death (5:21–24, 35–43). For Mark, the story of the demoniac demonstrates once again that Jesus is the Son of God (Mark 1:1; 15:39) who has absolute authority over the spiritual realm. Details such as how strong the demonized man was (Mark 5:3–5) or how many pigs the demons drove into the sea (Mark 5:13) only serve to highlight how powerful the one who defeated them is.

Below are guidelines that aid in interpreting historical narrative.[3]

1. *Context.* While context is important for all interpretation, it is especially important for the more indirect genre of historical narrative. The author of the biblical book did, in fact, intend his audience to read the whole account, so each minor section needs to be read in light of the whole and vice versa. In Mark 1:1, Mark tells us that the purpose of his account is to relate the good news about Messiah Jesus, the Son

---

3. These guidelines are adapted from Stein, *A Basic Guide to Interpreting the Bible*, 157–65.

of God. All the material that follows should be read in light of Mark's opening statement.

2. *Editorial Comments.* Sometimes the author will give explicit editorial comments as to the meaning or importance of an event. This is especially helpful to the reader and should not be overlooked. In Mark 7:19, for example, Mark notes that Jesus' comments about food and purity should be understood as declaring "all foods clean." Also, Mark notes that when the evil spirits cry out in Jesus' presence with expressions such as, "You are the Son of God" (Mark 3:11–12; cf. Mark 1:23–24; 5:7), they are accurately identifying who Jesus is. In the account of the demoniac discussed above, this point is significant because the demonized man cries out, "What do you want with me, Jesus, Son of the Most High God? Swear to God that you won't torture me!" (Mark 5:7) In this statement, the identity and authority of Jesus are highlighted, as Mark has prepared us to "trust" such demonic spokesmen.[4] One should be wary of any overly subtle interpretation for which the author has not prepared his readers.

3. *Thematic Statements.* Sometimes an author will begin his work or a section of his work with a thematic statement that helps us to understand the remainder of the work. An example of this would be Acts 1:8: "But you will receive power when the Holy Spirit comes on you; and you will be my witnesses in Jerusalem, and in all Judea and Samaria, and to the ends of the earth." As we see, the remainder of the book of Acts traces the Holy Spirit propelling the church outward in witness to the gospel of Christ in ever-widening geographic venues (e.g., Acts 2:14–42; 8:1–25, 26–40; 10:1–48; 11:19–21; 13:1–3; 28:28–31).

4. *Repetition.* Biblical authors did not have the luxury of bold script or impressive graphics. When they wanted to emphasize something, they often used repetition. As is clear from Mark's frequent summary statements on the matter, he wanted to emphasize the massive crowds that were drawn to Jesus, as well as their utter amazement at his teaching and miracles (e.g., Mark 1:27–28, 45; 2:12; 3:7–12; 4:1).

5. *Trustworthy Characters.* Whether directly or indirectly, the author clues the reader as to which characters are to be believed or imitated.

---

4. In his classroom lectures, Stein recommends highlighting (e.g., with a yellow marker) all such editorial comments and authorial summary statements within a work to look for repeated patterns.

So, for example, when an angel from God speaks to a character, there is no doubt that the angel is conveying trustworthy information (e.g., Matt. 1:20–25). As noted above, even demons can be considered trustworthy when they are overwhelmed by the powerful presence of Jesus and, in submissive spiritual reflex, declare his true identity (e.g., Mark 5:7).

One of the most helpful ways to learn how to interpret historical narrative is to listen to or read numerous examples of judicious interpretation. The wise interpreter is always seeking the authorial meaning of the text and does not use extraneous details for his own sermonizing flights of fancy. Such careful interpretative skill is more often caught than taught. For that reason, it is helpful to read commentaries by skillful interpreters.[5] By reading such commentaries, one will begin to absorb both the artistic touch and the analytic mind that are essential to careful interpretation. The beginning interpreter of narratives is also encouraged to find a wiser, more experienced reader who can offer critique and correction. Such solicited feedback, albeit immediately painful, will in the long run be quite salutary.

REFLECTION QUESTIONS

1. Have you ever heard someone employ a story as an especially effective form of communication? If so, when?

2. Do you recall a sermon or Bible lesson in which the speaker/author illegitimately interpreted a biblical narrative?

3. Do you know a trusted interpreter (a more experienced friend, for example) who would be willing to offer critical feedback on your sermons or Bible lessons?

4. In the next sermon you hear on a narrative passage, ask yourself these questions: Did the speaker arrive at the correct meaning of the text? If he did not interpret the text correctly, what interpretive principles discussed above aid in properly understanding the text?

5. Choose a narrative book in the Bible, photocopy it, and highlight all authorial comments or summary statements. At the end, look back over the highlighted portions. What was the author emphasizing?

---

5. See the commentaries recommended in the "For Further Study" section below.

FOR FURTHER STUDY

Carson, D. A. *Matthew, Chapters 1–12*. Expositor's Bible Commentary. Grand Rapids: Zondervan, 1995.

_____. *Matthew, Chapters 13–28*. Expositor's Bible Commentary. Grand Rapids: Zondervan, 1995.

Frei, Hans W. *The Eclipse of Biblical Narrative: A Study in Eighteenth and Nineteenth Century Hermeneutics*. New Haven, CT: Yale University Press, 1974.

Stein, Robert H. *Mark*. BECNT. Grand Rapids: Baker, 2008.

_____. *Luke*. The NAC 24. Nashville: Broadman, 1992.

How Do We Interpret Prophecy? (General Guidelines)

To many people the word *prophecy* brings to mind the picture of a wide-eyed harbinger of doom, someone walking the streets with a sign that says, "REPENT! THE WORLD WILL END TOMORROW!" Nevertheless, we must set aside our biases and turn to the Scriptures for a true understanding of prophecy. Indeed, what is *biblical* prophecy, and what are some principles that will help us understand it? In this question, we will present a broad survey of prophecy and then offer guidelines that will help in interpreting most prophecy. In the next question, we will discuss a subsection of prophecy known as typology.

Defining Prophet and Prophecy

The words *prophet* and *prophecy* have a range of meaning within the Bible. At the most fundamental level, a prophet is someone who is sent by God with a prophecy—that is, a message from him (Jer. 1:4–10; Matt. 23:34). As we continue to explain these terms below, we will inevitably move back and forth between discussing the agent (prophet) and his divine message (prophecy).

The Old Testament's use of the term *prophet* exhibits a range of meaning. Moses says, "I wish that all the LORD's people were prophets and that the LORD would put his Spirit on them!" (Num. 11:29) Yet such is clearly not the case. The author of Hebrews describes all the previous divine spokesmen and inspired authors of the old covenant era as "prophets" (Heb. 1:1). It seems that "schools," or communities, of prophets existed (e.g., 1 Kings 18:4, 19; 20:35; 2 Kings 2:3–7, 15; 4:1, 38; 5:22; 6:1; 9:1) and that such groups were known for their music-accompanied itinerant worship (1 Sam. 10:5), eccentric behavior (1 Kings 20:35–43; 2 Kings 9:11; Ezek. 4–5), fearless proclamation of the truth to disobedient Israel (I Kings 22:6–28), and the God-given ability to predict the future, explain dreams, or have access to other hidden information (1 Sam. 9:19–20; Ezek. 8; Dan. 2:27–28). The prophets denounce

Israel and/or surrounding nations for their disobedience to God. Judgment is threatened; blessings are promised. Sometimes specific prophecies related to battles (Dan. 11), or rulers (Isa. 45:1), or the coming Messiah (Mic. 5:2–3) describe events dozens or even hundreds of years in advance.

In the new covenant era (inaugurated by Jesus), all God's people are considered prophets in some sense, for all have the Lord's word on their heart and speak it to their neighbor (Joel 2:28–29; Heb. 8:11; Acts 2:16–18; cf. Matt. 5:12). Yet even in this era of fulfillment, there remains a unique gift of prophecy that is given to only some of God's people (Rom. 12:6; 1 Cor. 12:10, 29; 14:29–32). Such prophecy apparently includes both predictions of coming events and timely exhortations that demonstrate insight beyond that which is natural (1 Cor. 14:25–30; Acts 2:30; 11:27–28). Both men and women are described as having the spiritual gift of prophecy (Luke 2:36; Acts 2:17; 11:27–28; 21:9).

Prophecy is Spirit-inspired utterance. Thus, the Old Testament authors describe the Spirit as both coming upon and departing from persons as their prophetic activity is respectively enabled or ceased (1 Sam. 10:10–13; 19:20–23; Ps. 51:11). The New Testament, by contrast, emphasizes new covenant believers' eternal possession of the Spirit (John 14:16–17; Rom. 8:9). But even in the new covenant era, believers can, depending on their response to God, be filled with the Spirit (Acts 4:31; Eph. 5:18) or grieve the Spirit (Eph. 4:30).

One paradigmatic passage for prophecy in the Bible is Deuteronomy 18:15–22. Here, Moses says:

> The LORD your God will raise up for you a prophet like me from among your own brothers. You must listen to him. For this is what you asked of the LORD your God at Horeb on the day of the assembly when you said, "Let us not hear the voice of the LORD our God nor see this great fire anymore, or we will die." The LORD said to me: "What they say is good. I will raise up for them a prophet like you from among their brothers; I will put my words in his mouth, and he will tell them everything I command him. If anyone does not listen to my words that the prophet speaks in my name, I myself will call him to account. But a prophet who presumes to speak in my name anything I have not commanded him to say, or a prophet who speaks in the name of other gods, must be put to death." You may say to yourselves, "How can we know when a message has not been spoken by the LORD?" If what a prophet proclaims in the name of the LORD does not take place or come true, that is a message the LORD has not spoken. That prophet has spoken presumptuously. Do not be afraid of him.

While this passage describes a succession of prophets after Moses, it also should be understood as referring to the climactic Prophet of prophets, Jesus of Nazareth, who as the unique Son of God, spoke the very words of God (John 3:34; Acts 3:22–23).

It is significant that in Deuteronomy 18:15–22, Moses also envisages the ongoing appearance of false prophets who seek to turn Israel to another god or declare false prophecies in the name of the true God. Israel's subsequent history proved Moses' prophecy true (e.g., 1 Kings 22:6–28; Jer. 23:9–21; Mic. 3:5–12). Likewise, Jesus predicted that before his second coming many false prophets would appear (Mark 13:22; Matt. 24:23–24), and the succession of years has shown his words to be true (1 John 4:1). Many people continue to claim to speak for God (that is, to be prophets), when in actuality they blaspheme God through the lies they declare about him.

Guidelines for Interpreting Prophecy

Just opening a book of prophecy to a random passage can be confusing. Below are some guidelines to help in the proper interpretation of prophecy.

1. *Investigate the book's background, date, and author.* To whom is the prophetic oracle addressed? Is there a unifying theme to the book? When were the prophecies proclaimed or written? Who is the author, and what do we know about him? How would the original hearers have understood the prophecies? To help answer these questions, consult a good study Bible (e.g., *The Zondervan NIV Study Bible* or *ESV Study Bible*) or an evangelical introduction to the Old Testament (e.g., Gleason Archer's *A Survey of Old Testament Introduction,* R. K. Harrison's *Introduction to the Old Testament,* or Raymond B. Dillard and Tremper Longman's *An Introduction to the Old Testament*).[1] Of course, as you work through the biblical text itself in greater detail, you should adjust your original understanding as the text demands. While availing ourselves of many excellent study tools, we must always remember that only the inspired biblical text has divine authority.

2. *Pay attention to context.* Allow the paragraph and section divisions of a modern Bible to help guide you. Modern editions of the Bible usually will add headings and subheadings to the text so that readers can follow more easily the author's unfolding message. When doing an in-depth study of a passage, it is advisable to compare several modern translations' segmentation of the text. If major modern translations disagree on the division of the text, the interpreter must investigate the reasons for the discrepancy and weigh the issues for himself.

3. *Expect figurative language.* Prophecy is the language of judgment, anguish, longing, and celebration. As an emotive genre, it is filled with poetic pictures and exaggerated expressions. In fact, many biblical

---

1. For full bibliographic information, see the "For Further Study" section below.

books of prophecy are written in Hebrew poetic meter. Modern English Bibles usually cue the reader to this fact by displaying the English text in poetic line (that is, leaving lots of white space around the text rather than just having blocks of black text, as in other portions of the Bible). The prophet's use of poetic meter is a further indication that one should be expecting figurative, poetic expressions and symbolism. If the author intended his language to be understood literally, we want to understand it literally. If he intended his words to be understood figuratively, likewise, we want to understand them that way. As we study the text, we are seeking the conscious intention of the divinely inspired author. Most modern Americans are prone to read all language literally. Undoubtedly, the Hebrew language of the Scriptures is much more likely to contain hyperbole and figurative language than the type of literature most modern Americans read regularly (e.g., newspapers, magazines).

4. *Distinguish conditional and unconditional prophecy.* Prophecies can be given as unalterable purposes of God (Gen. 12:1–3, Gal. 3:15–18), or they can be given as conditional promises or warnings (Jonah 3:4). Only additional statements in the context clarify whether the prophecy is unconditional or conditional. Conditional prophecies sometimes do not explicitly state implied conditions. Nevertheless, a foundational prophetic condition, at least for national judgment and blessing, is found in the book of Jeremiah.

> If at any time I announce that a nation or kingdom is to be uprooted, torn down and destroyed, and if that nation I warned repents of its evil, then I will relent and not inflict on it the disaster I had planned. And if at another time I announce that a nation or kingdom is to be built up and planted, and if it does evil in my sight and does not obey me, then I will reconsider the good I had intended to do for it. (18:7–10)

If such implied conditions for national judgment did not exist, the prophet Jonah would be a liar, for he proclaimed, "Forty more days and Nineveh will be overturned" (Jonah 3:4). Yet, when the city repents, the Lord relents (Jonah 3:10). Indeed, Jonah's awareness of God's merciful disposition is why he did not want to go to Nineveh in the first place. He hoped to avoid giving the Ninevites any chance at repentance (Jonah 4:1–2).

Such conditional prophecy demonstrates the mysterious way the sovereign, all-knowing God interacts with finite creatures. If God ultimately knows the Ninevites will repent, why does he have Jonah announce their destruction? It is because hearing the doom they deserve is the divinely appointed means to bring about their repentance. In God's sovereign purposes, the prophet's announcement of judgment sometimes serves to open the spigot of divine mercy. In other cases, the oracle serves only to increase the culpability of the rebellious humans (Isa. 6:9–13; Matt. 11:21–24; Mark 4:11–12).[2]

5. *Seek to understand what the inspired author is trying to convey to his original audience before seeking to determine the implications for us today.* One must be careful to distinguish prophecy of specific, unrepeatable events from the underlying patterns of God's dealings with humankind. God is not capricious, so the characteristics displayed by God in prophetic texts can be linked to similar situations today (for example, the ultimate accountability of wayward nations, the preservation of a faithful remnant, the apparent delay in God's judgment of the wicked, etc.). One specific example is the repeated prophetic declaration of God's faithfulness to Israel, even though they constantly abandon him. What analogous situation do we see today? The visible church fails to demonstrate consistently the truth of the gospel, but we know that Jesus has promised that he will build his church and that nothing can stop its ultimate advance and the coming consummation of his kingdom (Matt. 16:18).

6. *Determine whether the prophetic predictions are fulfilled or unfulfilled.* If there is an eschatological referent in the text, it may be difficult in some cases to determine the state of fulfillment. When possible, allow the New Testament to be your guide on the fulfillment of messianic and eschatological Old Testament prophecies. Sometimes, New Testament authors inform us that Old Testament prophecies were fulfilled in unexpected ways, finding ultimate expression in Jesus and the church (e.g., Acts 2:17–21; 15:16–18; Heb. 8:8–12).

7. *Note the apologetic value of prophecy.* In the earliest Christian preaching, the apostles appealed to the fulfillment of prophecy as the divine imprimatur of the Christian gospel (Acts 2:17–21). Centuries later, the mathematician and French philosopher Blaise Pascal (1623–1662) appealed to fulfilled prophecy as proof of Christianity's truthfulness.[3]

---

2. Other clear instances of conditional prophecies include the destruction of Jerusalem (Mic. 3:12; Jer. 26:18–19), the judgment on Ahab and his family (1 Kings 21:20–29), and the sickness of Hezekiah (2 Kings 20:1–5).

3. Pascal writes, "I see many contradictory religions, and consequently all false save one. Each wants to be believed on its own authority, and threatens unbelievers. I do not therefore believe them. Every one can say this; every one can call himself a prophet. But I see that Christian religion wherein prophecies are fulfilled; and that is what every one cannot do" (*Pensées*, fragment 693 in *Great Books of the Western World: Pascal*, ed. Mortimer J. Adler,

Still today, as Christians appeal to outsiders for a hearing, they point to the miraculous fulfillment of predictions in the Bible.[4]

I recall a conversation I had with a religion professor in college. As he assumed a late date for the book of Daniel, I asked, "Don't scholars date the book of Daniel late because they assume that the prophecies of various battles and rulers are too accurate to have been uttered hundreds of years prior to those events?" He admitted that such was the case. Skeptical scholars label such a prophecy with the Latin phrase *vaticinium ex eventu*, meaning "foretelling after the event," because they claim that the prophecies were fabricated to appear as predictions but were actually written after the events described.

I remember another situation in college where I was sitting with a Turkish (Muslim) young lady on the school courtyard. We had a class on Islam together and were continuing a conversation begun in class. I asked her to read Isaiah 53. After she read it, I inquired, "What is that about?" "Well, it's about Jesus, obviously," she said.

"It was written more than seven hundred years before Jesus was born," I said.

She was stunned.

8. *Understand the difference between Old Testament-era and New Testament-era prophecy.* As prophets sometimes spoke to unspectacular daily issues in the Old Testament era (e.g., lost donkeys, 1 Sam. 9:20), there were undoubtedly many prophecies that were never written down. The ones that have been recorded and preserved, however, are recognized as "God-breathed" (2 Tim. 3:16). Similarly, the early Christian writings of the apostles and their companions/associates are received as uniquely inspired and authoritative (see question 6, "Who determined what books would be included in the Bible?"). As prophecies continued during and after the writing of the New Testament (and even today), we need to note that the ongoing gift of Christian prophecy is different from the inscripturated prophecies we have in the Bible. All post-New Testament prophecy must be weighed and sifted by the church according to the standard of Scripture (1 Cor. 14:29; 1 John 4:1). Paul writes, "Do not treat prophecies with contempt. Test everything. Hold on to the good" (1 Thess. 5:20–21).[5]

2nd ed. [Chicago: Encyclopedia Britannica, 1990], 30:301–2). Within the volume, *Pensées* was translated by W. F. Trotter.

4. Josh McDowell, *Evidence for Christianity: Historical Evidences for the Christian Faith* (Nashville: Thomas Nelson, 2006), 193–243.

5. For more on the spiritual gift of prophecy, see Wayne Grudem, *Systematic Theology: An Introduction to Biblical Doctrine* (Grand Rapids: Zondervan; Leicester: Inter-Varsity Press, 1994), 1049–61; idem, *The Gift of Prophecy in 1 Corinthians* (Lanham, MD: University

REFLECTION QUESTIONS

1. How is biblical prophecy different stylistically from the normal language you use in everyday conversation?

2. Are there any prophecies in Scripture that have encouraged your faith in the divine origin of the Bible?

3. Do you feel confident detecting figurative language in prophecy? If not, what would aid you in doing so?

4. What do you believe about the gift of prophecy mentioned in the New Testament? Is it still operative today? What does it look like?

5. Have you ever appealed to biblical prophecy to commend or defend the trustworthiness of the Bible?

FOR FURTHER STUDY

Archer, Gleason L. *A Survey of Old Testament Introduction.* Rev. ed. Chicago: Moody Press, 1994.

Dillard, Raymond B., and Tremper Longman. *An Introduction to the Old Testament.* Grand Rapids: Zondervan, 1994.

Harrison, R. K. *Introduction to the Old Testament.* Grand Rapids: Eerdmans, 1969; reprint, Peabody, MA: Prince (Hendrickson), 1999.

McDowell, Josh. *Evidence for Christianity: Historical Evidences for the Christian Faith.* Nashville: Thomas Nelson, 2006.

Press of America, 1982); idem, *The Gift of Prophecy in the New Testament and Today,* rev. ed. (Wheaton, IL: Crossway, 2000); and idem, "Prophecy—Yes, but Teaching—No: Paul's Consistent Advocacy of Women's Participation Without Governing Authority," *JETS* 30, no. 1 (1987): 1–23.

How Do We Interpret Prophecy? (Typology)

In the previous question, we surveyed the terms *prophet* and *prophecy* and offered eight guidelines for interpreting prophecy. There is, however, a subset of prophecy known as typology, which deserves special attention. In this question, we will focus on how to interpret biblical typology.

What Is Typology?

In parts of the New Testament, the Old Testament is quoted in unexpected ways. For example, in Matthew 2:13–15, we read:

> When [the magi] had gone, an angel of the Lord appeared to Joseph in a dream. "Get up," he said, "take the child and his mother and escape to Egypt. Stay there until I tell you, for Herod is going to search for the child to kill him." So he got up, took the child and his mother during the night and left for Egypt, where he stayed until the death of Herod. And so was fulfilled what the Lord had said through the prophet: "Out of Egypt I called my son."

The last sentence quoted in this passage, is from Hosea 11:1. Most Christians assume that if they were to look up Hosea 11:1, they would find something like this:

> One day, promises the Lord, I will send my Messiah, the Christ, the Son of God. And even at his birth, the rulers will rage against him, and he will flee to Egypt. But, I will call him back to accomplish my purposes. Yes, and then it will be said, "Out of Egypt I called my son."

In fact, in the context of Hosea, the passage is addressed to disobedient Israel. Hosea proclaims that just as Israel (God's "son") was once "exiled" to slavery in Egypt, so in the prophet's day, the nation will be exiled to Assyria for their sins. Yet, in the same way that God delivered the Israelites out of that seemingly never-ending Egyptian slavery, so in Hosea's day, God will again deliver them out of bondage in Assyria.

Against initial appearances, Matthew is not haphazardly citing a text from the Old Testament. Along with the other inspired authors of Scripture and the Jews of his day, Matthew affirmed a providential understanding of history. Moreover, he believed that history recorded a series of successive, corresponding saving events moving toward a divine climactic intervention in Christ. The earlier divine interventions served as types (corresponding anticipations) for the final antitype (fulfillment). Because God is completely sovereign over history, *all* Old Testament-era saving events, institutions, persons, offices, holidays, and ceremonies served to anticipate the final saving event, the final saving person, the final saving ceremony, etc. This style of citing the Old Testament is known as typological interpretation. It occurs frequently in Matthew and Hebrews, both originally addressed to Jewish readers, who would have shared the authors' typological assumptions. For the original audiences, Matthew and the author of Hebrews unfolded the stereoscopic Christological depth of Old Testament history. Not only specific predictions, but also all of Israel's history, pointed to Jesus. The two-dimensional history of Israel became a three-dimensional living reality as it found its climactic reenactment in the Messiah.

Assumptions of Typological Interpretation

To better understand the New Testament authors' typological use of the Old Testament, it is important to make explicit the assumptions the biblical authors and their original audiences shared. Below is a list of such assumptions with brief explanatory comments.

1. *The authors of Scripture had a concept of corporate solidarity.* Klyne Snodgrass explains:

> [The expression "corporate solidarity"] refers to the oscillation or reciprocal relation between the individual and the community that existed in the Semitic mind. The act of the individual is not merely an individual act, for it affects the community and vice versa. The individual is often representative of the community and vice versa. Achan sinned and the whole nation suffered [Josh. 7].[1]

---

1. Klyne Snodgrass, "The Use of the Old Testament in the New," in *New Testament Criticism and Interpretation*, ed. David Alan Black and David S. Dockery (Grand Rapids: Zondervan, 1991), 416.

Christians should not balk at the concept of corporate solidarity, for it is the basis for our salvation! As Paul remarks, "One [i.e., Jesus] died for all, and therefore all died" (2 Cor. 5:14). Snodgrass comments further:

> The representative character of Jesus' ministry, which is closely related to corporate solidarity, is one of the most important keys in understanding him and the way Old Testament texts are applied to him. The Christological titles "Servant," "Son of Man," and "Son of God" were all representative titles that were applied to Israel first. Jesus took on these titles because he had taken Israel's task. He was representative of Israel and in solidarity with her. God's purposes for Israel were now taken up in his ministry. If this were true, what had been used to describe Israel could legitimately be used of him.[2]

In Matthew's citation of Hosea 11:1, we see that the unique Son, Jesus, is compared with the nation of Israel (also called God's "son"). Although Israel the son chased after foreign idols (Hos. 11:2), the unique Son was faithful in all things. Even so, just as the promises to Israel the son appeared endangered by Egyptian slavery and Assyrian exile, so the unique Son's role appeared threatened. How could Jesus fulfill his messianic calling while a refugee in Egypt? Even so, God's purposes and promises for his son/Son (Israel and ultimately Jesus) always prevail.

2. *Biblical authors assumed "a continuity in God's dealings with Israel, so that earlier events foreshadow later ones."*[3] We can compare Israel's view of history with a dimly lit stairway. As we make our way up those stairs (possibly feeling along the wall to steady ourselves), we expect the steps to follow a recognizable, repeated pattern. And though it is too dark to see clearly, we know that we are moving toward the top, although we don't know how close we are until we actually arrive. Similarly, the Jews expected God's later divine interventions to mirror his earlier ones, knowing that ultimately the climactic apex of saving history, the Messiah, would come. At that point, the Jews expected to look back over all prior salvation history and see the anticipatory patterns that led to that deliverer—the Christ. In fact, this is the very ap-

---

2. Ibid.
3. Mark Seifrid, "Introduction to the New Testament: Historical Background and Gospels, Course Number NT 22200" (unpublished notes, Southern Baptist Theological Seminary, fall 1998), 73.

proach the New Testament writers follow in their typological citations of the Old Testament.

To further illustrate this concept to my classes, I will sometimes ask, "Who in here became a Christian after age twenty?" A few people will raise their hands. Then I will choose one and ask, "When you were six years old, were you thinking, 'God is having this happen in my life so that I will seek him one day'? Or, when you were eighteen, did you think, 'God is having me go to this college, so I will hear the message of salvation'? No, you did not, but once you came to know Christ, did you not look back over your life and see how God was working to bring about your salvation? Typological interpretation is similar to that— looking back to see the providential foreshadowing of God."

3. *The New Testament authors understood themselves as living in days of eschatological fulfillment.* In other words (to continue the analogy proposed above), the New Testament authors believed they were at the top of the stairs. The climax had come. The apex of salvation, Jesus, the Messiah, had been revealed. Thus, it was not only hermeneutically appropriate but also interpretively incumbent to look back over God's prior saving interventions and see how this climax was anticipated.

4. *The New Testament authors believed that all the Scriptures were about the Christ* (Luke 24:27; 2 Cor. 1:20; 1 Peter 1:10–12). Salvation had arrived, and all God's promises were fulfilled in Jesus. Because God's salvation is found ultimately in a person (the Christ, Jesus), then all of God's prior saving work and revelations anticipate in some way the coming of this Messiah.

5. *For biblical authors, the concept of fulfillment was broader than our normal English usage of that term.* Henry Virkler lists the range of meaning for the Hebrew and Greek words underlying "fulfill" in our English versions.

   - Drawing out the full implications of something (Matt. 5:17; cf. verses 18–48).

   - Completion of a fixed time (Mark 1:15; Luke 21:24).

   - Satisfying a request or desire (Esther 5:8; Ps. 145:19; Prov. 13:19).

   - Carrying out what is promised (Lev. 22:21).

   - Conforming to or obeying a requirement (Gal. 5:14; James 2:8; Matt. 3:15).

- Corresponding of phrases, illustrations, or events between one historical period and another (Matt. 2:23; cf. Isa. 11:1; Jer. 31:15; cf. Matt. 2:17–18; Isa. 9:1–2; cf. Matt. 4:13–16).[4]

When an ordinary modern American reads a passage from Matthew that says that Jesus fulfilled an Old Testament prophecy, that person assumes that Matthew is referring to the fulfillment of a unique, unrepeatable propositional prediction. In actuality, Matthew could mean that, or he could be using the word in another way—possibly referring more broadly to the fulfillment of typological patterns in Israel's history (the last meaning in Virkler's list above). If we struggle to understand this concept, the problem is not with the Bible but with our narrow understanding of prophecy, which needs to be properly informed by the actual biblical usage.

Is Typological Interpretation a Reproducible Model?

In a famous lecture (and subsequently published article), New Testament scholar Richard Longenecker asked, "Can we reproduce the exegesis of the New Testament?"[5] Longenecker was asking whether we, as modern interpreters, can apply typological interpretive methods to passages not so cited by New Testament authors. Bible-believing Christians have reached a variety of conclusions on the matter. In my opinion, it is necessary to ask how any part of Scripture points to Christ. We must be cautious, however, in proposing any typological correspondences that are not explicitly mentioned in Scripture. In other words, we should keep the surface-level meaning of the text the primary focus of our exposition and give appropriate interpretive caveats when suggesting a Christological application not found explicitly in the Bible. Obscure symbolic interpretations of Old Testament laws should be avoided. It is probably wise to ask a friend who is more experienced in biblical interpretation to critique any newly proposed Christological typology before publicly proclaiming it.

Other Options for Interpreting Puzzling Prophecies

Sometimes the New Testament authors cite straightforward propositional predictions from the Old Testament (Matt. 8:17; cf. Isa. 53:4). At other times, their citations are better explained as typology (Matt. 2:13–15; cf. Hos. 11:1).

---

4. Henry Virkler, *Hermeneutics: Principles and Processes of Biblical Interpretation*, 1st ed. (Grand Rapids: Baker, 1981), 204–5. This information is not in the revised edition of this book.
5. R. N. Longenecker, "Can We Reproduce the Exegesis of the New Testament?" *TynBul* 21 (1970): 3–38. Longenecker questions not only whether modern interpreters can interpret the Old Testament typologically but, more broadly, whether they can apply a variety of early Jewish hermeneutical methods.

Still other New Testament citations may be better explained by one of the following options.

1. *The New Testament authors occasionally cite the Old Testament in rhetorical fashion, not meaning to assert any prophetic fulfillment.* For example, it is not clear that by citing a phrase from Numbers 16:5 in 2 Timothy 2:19 ("The Lord knows those who are his") that Paul is intending his reader(s) to assume the context of Numbers 16:5 in understanding that phrase.

2. *Sometimes a single prophecy will include multiple events.* Chronological distance between multiple events is often not made clear in the original prediction. For example, the first and second comings of Christ (to save and to judge) are blended together in Isaiah 61:1–2. Only with further revelation at Christ's first coming are we made aware that a distance of time will separate his coming to save and coming to judge (Luke 4:18–19, Matt. 25:31–46). This blending of multiple events in one prophecy is called prophetic foreshortening. This style of prophecy has been compared with multiple transparencies laid on top of each other on an overhead projector. The image projected on the wall appears as a unified whole, even though it is made up of several layers. Similarly, a mountain chain seen from a distance appears almost two-dimensional. Only as we draw near to the first mountain do we see that the other mountains lie stretched out before us in the distance.

3. *A number of interpreters claim that the only way to understand some New Testament citations of the Old Testament is to appeal to sensus plenior* (Latin: "fuller sense"). That is, the Holy Spirit revealed a hidden meaning of which no human author was aware until the Spirit revealed it. An example of this would be John Broadus's explanation of Matthew 1:22–23. He writes:

> It is often unnecessary, and sometimes impossible, to suppose that the prophet himself had in mind that which the New Testament writer calls a fulfillment of his prediction. Some predictions were involuntary, as that of Caiaphas (John 11:50). Many prophecies received fulfillments which the prophet does not appear to have at all contemplated. But as God's providence often brought about the fulfillment though the human actors were heedless or even ignorant of the predictions they fulfilled (e.g., John 19:24), so God's Spirit often contemplated fulfillments of which the prophet had no conception, but which the Evangelist makes known. And it is of a piece with the general development of revelation that the later inspiration

should explain the records of earlier inspiration, and that only after events have occurred should the early predictions of them be fully understood.[6]

Though many skilled interpreters appeal to *sensus plenior*, I believe all New Testament citations of the Old Testament can be explained without recourse to it.

REFLECTION QUESTIONS

1. When reading the New Testament, do you ever look up Old Testament verses that are quoted?

2. Which is a more convincing way to understand Matthew 2:13–15, as typology or *sensus plenior*? Why?

3. Have you ever heard or read a typological interpretation that you considered invalid?

4. Explain the use of Jeremiah 31:15 in Matthew 2:18. (You may need to consult a study Bible or commentary to understand the context of Jeremiah 31.)

5. Does the understanding of typology presented above challenge you to read your Bible differently? If so, how?

FOR FURTHER STUDY

Davidson, Richard M. *Typology in Scripture: A Study of Hermeneutical* Tupos *Structures*. Berrien Springs, MI: Andrews University Press, 1981.
Fairbairn, Patrick. *Typology of Scripture: Two Volumes in One*. New York: Funk & Wagnalls, 1900; reprint, Grand Rapids: Kregel, 2000.
Goppelt, Leonhard. *Typos: The Typological Interpretation of the Old Testament in the New*. Translated by Donald H. Madvig. Grand Rapids: Eerdmans, 1982.
Johnson, S. Lewis. *The Old Testament in the New*. Grand Rapids: Zondervan, 1980.

---

6. John A. Broadus, *Commentary on the Gospel of Matthew. An American Commentary on the New Testament* (London: Baptist Tract and Book Society; Philadelphia: American Baptist Publication Society, 1886), 11–12.

Moo, Douglas J. "The Problem of *Sensus Plenior*." In *Hermeneutics, Authority, and Canon,* 175–211. Grand Rapids: Zondervan, 1986; reprint, Eugene, OR: Wipf & Stock, 2005.

Snodgrass, Klyne. "The Use of the Old Testament in the New." In *New Testament Criticism and Interpretation,* 408–34. Edited by David Alan Black and David S. Dockery. Grand Rapids: Zondervan, 1991.

How Do We Interpret Apocalyptic Literature?

The English word *apocalyptic* comes from the Greek word *apokaluptō*, meaning "to reveal" or "to unveil." Apocalyptic literature is a genre of Jewish literature characterized by its use of symbolic imagery to reveal God's mysterious, providential workings behind the scenes and his coming plans for the future. Apocalyptic literature generally appears within a four-hundred-year span, from the second century B.C. to the second century A.D. (though Daniel is written before this time frame and is often classified as apocalyptic). Most, if not all, nonbiblical apocalypses are pseudonymous (i.e., written under a false name).

Characteristics of Apocalyptic Literature

While there is a good deal of variety among apocalyptic writings, some common characteristics include the following.

1. The expectation of the inbreaking of God into the present age to usher in a qualitatively different existence in the age to come.

2. The use of an angelic mediator or mediators to communicate God's message to a chosen recipient/spokesman.

3. The journey of the chosen human recipient into the heavenly realms, with ongoing interaction and communication with the angelic mediator(s).

4. Highly symbolic visions or dreams that describe both current hidden spiritual realities and future divine interventions.

5. Visions of final, divine judgment.

6. Warnings of coming distresses and trials to be faced by the faithful.

7. Encouragements to the faithful to persevere in light of the true spiritual realities and coming divine interventions.

Within the Bible there are isolated elements that might be classified as apocalyptic (e.g., Isa. 24–27; Ezek. 38–39; Zech. 1–6; Mark 13), but the only canonical books with enough relevant content to be considered part of the apocalyptic genre are Daniel and Revelation. The English word *revelation* is a synonym for *apocalypse,* which is itself a transliteration of one word from the underlying Greek title, *Apokalupsis Iōannou* ("The Apocalypse/Revelation of John"). Although much of Revelation does fit the standard description of an apocalypse, it is, in fact, more of a composite work. Part of the book is made up of letters (Rev. 2:1–3:22), while other parts seem to mirror Old Testament prophecy (cf. Rev. 1:3).[1] Similarly, the first half of Daniel is composed of narratives about faithful Jews in Babylonian exile, while the latter half records Daniel's apocalyptic visions about coming earthly battles and, finally, the end of the age. Without some understanding of the genre of apocalypse, both Daniel and Revelation will remain enigmas to modern readers.

It is also important to note how Daniel and Revelation differ from other apocalyptic works in a fundamental way. As Christians, we recognize the books of Daniel and Revelation as inerrant Scripture. No other apocalypse can claim this status.

Interpreting Daniel

First transcribed in the sixth century B.C., Daniel's visions in chapters 7–12 describe great shifts of international power in the coming centuries, with special emphasis on battles in the second century B.C.[2] Also, Daniel's visions anticipate the climax of history and the resurrection of the dead (Dan. 12:1–4). A good study Bible or commentary on Daniel will assist the modern reader in understanding the sometimes obscure imagery and historical allusions (see question 13, "What are some helpful books or tools for interpreting the Bible?").

Interpreting the Book of Revelation

Recognizing the book of Revelation as apocalyptic literature leads us to begin with a major interpretive caveat: we must be careful to interpret the

---

1. J. J. Collins notes, "There is obvious continuity between the Jewish and Christian apocalypses and the Hebrew prophets, in their concern with history and expectation of divine intervention and judgment" ("Apocalyptic Literature," in *DNTB*, 42).

2. Because of these detailed predictions, some scholars claim that Daniel was written pseudonymously during the second century B.C. Such an approach, however, is not necessitated unless one rules out divine intervention *a priori.* See Gleason L. Archer, *A Survey of Old Testament Introduction,* rev. ed. (Chicago: Moody Press, 1994), 421–47.

symbolic images according to the author's intent. Because of the difficulty in understanding some parts of Revelation, we should not adopt any interpretation that is out of harmony with the rest of the Bible. We must have great humility. A godly, learned pastor once told me that he was preaching through Revelation at his church, but when he arrived at Revelation 11 he did not feel that he could go any farther. He was at a loss as to the true interpretation of the text. He humbly explained the situation to his congregation and said that he would return when he felt that he could proclaim the message of the text with authority.

There are several distinct interpretive approaches to the book of Revelation.

1. *Preterist.* According to preterists, while portions of Revelation may have been forward-looking when initially written, almost all events described in Revelation already have taken place, most in the first century or soon thereafter. Preterists tie much of the cataclysmic symbols in Revelation to the destruction of the Jewish temple in Jerusalem in A.D. 70.

2. *Historicist.* Historicists approach Revelation as a blueprint of the entire span of church history. Thus, portions of the book describe the past, while others look to the future.[3]

3. *Idealist.* Idealists see Revelation as describing the spiritual realities that reoccur throughout history until the final consummation. It is erroneous, then, to seek particular rulers or events that uniquely correspond with the beasts or images and events in Revelation. Many events throughout history correspond to these same symbols.

4. *Futurist.* The futurist view sees the majority of Revelation as applying to future end-time events that occur directly prior to Christ's return.

Scholars also sometimes adopt a combination of the views above. In my opinion, parts of Revelation are read best through the preterist lens (e.g., Rev. 2–3), but most of the book should be understood according to the idealist approach. Still, in accord with futurist interpretations, some portions of Revelation await a one-time fulfillment at the end of time (e.g., Rev. 20:7–22:21). Regardless of their approach, most interpreters should be able to agree to these helpful guidelines.

---

3. L. L. Morris notes, "Such [historicist] views were held by most of the Reformers, who identified papal Rome with the beast. But the difficulties seem insuperable, and it is significant that, while stoutly maintaining that all history is here set forth, historicists have not been able to agree among themselves as to the precise episodes in history which the various visions symbolize" ("Revelation, Book of," in *The Illustrated Bible Dictionary,* ed. J. D. Douglas [Leicester: Inter-Varsity Press, 1980], 3:1338).

1. Old Testament apocalyptic passages provide the most helpful background to understanding Revelation (e.g., Isa. 24–27; Ezek. 38–39; Zech. 1–6; Dan. 7–12). Of 405 verses in Revelation, 278 contain allusions to the Old Testament.

2. The book of Revelation should be read from the perspective of the original audience. How would the early Christians of Asia Minor addressed in Revelation 1–3 have understood the later portions of the book?

3. In accord with the standards of apocalyptic literature, the symbolic images in Revelation must not be taken literally. This does not mean, however, that they are not important, meaningful, or authoritative descriptions of reality. Yet, the symbols point to reality in a figurative way. For example, the walls of unimaginable thickness in Revelation 21:17 point to the splendor of the heavenly city and the complete safety of all who dwell there.

4. Revelation is not intended to be read chronologically. This is made clear by the fact that Christ's birth is not reported until Revelation 12, and various sequences of visions repeat nearly identical judgment language (e.g., Rev. 6:12–17; 11:19; 16:18–21). The certainty and truth of God's coming judgment is emphasized in these prophetic recapitulations.

Extrabiblical Apocalyptic Literature

It is also beneficial to peruse nonbiblical apocalyptic works in order to gain a better understanding of a genre that is quite foreign to most modern readers. Both early Jews and Christians produced apocalyptic works. Below is a list of some nonbiblical apocalyptic works with brief descriptions of their contents.

1. *Book of Enoch (1 Enoch)*. Written between 200 B.C. and A.D. 50, 1 Enoch is one of the best known nonbiblical apocalyptic works. It is composed of five distinct portions: (a) The Book of the Watchers, chapters 1–36; (b) The Book of the Similitudes, chapters 37–71; (c) The Book of Astronomical Writings, chapters 72–82; (d) The Book of Dream Visions, chapters 83–90; and (e) The Book of the Epistle of Enoch, chapters 91–107.[4]

2. *Baruch (Syriac Apocalypse of Baruch)*. Written in the early second century A.D., this work attempts to understand why the Romans were allowed to conquer Jerusalem in A.D. 70. While a future judgment of the

---

4. To read an English translation of *1 Enoch*, see *OTP* 1:13–89.

wicked is expected, readers also are reassured that "the real Jerusalem is still intact in heaven."[5]

3. *Apocalypse of Abraham.* Written sometime between A.D. 70 to 200, the *Apocalypse of Abraham* reports Abraham's conversion from paganism, followed by "an apocalyptic vision purportedly given to Abraham that expands at great length upon the vision of the patriarch recorded in Genesis 15 and adds to it a wealth of theological, cosmological, and eschatological details."[6]

4. *Apocalypse of Zephaniah.* Written between 100 B.C. and A.D. 100, the *Apocalypse of Zephaniah* claims to report the visionary experiences of the Old Testament prophet Zephaniah.[7] "This book is typical of the heavenly journey theme in which the seer witnesses the judgment and punishment of sinners and the vindication of the righteous."[8] The work is only partially preserved.

5. *Shepherd of Hermas.* Part of the apostolic fathers (i.e., the earliest post-New Testament Christian writings), the Shepherd of Hermas is comprised of two main sections: (a) visions 1–4 and (b) the mandates and parables, with vision 5 as an introduction. The Shepherd apparently was composed and edited over a period of time, possibly from A.D. 100 to 160.[9] The first part of the work (visions 1–4) is especially typical of the apocalyptic genre.

REFLECTION QUESTIONS

1. Challenge: If you have never read through Daniel and/or the book of Revelation, do so during the next week.

2. Challenge: Choose one of the extrabiblical apocalypses, find it at a local library or through an Internet search, and read it. How is it similar to Daniel and the book of Revelation? How is it different?

---

5. J. J. Collins, "Apocalyptic Literature," 44. To read this work (or the following works listed in this section) in English, see *OTP.*

6. S. E. Robinson, "Apocalypse of Abraham" in *DNTB*, 37.

7. Ibid., 39.

8. Craig A. Evans, *Ancient Texts for New Testament Studies: A Guide to the Background Literature* (Peabody, MA: Hendrickson, 2005), 33.

9. *The Apostolic Fathers: Greek Texts and English Translations*, ed. and trans. Michael W. Holmes, 3rd ed. (Grand Rapids: Baker, 2007), 445–47.

3. Have you ever encountered the view that Daniel was not written until the second century B.C.? How would you respond to such a view? (See footnotes above for additional recommended resources.)

4. Of the four major approaches to the book of Revelation (preterist, historicist, idealist, futurist), which approach seems most convincing to you? Why?

5. Of the various literary genres that modern Americans read today, which is the closest to apocalyptic?

FOR FURTHER STUDY

Evans, Craig A. *Ancient Texts for New Testament Studies: A Guide to the Background Literature*. Peabody, MA: Hendrickson, 2005.
Metzger, Bruce M. *Breaking the Code: Understanding the Book of Revelation*. Nashville: Abingdon, 1993.

How Do We Interpret Exaggerated or Hyperbolic Language?

If your daughter were to come home from school and complain, "I'm starving," you would not proceed to rush her to the hospital and demand emergency care for malnourishment. We comprehend the statement, "I'm starving," as hyperbolic language to express strong emotion. Biblical characters and authors used exaggerated language as well, and it is important for us to recognize it so that we properly understand the text's meaning.

The Form and Purpose of Exaggeration

Exaggeration occurs within various literary genres in the Bible. It is especially common in poetry, proverbs, and the historical narratives of Jesus. Jesus was a master teacher. Crowds hung on his every word (Mark 2:13; Matt. 7:28–29). One of the literary devices he used to make his teaching memorable and emphatic was exaggeration. Understanding the genre of exaggeration should not inoculate us against it but rather challenge us to present these truths with appropriate emphasis. For example, in teaching on lust, Jesus said, "If your right eye causes you to sin, gouge it out and throw it away" (Matt. 5:29). As Jesus' followers did not become known as "The Assembly of the One-Eyed Disciples," it is clear that Jesus meant this language hyperbolically.[1] Jesus was calling his disciples to act radically in self-denial to avoid lust. So, in teaching on Matthew 5:29 today, we might challenge those struggling with pornography to cut (literally!) the Internet cable, to cancel the iPhone service, to smash the DVD player, etc. In other words, we call people not to literal self-mutilation but to genuine and severe personal inconvenience to steer clear of sin.

---

1. Here, I am drawing upon a classroom example from Robert Stein.

There are two interpretive dangers to avoid here. One is the danger of understanding exaggerated language literally. To obey the language *literally* is actually to disobey. For example, if a person struggling with lust gouged out his right eye, his left eye would still be just as lustful! A second danger is to appeal to one's understanding of the hyperbolic nature of the teaching as a rationalization for disobedience. "Oh that's just hyperbolic language! Jesus doesn't really want me to gouge my eye out. I sure am glad I studied hermeneutics," the lustful sinner may say as he blissfully continues down the path of destruction.

Principles for Recognizing Exaggeration

To label a teaching in Scripture as "exaggeration," one should have clear textual justification. Below are eight principles to help the interpreter recognize exaggeration. The examples are mostly limited to Jesus' teaching, but they apply easily to other genres.[2]

1. *The statement is literally impossible.* If a text describes something that is literally impossible, yet the author seems to assume that the event is, in fact, a real possibility, we are inclined to understand it as hyperbole.[3] For example, in Matthew 19:24, Jesus says, "Again I tell you, it is easier for a camel to go through the eye of a needle than for a rich man to enter the kingdom of God." (And, yes, in case you didn't know, it is impossible for a camel to go through the eye of a needle.) Jesus employs hyperbolic language to emphasize how difficult it is for persons ensconced with worldly comforts to be saved (cf. 1 Tim. 6:10). In the end, however, Jesus says that God's grace can overpower even a wealth-encrusted heart (Matt. 19:26; cf. 1 Cor. 1:26; 1 Tim. 6:17–19).

   There is a long tradition of interpreters who speak of a Needle's Eye gate in Jerusalem, which was so small that only unladed camels could barely squeeze through it. Though a memorable sermon illustration, the Needle's Eye gate has no historical basis. It is a fiction birthed out of a misunderstanding of biblical hyperbole. Other literally impossible examples of exaggeration include Matthew 6:3 ("do not let your left hand know what your right hand is doing") and Matthew 7:3–5 ("plank in your own eye").

2. *The statement conflicts with what Jesus says elsewhere.* Jesus said, "Do not call anyone on earth 'father,' for you have one Father, and he is

---

2. In these guidelines, I am directly dependent upon Robert H. Stein, *A Basic Guide to Interpreting the Bible: Playing by the Rules* (Grand Rapids: Baker, 1994), 123–35.
3. In the case of the Old Testament law, however, we find a literally impossible demand (perfect holiness, Lev. 11:45) that points beyond itself to the divine provision of righteousness in Christ (Rom. 3:9–31).

in heaven" (Matt. 23:9). Yet, elsewhere, Jesus instructed a young man, "Honor your father and mother" (Matt. 19:19). Note that Jesus did not say, "Honor your male parent and your mother." Jesus did not hesitate to call the young man's male parent "father."

The point of Jesus' teaching in Matthew 23:9 is not to prevent our mouths from pronouncing the two syllables for "fa-ther" (or the Greek and Aramaic equivalents) when referring to or addressing our male parent. In Matthew 23:7–12, Jesus is denouncing the use of titles that exalt human religious leaders in a way that reduces God's glory and creates a high priestly class of religious professionals. As a man who is frequently addressed with the titles "Professor" and "Doctor," I need to hear this teaching. Are the titles in front of my name simply polite and respectful social conventions or idolatrous exaltations?

When I was first hired as an assistant professor at the seminary where I teach, the dean's secretary discovered that I was often in my office. My availability and low professional rank resulted in the frequent transfer of outside telephone inquiries.[4] One such caller was having trouble understanding a hyperbolic text, so I appealed to what I thought was an unmistakable example of exaggeration. I said, "See in Matthew 23:9 how Jesus said not to call anyone, 'Father.' Now, certainly, you let your children call you 'Father,' don't you? Do you see that Jesus' real concern was with the use of titles to exalt ourselves sinfully above others?"

His response was, "I have never let my children call me, 'Father.'" I was stunned. We can at least say this man was consistent in his literalistic hermeneutic. I didn't ask him if he still had his right eye and right hand (Matt. 5:29–30)! Other examples of exaggerated statements that conflict with Jesus' teaching elsewhere include: Matthew 6:6 ("when you pray, go into your room, close the door and pray to your Father" [cf. Matt. 6:9–13]) and Luke 14:26 ("If anyone comes to me and does not hate his father and mother . . . he cannot be my disciple" [cf. Luke 6:27]).

3. *The statement conflicts with the actions of Jesus elsewhere.* In Luke 14:26, Jesus says, "If anyone comes to me and does not hate his father and mother, his wife and children, his brothers and sisters—yes, even his own life—he cannot be my disciple." So, are we to hate our own family? That statement clearly conflicts with Jesus teaching elsewhere (Mark 7:9–13). Moreover, Jesus does not act hatefully toward Mary, his mother. Indeed, on the cross, in his dying moments, he makes sure that Mary

---

4. On the basis of some of those phone calls, I could write another book titled *40 Unusual Questions about the Bible.*

will be provided for (John 19:26–27). The fact that Jesus' statement in Luke 14:26 (on hating family) conflicts with his words and actions elsewhere indicates that we should understand Luke 14:26 as hyperbole. Jesus is saying categorically that our devotion to him should be far greater than any other relationship. Other examples of exaggeration that conflict with Jesus' behavior include Matthew 5:33–37 ("Do not swear at all" [cf. Matt. 26:63–64]) and Matthew 10:34 ("I did not come to bring peace, but a sword" [cf. Mark 14:43–50; Luke 23:14; Matt. 5:9]).

4. *The statement conflicts with the broader teaching of Scripture.* Looking at the same verse again (Luke 14:26), we note that Jesus' command to hate one's family is at odds with Old Testament teaching on honoring, loving, and obeying one's parents (Exod. 20:12; Deut. 5:16; Prov. 23:22). Of course, in some instances, Jesus intensifies or modifies Old Testament teaching (Matt. 5:33–37), but on this particular topic, his words elsewhere unequivocally affirm the Old Testament's commands about honoring one's parents (Matt. 15:3–6; 19:19). Thus, a conflict between a literalistic reading of Jesus' words (hating parents) and the words of the Old Testament (honoring parents) provides evidence that Jesus intended his teaching to be understood as hyperbole.

A literalistic reading of Luke 14:26 (the command to hate one's family) also conflicts with broader New Testament teaching. Paul writes, "But if a widow has children or grandchildren, these should learn first of all to put their religion into practice by caring for their own family and so repaying their parents and grandparents, for this is pleasing to God" (1 Tim. 5:4). Paul, an inspired apostle, did not understand Jesus to have instructed us to literally hate our family. As messengers commissioned personally by Jesus, the apostles are the best guides to understanding the meaning of Jesus' teaching. Moreover, as Christians, we believe the apostles' inscripturated words are inspired and preserved from all error (see question 4, "Does the Bible contain error?").

Sometimes the Gospel authors, as inspired summarizers, conveyors, and translators of Jesus' teaching, give us clues as to his nonliteral intentions. It is important to remember that Jesus taught mostly, if not exclusively, in the Aramaic language.[5] The Gospels, however, were written in Greek, the *lingua franca* of the day. Sometimes the

---

5. M. O. Wise offers a conservative assessment of the language[s] of Jesus. He writes, "Based on Mark 5:41 one can only say that Jesus certainly spoke Aramaic on occasion. This much was to be expected on the basis of our knowledge of the dominant language among the Jews of Galilee. The question whether he also knew Hebrew and Greek can only be answered on theoretical grounds" ("Languages of Palestine," in *DJG*, 442).

Gospel authors give us a more literal (word-for-word) translation of Jesus' Aramaic teaching, and sometimes they give us a more dynamic (thought-for-thought) translation. Luke's recording of Jesus' command to "hate family" in 14:26 is a word-for-word translation, which is paralleled by a thought-for-thought translation in Matthew 10:37, which reads, "Anyone who loves his father or mother more than me is not worthy of me; anyone who loves his son or daughter more than me is not worthy of me." As we see in this thought-for-thought translation, Matthew did not understand Jesus to be commanding literal hatred of family.

Another example where a literal reading of Jesus' words conflicts with the broader teaching of the New Testament is over the issue of swearing oaths. Jesus forbids the swearing of any oaths (Matt. 5:33–37), but elsewhere the apostle Paul swears oaths to affirm the truthfulness of his writing (2 Cor. 11:31; Gal. 1:20; Phil. 1:8). Jesus testifies under oath at his trial (Matt. 26:63), and God is described as swearing an oath by the author of Hebrews (Heb. 6:13–14). Looking at Matthew 23:16–20, it appears that Jesus' concern with oaths was the sinful misuse of them to justify dishonesty (for example, "I don't have to keep my word to you because I had my fingers crossed when I said that"). Considering the evidence of the entire New Testament, it does not seem that Jesus intended to forbid oaths categorically but rather to prohibit their disingenuous employment.

So, if asked to swear an oath in court, what should you do? If you wanted to be dramatic, you could say, "As a follower of Jesus, all my words are to be completely truthful. Placing my hand on the Bible and saying an oath will not make me any more truthful, for God always demands my complete honesty. If, however, it pleases the court for me to swear this oath as a public record of my intent to speak honestly, I will do so."

5. *The statement is not always literally fulfilled in practice.* Sometimes the fact that a statement is not literally fulfilled cues us that it should be understood hyperbolically. For example, in reference to the temple, Jesus says, "Do you see all these great buildings? . . . Not one stone here will be left on another; every one will be thrown down" (Mark 13:2). Of course, if one goes to the ruins of the ancient Jewish temple in Jerusalem today, one can still see a large section of stones stacked on each other as they were two thousand years ago. Looking at this evidence, Bible-believing Christians face two options. (1) They can understand Jesus' language as hyperbolic. Similarly, if on September 10, 2001, a modern prophet in New York had declared, "The World Trade Centers will be flattened tomorrow," no one would accuse him of falsehood because a

small section of a stairway was still standing at the end of September 11. Indeed, it would have been a bit odd for Jesus to say, "Do you see all these great buildings? Only 0.97 percent of the stones will be left on top of each other." (2) Another option is to see Jesus' statement as not including the ancient retaining wall (the remains of which make up the Western or Wailing Wall). This meaning is possible, though I do not see adopting option 1 as impinging in any way on the truth of Jesus' prophecy. Indeed, Jesus' prophecy was so strikingly fulfilled that skeptical scholars have accused it of being written after the fact (a *vaticinium ex eventu*, see question 23 on prophecy). Another example of an exaggerated statement not literally fulfilled in practice is Mark 11:22–24 ("if anyone says to this mountain, 'Go, throw yourself into the sea,' and does not doubt in his heart but believes . . . it will be done for him").

6. *The statement's literal fulfillment would not achieve the desired goal.* In teaching on lust, Jesus said,

> If your right eye causes you to sin, gouge it out and throw it away. It is better for you to lose one part of your body than for your whole body to be thrown into hell. And if your right hand causes you to sin, cut it off and throw it away. It is better for you to lose one part of your body than for your whole body to go into hell. (Matt. 5:29–30)

Lust is ultimately a matter of the heart (Mark 7:20–23), and the removal of an eye or an appendage will not cleanse the heart. Radical steps of self-denial, however, demonstrate a heart responding to God's grace in repentance. Jesus calls his disciples to this sort of denial.

7. *The statement uses a particular literary form prone to exaggeration.* Some emotion-laden literary genres such as proverbs, poetry, and prophecy are especially prone to using exaggerated language. For example, in David's lament over the death of Saul and Jonathan, he said, "They were swifter than eagles, they were stronger than lions" (2 Sam. 1:23). David did not intend to say that Saul and Jonathan really could outrun eagles or that they were literally stronger than lions. Poetry does not work that way. One might compare a modern-day love poem in which the poet declares that he has been thinking of his beloved "every second of the day." We expect exaggeration in poems, so a woman addressed by such verse would not protest, "I don't believe that you think of me 86,400 seconds per day."

An idiom is an expression whose nonliteral meanings have become customary in a language. We have many idioms in English. For example, if I ask you to "hit the lights," you do not climb a ladder and hit the light fixture with your fist. Likewise, the authors of Scripture used various idioms current in the language and culture of their day. Many times these idioms are translated in a thought-for-thought way in our modern English translations so that we do not face potential misunderstanding (for example, 1 John 3:17 translates the Greek word for "bowels" [idiomatic seat of emotion] with the modern English word *heart*). In Jesus' day, a number of Jewish texts speak of "moving mountains" as a feat done by persons with great faith (cf. Zech. 14:4; 1 Cor. 13:2).[6] Thus, we should not understand Jesus literally when he says, "I tell you the truth, if you have faith as small as a mustard seed, you can say to this mountain, 'Move from here to there' and it will move. Nothing will be impossible for you" (Matt. 17:20). Jesus is not preparing his followers to work for coal-mining companies—moving the tops of physical mountains. Rather, through faith in God, Jesus' followers will overcome seemingly impossible obstacles.

I once heard a lecture in which the idiomatic nature of this "moving mountains" expression was not clearly understood. The professor discussed at great length Jesus' supposed allusion to Herod the Great's removal of a hilltop to build the Herodium, one of his palaces. The lecture, while interesting, seemed to miss the intent of Jesus' idiomatic expression.

8. *The statement uses all-inclusive or universal language.* Sometimes the word *all* means literally "all," but not always. Let us turn to an example outside the Gospels. In Colossians 1:23, Paul writes, "This is the gospel that you heard and that has been proclaimed to every creature under heaven." Proclaimed to *every creature* under heaven? Birds? Reptiles? Insects? Possibly just all human creatures? If so, why does Paul make it his ambition to continue preaching where Christ is unknown (Rom. 15:20)? Clearly, Paul is using universal language in a hyperbolic way. We might say something similar in modern English, such as, "That church is influencing every part of that city," or, "In our day, the gospel is going out into all of China."

We also might think of the expressions "all" and "every" as expressing "all without distinction" but not "all without exception." In Paul's case, the gospel is going to all sorts of persons without

---

6. For rabbinic parallels see J. B. Lightfoot, *A Commentary on the New Testament from the Talmud and Hebraica* (Oxford: Oxford University Press, 1859; reprint, Peabody, MA: Hendrickson, 1997), 2:283. D. A. Carson writes, "Removal of mountains was proverbial for overcoming great difficulties (cf. Isa 40:4; 49:11; 54:10; Matt 21:21–22; Mark 11:23; Luke 17:6; 1 Cor 13:2)" (*Matthew, Chapters 13–28*, EBC [Grand Rapids: Zondervan, 1995], 391).

distinction—slaves, free, women, men, poor, rich, Jew, Gentile. There are no classes or races the gospel has failed to reach.

REFLECTION QUESTIONS

1. Have you ever heard a hyperbolic statement in Scripture wrongly taught as literal language? Relate the incident.

2. Are there any hyperbolic statements in Scripture that you initially misunderstood but later came to understand rightly as exaggerated in form?

3. Can you think of two or three examples of exaggerated language commonly used in modern English?

4. Of the two interpretive dangers of exaggerated language presented above (overly literal application vs. dismissing the teaching), of which are you most in danger?

5. Choose one of Jesus' exaggerated statements, and ask several people what they think the teaching means.

FOR FURTHER STUDY

Bullinger, E. W. *Figures of Speech Used in the Bible*. London: Eyre and Spottiswoorde, 1898; reprint, Grand Rapids: Baker, 2003. (See "Hyperbole or Exaggeration," 423–28).

Efird, James M. *How to Interpret the Bible*. Atlanta: John Knox, 1984. (See "Hyperbole," 69–72).

Stein, Robert H. *A Basic Guide to Interpreting the Bible: Playing by the Rules*. Grand Rapids: Baker, 1994. (See chap. 9, "The Game of Exaggeration—Hyperbole," 123–35).

How Do We Interpret Figures of Speech?

A figure of speech is an expression that, at its base, is to be understood non-literally. Speakers and authors employ figures of speech for "emphasis, clarity, or freshness of thought."[1] For example, this English sentence uses a figure of speech: "Bubba, hit the lights" (unless, of course, you are asking Bubba to assault the chandelier, in which case this would be literal language). Such a figurative expression conveys a bit more emotion in compact form, as compared with: "Bubba, flip down the light switch to the off position."

All languages and cultures have figures of speech. Figures of speech are sometimes difficult for nonnative speakers to understand because of our natural propensity to understand new expressions literally. Examples of some common figures of speech from both the Old and New Testaments will be listed and briefly explained below.

Metaphor

In a metaphor, a figurative description is applied to a person or thing without overt terms of comparison. For example, in Amos 4:1, the prophet addresses the sinfully luxurious women of Israel, saying,

> Hear this word, you cows of Bashan on Mount Samaria, you women who oppress the poor and crush the needy and say to your husbands, "Bring us some drinks!"

---

1. Richard A. Young, *Intermediate New Testament Greek: A Linguistic and Exegetical Approach* (Nashville: Broadman & Holman, 1994), 235. I found Young's discussion of figurative language very helpful.

We note that Amos does not say, "You rich, proud women are *like* fat cows." That would be a simile, with the word *like* used as an explicit signification of comparison.

Simile

A simile is similar to a metaphor in that a figurative description is applied to a person or thing. The only difference is that, in a simile, comparison words such as *like* or *as* are used. For example, in Psalm 1:3, we find a simile to describe the wise man who meditates on God's Word.

> He is like a tree planted by streams of water, which yields its fruit in season and whose leaf does not wither. Whatever he does prospers.

Another example is Matthew 24:27, where Jesus declares:

> For as lightning that comes from the east is visible even in the west, so will be the coming of the Son of Man.

As in all similes and metaphors, we have (a) the topic discussed (the coming of the Son of Man), (b) the image compared with the topic (lightning), and (c) the point of comparison (undeniable visibility).[2] An author using a metaphor or simile may choose to imply one or more of these three items.

Merism[3]

A merism is a figure of speech in which two elements together stand for the totality of something. For example, in Genesis 1:1 God is described as creating "the heavens and the earth." This expression is best understood as a merism for the entire created order. Likewise, in Psalm 105:14, "*'adam* ('man') and *melakim* ('kings') denote any and everybody."[4]

Hendiadys[5]

A "hendiadys is the expression of one idea with two or more similar words; that is, two words are used for the same thing."[6] In 2 Timothy 1:10, for example, Paul says that Jesus "has destroyed death and has brought life and immortality to light through the gospel." Here, "life" and "immortality" refer to the same reality

---

2. Ibid., 236.
3. Pronunciation: mer-ism. For pronunciation of the terms in this chapter, also see Webster's Third New International Dictionary, Unabridged. Merriam-Webster, 2002. http://unabridged.merriam-webster.com.
4. Willem A. VanGemeren, "Psalms," in EBC 5 (Grand Rapids: Zondervan, 1991), 26.
5. Pronunciation: hen-di-a-dys.
6. Young, *Intermediate New Testament Greek*, 243.

of eternal life.[7] Another example is found in James 4:2, where the literal Greek expression, "You kill, and you are jealous," possibly should be understood as the hendiadys, "you are filled with deadly jealousy" or "you murderously envy."[8]

Synecdoche[9]

Synecdoche is a literary expression in which the part represents the whole or the whole stands for the part. For example, when a sea captain cries, "All hands on deck," he is not calling for dozens of severed hands to come to his assistance. Likewise, when we read, "How beautiful on the mountains are the feet of those who bring good news" (Isa. 52:7; cf. Rom. 10:15), we understand that feet are a synecdoche for the person heralding the gospel. The author of Isaiah is not really so interested in the feet of the preacher. As a part of the preacher's body that represents the coming with good news, the feet are selected to highlight delight in the herald's arrival.

Another example of synecdoche is found in the well-known petition of the Lord's Prayer, "Give us today our daily bread" (Matt. 6:11). Here, "bread," as a commonly consumed staple, serves as a synecdoche for the entire category of food—or possibly a synecdoche for all daily needs.

Metonymy[10]

Metonymy is an expression in which one word or phrase stands in for another with which it is closely associated. For example, in English, we might say, "The White House vetoed the bill." The White House, of course, is the stone-and-mortar residence of the president of the United States of America. A house cannot actually veto anything. But, because of our close mental association between the president and his official residence, we use "White House" as a metonymy for "U.S. president."

The Greek and Hebrew of the Bible have similar, cultural-specific examples of metonymy. For example, in the parable of the rich man and Lazarus (Luke 16:19–31), after the rich man begs Abraham to send Lazarus back from the dead to warn his brothers, we read:

> Abraham replied, "They have Moses and the Prophets; let them listen to them." "No, father Abraham," [the rich man] said, "but if someone from the dead goes to them, they will repent." [Abraham] said to him, "If they do not listen to Moses and the Prophets, they will not be convinced even if someone rises from the dead." (Luke 16:29–31)

---

7. Ibid.
8. Joseph B. Mayor notes this possibility (*The Epistle of St. James*, 2nd ed. [New York: Macmillan, 1897], 130).
9. Pronunciation: syn-ec-do-che.
10. Pronunciation: me-ton-y-my.

The brothers of the rich man did not really possess the person of Moses, who had long since died (Deut. 34:7). Neither did they have his skeleton or mummified body in their possession. No, here the name "Moses" (the author of the Pentateuch) clearly serves as a metonymy for the writings he produced.[11] Similarly, sometimes in the New Testament, "the cross" serves as a metonymy for the atoning death of Jesus (e.g., Gal. 6:14; Eph. 2:16; Phil. 3:18).

Personification

Personification is the presentation of a thing (an inanimate object) or idea as having the qualities or actions of a person. For example, Jesus said,

> But when you give to the needy, do not let your left hand know what your right hand is doing, so that your giving may be in secret. Then your Father, who sees what is done in secret, will reward you. (Matt. 6:3–4)

It is not possible, of course, for the limbs or appendages of our bodies to actually know anything. But in this personification of a person's right and left hand, Jesus makes a memorable and emphatic appeal to self-forgetful giving. A subset of personification, apostrophe, is a figure of speech in which the personified thing is addressed as a person. Below is an example of apostrophe from the Psalms, in which personified mountains are addressed.

> Why gaze in envy, O rugged mountains, at the mountain where God chooses to reign, where the LORD himself will dwell forever? (Ps. 68:16)

Anthropomorphism

An anthropomorphism is a presentation of God as having human characteristics or actions. For example, in 2 Chronicles 16:9, we read:

> For the eyes of the LORD range throughout the earth to strengthen those whose hearts are fully committed to him.

Of course, as a spiritual being (John 4:24), God does not have physical eyes that literally rove throughout the earth. How else, though, can humans, who know visual sight only in the concreteness of our own physical existence, describe God's sight of all things? Likewise, biblical passages that speak of God's arm or hand are not physical descriptions of God's appearance (e.g., Ps. 98:1) but anthropomorphisms (cf. Exod. 33:18–23).

---

11. The examples of the White House and Moses are from Richard Young, *Intermediate New Testament Greek*, 237.

Litotes[12]

"Litotes occurs when an assertion is made by negating the opposite."[13] For example, if someone asks, "How much did you decorate your house for Christmas this year?" and you respond, "I didn't hold back," in reality you mean, "I decorated extensively." Similarly, in Acts 15:2, when Luke says that Paul and Barnabas "had no small dissension and debate with [the false teachers who were demanding that Gentiles be circumcised]" (NRSV), he is employing litotes to mean that there was "sharp dispute and debate" (NIV).

Idioms

It is important to note the difference between one-time or rare occurrences and commonplace expressions. Anyone can coin a new figure of speech, and sometimes the originality of the expression is especially effective in jarring the listener. For example, someone might say, "I weigh more than an aircraft carrier. I'd better start exercising." While this hyperbolic expression conveys the intensity of the speaker's thought, it is doubtful that others will repeat it. However, if the expression becomes repeated and commonplace (e.g., "I weigh a ton"), it then becomes not only an example of hyperbole but also an idiom.

Many idioms in the Bible are smoothed out by modern English translations so that the modern reader never notices them. For example, E. W. Bullinger notes that the phrase, "answered and said" is an idiomatic Hebraic phrase to introduce any kind of speech (i.e., not simply a reply). Bullinger writes, "[The phrase] should therefore not be rendered literally, 'Answered and said,' but translated so as to express whatever may be the particular kind of speech referred to in the verb 'said.'"[14] Another example of a common biblical idiom is the Hebraic phrase, "break bread," which means "to consume food" and is frequently used in reference to the eating of a meal.[15]

REFLECTION QUESTIONS

1. Can you define "figure of speech"?

2. Give an example of some figures of speech from the English language.

---

12. Pronunciation: li-to-tes.
13. Young, *Intermediate New Testament Greek*, 241.
14. E. W. Bullinger, *Figures of Speech Used in the Bible* (London: Eyre and Spottiswoorde, 1898; reprint, Grand Rapids: Baker, 2003), 837. Bullinger gives many examples of biblical idioms (ibid., 819–60).
15. Ibid., 839.

3. Were any of the figures of speech described above new to you? Which one(s)?

4. Choose a figurative expression from the Bible discussed above. How would a literal reading of this expression result in misunderstanding?

5. Why do persons use figures of speech instead of more straightforward, easily translatable expressions?

FOR FURTHER STUDY

Bullinger, E. W. *Figures of Speech Used in the Bible.* London: Eyre and Spottiswoorde, 1898; reprint, Grand Rapids: Baker, 2003.
Young, Richard A. *Intermediate New Testament Greek: A Linguistic and Exegetical Approach.* Nashville: Broadman & Holman, 1994.

Primarily Old Testament Genres

How Do We Interpret Proverbs?

Soon after our first child was born, I received an e-mail from a friend in which I was challenged to "claim the promise" of Proverbs 22:6 ("Train a child in the way he should go, and when he is old he will not turn from it"). Is this in fact a "promise"? If, upon reaching adulthood, my daughter were to turn away from the Lord, does that mean that ultimately my training is to blame? Rightly understanding the genre of proverbs will enable us to answer these questions.

Most Proverbs Are General Truths That Assume Exceptions

A proverb is a subset of wisdom literature. Wisdom literature is a broad genre in which the sayings and reflections of the wise are recorded. Such sayings can take the form of disputations (Job), poetical self-reflection and lament (Ecclesiastes), or pithy observations on the normal workings of life (Proverbs).[1] In this question, we will focus on proverbs, which not only occur in the book by that name but are also found scattered throughout other biblical genres (e.g., 1 Kings 20:11; Matt. 26:52).

The latter two-thirds of the book of Proverbs (chapters 10–31) is made up of brief sayings we would readily recognize as proverbs in English. The

---

1. D. A. Hubbard writes, "[Wisdom literature is] a family of literary *genres* common in the ancient Near East in which instructions for successful living are given or the perplexities of human existence are contemplated. There are two broad types: proverbial wisdom—short, pithy sayings which state rules for personal happiness and welfare (e.g., Proverbs), and speculative wisdom—monologues (e.g., Ecclesiastes) or dialogues (e.g., Job) which attempt to delve into such problems as the meaning of existence and the relationship between God and man. This speculative wisdom is practical and empirical, not theoretical. Problems of human existence are discussed in terms of concrete examples: 'There was a man . . . whose name was Job'" ("Wisdom Literature," in *The Illustrated Bible Dictionary, vol. 3*, ed. J. D. Douglas [Leicester: Inter-Varsity Press, 1980], 1651).

first nine chapters of Proverbs, however, consists mainly of longer discourses, with a father giving advice to his son or personified "Lady Wisdom" calling out to persons passing by. In many ways, these initial nine chapters provide a grid through which we understand the later material in the book. True wise living, however pragmatic, is always grounded in "the fear of the LORD" (Prov. 1:7).[2]

All languages and cultures have proverbs—wise advice in short, memorable expressions. Possibly due to the American fixation on productivity, many American proverbs deal with efficiency, money, employment, or contentment. For example, one common proverb is, "A stitch, in time, saves nine." In other words, if you see a cloth beginning to tear and you stop to repair it now, it will prevent you from having to make a much larger repair later. This proverb, while using the language of needlework, applies to any situation in which a little forethought and intervention will prevent a larger cleanup later on (car maintenance, home repair, human relationship issues, etc.). Also, we recognize that the proverb is not a fail-proof promise. It describes the way things normally work. One might put a stitch in a shirt that is beginning to tear, only to find out later that the tear has gotten worse. Poorly made fabric cannot be rescued by an early stitch. Even with such exceptions, however, the proverb is not false. It describes the way things normally work.

How are biblical proverbs different from any other proverbs? To begin with, the proverbs in the Bible are divinely inspired (2 Tim. 3:16). Thus, such proverbs will approve what God approves and condemn what God condemns. Moreover, they will be free from all error (see question 4, "Does the Bible contain error?"). Although many nonbiblical proverbs demonstrate insight, they also sometimes exalt wickedness and misrepresent God and his creation. The Chinese sage Confucius (551–479 B.C.) said many wise things. For example, he said, "He who is too ready to speak of it will have difficulties carrying it out."[3] He also said, "With coarse food to eat, cold water to drink, and the bended arm as a pillow, happiness may still exist. Wealth and rank unrighteously obtained seem to me as insubstantial as floating clouds."[4] Yet, Confucius also is credited with this horrendous maxim: "One hundred women are not worth a

---

2. Longman writes, "Chaps. 1–9 serve as an introduction, even a kind of hermeneutical prism, through which we should read the rest of the book. The first part of the book requires a decision of the young men, who represent the reader. With whom will one dine, with Wisdom or with Folly? This calls for a religious decision, a decision between the true God and false gods" (Tremper Longman, *Proverbs,* Baker Commentary on the Old Testament [Grand Rapids: Baker, 2006], 61).
3. Luo Chenglie, Liangwen Guo, Tianchen Li, and Jiasen Zhang, *A Collection of Confucius' Sayings: An English-Chinese Bilingual Textbook* (Jinan: Qi Lu, 1988), 65.
4. Ibid., 35.

single testicle."[5] While the former two Confucian proverbs are in accord with biblical revelation, the latter is squarely opposed to the biblical teaching on the equal dignity and worth of the sexes (Gen. 1:26–27; 1 Cor. 11:11–12; Eph. 5:21–33).

How are biblical proverbs similar to other proverbs? Both generally assume exceptions. Such exceptions are inherent to the nature of wise sayings about the way life *normally* works. For example, in Proverbs 10:4, we read, "Lazy hands make a man poor, but diligent hands bring wealth." This is generally true. If you are lazy, after a while, you will be poor. Or as we read in Proverbs 6:10–11, "A little sleep, a little slumber, a little folding of the hands to rest—and poverty will come on you like a bandit and scarcity like an armed man." On the other hand, those who work diligently will gradually acquire wealth. But there are situations with extenuating circumstances when this general truth does not prove true. For example, some children are born into such immensely rich families that they are able to live lazily and luxuriously their entire lives and still die wealthy. There are other hardworking people who are unjustly denied the fruit of their labor. Indeed, other proverbs note such injustice. For example, Proverbs 13:23 states, "A poor man's field may produce abundant food, but injustice sweeps it away." The fact that some biblical proverbs on first glance conflict with each other reminds us that proverbs are situational or occasional. Each proverb addresses a certain occasion as we normally encounter it, but it does not intend to describe all exceptions. If all such exceptions were listed, the resulting proverb would be far from short or memorable! It would be more like an essay titled, "A General Truth, with All Conceivable Exceptions."

Here is an example of two side-by-side biblical proverbs that seem, on face value, to conflict:

Do not answer a fool according to his folly, or you will be like him yourself. (Prov. 26:4)[6]

Answer a fool according to his folly, or he will be wise in his own eyes. (Prov. 26:5)

We must realize the circumstantial nature of proverbs to affirm the truth of both these proverbs. Depending on the receptivity of the fool to rebuke,

---

5. I first encountered this Confucian proverb in a high school lecture on sexism. A search on the Internet shows that the proverb is widely quoted, though I do not have access to a print collection of Confucian proverbs that includes it.

6. It is important to note that in wisdom literature, the "fool" is an "unbelieving pagan who ignores God and follows self" (Grant R. Osborne, *The Hermeneutical Spiral: A Comprehensive Introduction to Biblical Interpretation*, rev. ed. [Downers Grove, IL: InterVarsity Press, 2006], 244).

one of these proverbs will apply to any fool's folly. In other words, if a fool is recklessly unwilling to listen to the input of others, you yourself don the fool's cap when you try to reason with him (Prov. 26:4). However, there are situations where calling out a person's foolish actions will prevent him from moving on in destructive self-deception (Prov. 26:5). Wisdom about the situation is needed to know which proverb applies.[7]

An important question to consider is the function of proverbs. A biblical proverb can help us here. Proverbs 26:7 says, "Like a lame man's legs that hang limp is a proverb in the mouth of a fool." In other words, simply knowing or reciting a proverb is useless if it does not result in changed behavior. Proverbs call us to action. Biblical proverbs call us to respond to God in faith and obedience.

Some Proverbs, However, Have No Exceptions

In attempting to correct the common misunderstanding of proverbs as promises, interpreters sometimes can miss the fact that some biblical proverbs are always true. Some proverbs *are* essentially promises. These proverbs deal with the nature of God. Insofar as a proverb describes a quality of God (holiness, knowledge, etc.), that proverb is true without exception, for God is not subject to human vicissitudes (Num. 23:19). For example, in Proverbs 11:1, we read, "The LORD abhors dishonest scales, but accurate weights are his delight." Because God is righteous, he always abhors cheating in business without exception.[8] Similarly, we see a list that has no exceptions in Proverbs 6:16–19:

> There are six things the LORD hates, seven that are detestable to him: haughty eyes, a lying tongue, hands that shed innocent blood, a heart that devises wicked schemes, feet that are quick to rush into evil, a false witness who pours out lies and a man who stirs up dissension among brothers.

God does not sometimes hate these things and at other times not hate these things. As a completely holy God, these are things he always hates.

---

7. Tremper Longman offers a similar understanding of these two proverbs: "This proverb pair [Prov. 26:4–5] is prime evidence leading toward the proper understanding of the proverb genre. Proverbs are not universally true laws but circumstantially relevant principles. . . . In short, the answer depends on the nature of the fool with whom one is engaged in conversation. In other words, the wise person must assess whether this is a fool who will simply drain one's energy with no positive results or whether an answer will prove fruitful to the fool or perhaps to those who overhear. The wise not only know the proverb but also can read the circumstances and the people with whom they dialogue" (*Proverbs*, 464). Osborne warns, "We dare not read more into the proverbial statement than is there. By their very nature they are generalized statements, intended to give advice rather than to establish rigid codes by which God works" (*Hermeneutical Spiral*, 247).
8. About this same proverb, Longman writes, "If there are any exceptions to this proverb, they are so rare as to be unimportant" (*Proverbs*, 33).

What about proverbs that describe God's interventions in this world? For example, in Proverbs 10:3, we read, "The LORD does not let the righteous go hungry but he thwarts the craving of the wicked." Are there any exceptions to this proverb? Do God's people (the righteous) ever go hungry? Most interpreters would acknowledge that some of God's people are occasionally hungry. The apostle Paul says he was sometimes without food (2 Cor. 11:27). The crowds listening to Jesus are described as hungry to the point that they would faint if they were sent away without food (Matt. 15:32). Yet, if you are a Christian, you have likely seen the Lord provide for your basic needs in miraculous ways. And you have likely heard of how he has done so for other believers. As we walk through life, we normally expect God to work in the way Proverbs 10:3 describes. But if he does not, we know "[his] power is made perfect in weakness" and his "grace is sufficient" for us (2 Cor. 12:9).

It is also worth noting that portions of wisdom literature point to God's final intervening justice as outside the short span of earthly human life. In other words, God's final settling of accounts awaits the afterlife and ultimately his wrapping up all things in a day of judgment. In Psalm 73 (a wisdom psalm), Asaph struggles to comprehend the injustices around him and finds resolution in the afterlife. He writes, "When I tried to understand all this, it was oppressive to me till I entered the sanctuary of God; then I understood [the wicked people's] final destiny" (Ps. 73:16–17).

Below are a few proverbs that imply divine intervention beyond this temporal life.[9]

Ill-gotten treasures are of no value, but righteousness delivers from death. (Prov. 10:2)

Wealth is worthless in the day of wrath, but righteousness delivers from death. (Prov. 11:4)

When a wicked man dies, his hope perishes; all he expected from his power comes to nothing. (Prov. 11:7)

Thus, while biblical proverbs usually speak about God's intervention on behalf of his people as experienced in normal, daily life, the proverbs allude to an eternal trajectory that points to the final day of judgment.

Interpreting Other Wisdom Literature

A few brief comments are in order regarding the interpretation of other wisdom literature. With both the disputations of Job and monologues of

---

9. See also Proverbs 12:28; 15:24; 23:13–14. Longman sees these verses as possibly pointing to an afterlife.

Ecclesiastes, context is more important than with the staccato style of proverbs. Ecclesiastes is intended to be interpreted in light of the final summary statement: "Now all has been heard; here is the conclusion of the matter: Fear God and keep his commandments, for this is the whole duty of man. For God will bring every deed into judgment, including every hidden thing, whether it is good or evil" (Eccl. 12:13–14). When one loses sight of this organizing truth, the vanities of life are attractive and seemingly reasonable to pursue, as earlier portions of the book indicate. Likewise with Job, one must read the entire work to discover that God discredits some of the seemingly wise advice of Job's friends (Job 42:7). Job's friends seem to have taken the ways God normally works (i.e., proverbs) and made them absolute laws with no exceptions (e.g., Job 4:7–9; 8:3–7). In the end, the book of Job lauds the mystery of God's providential workings (Job 42:1–6).

Longman argues that Ecclesiastes and Job are helpful canonical correctives to potential misunderstandings of biblical proverbs. They show us that proverbs are not promises, for there are many puzzling injustices and vagaries in this life. Ultimately, we all face situations in which we must submit to God's mysterious sovereignty.[10]

The Song of Solomon (or Song of Songs) is generally recognized as a hybrid of wisdom literature and poetic song. As one commentator aptly notes, "Wisdom is the application of God's will to the nitty-gritty of life."[11] Fittingly, then, the Song of Solomon offers a divine perspective on the experience of romantic love between a husband and wife. Despite many attempts to allegorize the text, it is best understood as a divinely inspired stamp of approval on the emotional and physical joys shared within marriage.

REFLECTION QUESTIONS

1. Do you have a favorite biblical proverb? If so, is it a proverb that assumes exceptions?

2. What are some modern (nonbiblical) proverbs?

3. Can you think of any nonbiblical proverbs that contradict the truths of Scripture?

---

10. Longman, *Proverbs*, 63.
11. Tremper Longman, *Song of Songs*, NICOT (Grand Rapids: Eerdmans, 2001), 49. For practical teaching on the Song of Songs, the reader is referred to Daniel Akin's *God on Sex: The Creator's Ideas about Love, Intimacy, and Marriage* (Nashville: Broadman & Holman, 2003).

4. Is Proverbs 22:6 ("Train a child in the way he should go, and when he is old he will not turn from it") a promise? If not, what are some possible exceptions?

5. Challenge: Beginning on the first day of the month, read a chapter of Proverbs every day for the whole month. (There are thirty-one chapters in the book of Proverbs.)

FOR FURTHER STUDY

Longman, Tremper. *Proverbs.* Baker Commentary on the Old Testament. Grand Rapids: Baker, 2006.

Osborne, Grant R. *The Hermeneutical Spiral: A Comprehensive Introduction to Biblical Interpretation.* Rev. ed. Downers Grove, IL: InterVarsity Press, 2006. (See chap. 9, "Wisdom.")

How Do We Interpret Poetry?

I once attended a Bible study where a person was puzzled by Proverbs 6:16–19 ("There are six things the LORD hates, seven that are detestable to him . . ."). Indeed, an untrained reader might well ask, "Did the author initially forget one thing in his list ('six things') and then quickly add the forgotten item ('seven')?" In fact, these verses demonstrate a common Semitic poetic style ("x, x + 1" poetic form). The author did not forget something and then add it. This poetic form, rather, was a recognized way of presenting a list in a memorable, emphatic way.

Poetry occurs within many biblical genres—in proverbs, historical narrative, prophecy, psalms, etc. To properly understand poetry, we must first recognize a text as poetic. Then, we must have some understanding of the assumptions underlying poetry. Finally, we must employ sound hermeneutical principles in interpreting various poetic forms.

Recognize When Poetry Is Employed

Ask a modern English speaker to recite a poem from memory, and the person will likely recall a nursery rhyme or the lyrics of a popular song. Although many English poems do not rhyme, the average person generally associates poetry with rhyme and regular meter (repeated syllable and stress patterns). Hebrew and Greek poetry, by contrast, rarely rhyme. Rather, such poetry is recognized by repeated syllables or stress patterns, parallel lines, the repetition of similar sounds (consonants, vowels, diphthongs), etc.[1] Most of these common poetic indicators do not readily translate into other languages. Thus, persons reading the Bible in languages other than Hebrew and Greek are dependent upon translators and Bible publishers to indicate poetry by the layout of the text. Almost all modern Bibles present poetry

---

1. There is considerable disagreement among scholars concerning the relation of syllables and stress patterns to demarcating Semitic meter.

in recognizable ways—spacing out stanzas, grouping parallel lines, leaving plenty of white space around the poetic passages so they are distinct from nonpoetic sections, etc. Flip through a modern Bible, and you will quickly see the distinct layout of poetic versus nonpoetic sections. The entire book of Psalms, along with many prophetic books, for example, is laid out poetically.

Note the Assumptions Underlying Poetry

Poetry may be employed by a writer or speaker for a number of reasons. Two chief reasons will be mentioned here. First, some writers/speakers employ poetry to make their words more memorable. Indeed, a large percentage of Jesus' teaching follows Semitic poetic forms. As the greatest teacher who ever lived, Jesus taught in engaging ways. Jesus intended for his teaching to be remembered, obeyed, and repeated (Matt. 7:24–29; Mark 6:7–13, 30). His teaching style made the task of remembering his words easier. Second, writers or speakers often employ poetry for affective reasons. That is, poetry is used to express and evoke strong emotions. Poetry employs stark imagery and hyperbolic language. When reading poetry, we do not find scientific, factual lists. We expect to be presented with a moving reality and to be moved ourselves. Of course, that is not to deny that the poem's author intends to convey factual information. However, we must expect figurative (nonliteral) and exaggerated language, which, if taken literally, would be wrongly understood (see question 26, "How do we interpret exaggerated or hyperbolic language?"). Indeed, the key hermeneutical question always is, "What did the inspired author intend to convey by these words and phrases?" For example, in Old Testament poetic descriptions of battle, cosmic imagery is sometimes used in a figurative way. Stars fall from the sky, the moon is darkened, and the sun is blotted out (Isa. 13:10; 34:4; Ezek. 32:7; Joel 2:10; 3:15). If the descriptions of such cosmic catastrophes occur within poetic sections and other textual markers indicate that life on this planet continued normally, then we likely should understand such cosmic language as figurative descriptions of national or international turmoil.

In my hermeneutics classes, I sometimes find that students who readily recognize figurative language in English poetry are resistant to recognizing it in the Bible. Such resistance often is grounded in a misguided piety that thinks that labeling a text as figurative is to deny its truthfulness. That is, "figurative" is seen as equivalent to "mythological"—an epithet used to deny the truthfulness and authority of Scripture while still trying to maintain its "meaningfulness." Again, the central question is, "What did the inspired author intend?" If the biblical author intended his words figuratively, we are, in fact, being unfaithful if we understand them literally. See question 27 ("How do we interpret figures of speech?") for more assistance in understanding some common biblical figures of speech.

Be Familiar with Common Poetic Forms

Part of the proper interpretation of poetry hinges on recognizing poetic forms and reading them in light of authorial assumptions associated with such forms. Below is a list of common biblical poetic forms with associated assumptions.

1. *Synonymous Parallelism.* Parallelism is one of the most common Semitic poetic forms. Dan McCartney and Charles Clayton define parallelism as follows:

> Parallelism occurs where two or more lines of approximately equal length (in number of syllables) and similar grammatical structure deal with the same subject. The second line provides a bit more information or a different depiction than the first line, either by addition, contrast, or specification.[2]

> Synonymous parallelism, a subset of parallelism, is characterized by two poetic lines that are very close in meaning, if not synonymous. An obscure initial line can be elucidated by a second, clearer one. For example, in Psalm 52:8, we read:

> But I am like an olive tree flourishing in the house of God; I trust in God's unfailing love for ever and ever.[3]

Without the second synonymous line, we might be left puzzling as to how David is like an olive tree. The second line seems to clarify that the first image is intended to paint a picture of reliance and sustained fruitfulness.

2. *Antithetical Parallelism.* A second common form of parallelism is antithetical parallelism, in which the second line contrasts with the first in asserting an opposing truth. For example in the Magnificat (Luke 1:46–55), Mary sings of God's humbling the proud (line 1) and exalting the humble (line 2):

> He has brought down rulers from their thrones but has lifted up the humble. (v. 52)

> Through such antithetical repetition, the initial assertion in the first line is further clarified and set in memorable relief.

---

2. Dan McCartney and Charles Clayton, *Let the Reader Understand: A Guide to Interpreting and Applying the Bible*, 2nd ed. (Phillipsburg, NJ: P&R, 2002), 230.
3. McCartney and Clayton also give this verse as an example of synonymous parallelism (ibid.).

3. *Synthetic Parallelism.* A third form of parallelism, synthetic parallelism, recognizes the addition of information or emphasis in the second line to a degree that the second line can no longer be called synonymous (sometimes also called step or climactic parallelism). There is a general trend among scholars to allow for more synthetic parallelism in the Bible. Interpreters fear the flattening out of nuances that biblical authors intended by too quickly labeling poetic lines as synonymous. An example of synthetic parallelism also can be drawn from the Magnificat.

> He has performed mighty deeds with his arm; he has scattered those who are proud in their inmost thoughts. (Luke 1:51)

Here the second line does more than restate the first. The second line gives a specific example of a mighty deed the Lord has done—the scattering of the proud.[4]

4. *"X, X+1" Poetic Form.* As mentioned in the introduction to this question, Semitic poetry sometimes uses the "x, x+1" form to emphasize a list of two or more items. For example, Proverbs 30:18–19 reads,

> There are three things that are too amazing for me, four that I do not understand: the way of an eagle in the sky, the way of a snake on a rock, the way of a ship on the high seas, and the way of a man with a maiden.

There are numerous other biblical examples of this "x, x+1" configuration (Ps. 62:11; Prov. 30:15–16, 21–23, 29–31; Mic. 5:5).

5. *Repetition of Similar Sounds.* An author may choose to repeat similar sounds (i.e., consonants, vowels, or diphthongs) as a memory device, for literary artistry, humor, or some other reason. Of course, it is usually not possible to maintain a similar repetition of sounds in a translation of the text. For example, in James 1:1–2, the words in Greek for "greetings" (*chairein*) and "joy" (*charan*) sound very similar. James sometimes stitches together his sections by repeating words with a similar sound. This organizational device is lost to the non-Greek reader, though the footnotes of a study Bible or a commentary should

---

4. For a more detailed subdividing of Hebrew parallelism, see the chart, "Types of Hebrew Parallelism," in *Chronological and Background Charts of the Old Testament*, by John H. Walton, rev. ed. (Grand Rapids: Zondervan, 1994), 47.

inform the reader of such literary devices (see question 13, "What are some helpful books or tools for interpreting the Bible?").

6. *Acrostic.* In several passages in the Old Testament, we find acrostics. An acrostic is "a composition in verse in which sets of letters (as the initial or final letters of the lines) taken in order form a word or phrase or a regular sequence of letters of the alphabet."[5] For example, in English, an acrostic poem based on the name "Chloe" would begin line one with a *c,* line two with an *h,* and so on (C.H.L.O.E.). An acrostic poem also can repeat letters at the beginning of each stanza. Acrostics in the Bible are based on the regular order of the letters of the Hebrew alphabet (e.g., Pss. 9; 10; 25; 34; 37; 111; 112; 119; 145; Prov. 31:10–31; Lam. 1–4; Nah. 1:2–10).

7. *Chiasm.* A chiasm "is a series of two or more elements followed by a series of corresponding elements in reverse order."[6] A visual representation of the simplest form of this structure is:

A
A^1
B^1
B

An example from the New Testament, Mark 2:27, is printed below in chiasmic form:

The Sabbath was made
for man,
not man
For the Sabbath.[7]

REFLECTION QUESTIONS

1. Do you find yourself resistant to reading biblical passages as figurative? Why or why not?

2. Does your Bible clearly distinguish which texts are poetic? How?

---

5. Merriam-Webster online dictionary (accessed October 14, 2008).
6. Richard A. Young, *Intermediate New Testament Greek: A Linguistic and Exegetical Approach* (Nashville: Broadman & Holman, 1994), 243.
7. Richard Young also gives this verse as an example of a chiasm (ibid.).

3. Of the common poetic forms found in the Bible and discussed above, were any unfamiliar to you?

4. How is the modern American use of poetry different from that of biblical poetry?

5. How many English poems can you recite from memory? Why, in your opinion, is poetry so rarely employed in our modern American culture?

FOR FURTHER STUDY

Fokkelman, J. P. *Reading Biblical Poetry: An Introductory Guide.* Louisville, KY: Westminster John Knox, 2001.
Watson, Wilfred G. E. *Classical Hebrew Poetry: A Guide to Its Techniques.* Sheffield: JSOT Press, 1984.

How Do We Interpret the Psalms?
(Classification of Psalms)

Growing up on a farm in Tennessee, I learned how to identify common trees—maples, oaks, tulip poplars, dogwoods, redbuds, etc. I'm always surprised to find people who see each unique arboreal specimen as "just another tree." Similarly, many people come to the book of Psalms assuming that each psalm is "just another worship song." In reality, there are recognizable forms (subgenres) that we find repeated among the psalms. In this initial question, we will list and briefly explain common psalm types. Then, in the next question, we will deal with strategies for interpreting the psalms.

Although part of the broader genre of poetry, the book of Psalms (150 individual songs) makes up a distinct and well-known portion of Scripture that deserves special attention. In this section, we will see how the Psalms can be organized into subgroupings based on common characteristics. Below are brief discussions of seven of the most common types of psalms.[1]

Lament Psalms

Lament psalms are the most widespread subgenre of psalm. About one-third of the Psalter is composed of lament psalms (Pss. 3; 9; 12; 13; 17; 42; 60; 74; 94; 139). In a lament, an individual or a group cries out to God in distress. In light of how much current Christian worship music ignores the difficulties of life, it is instructive to see the prominence Psalms gives to speaking honestly about one's troubles to God. John Hayes lists seven parts commonly found in lament psalms: (1) address to God; (2) description of distress; (3) plea for deliverance; (4) statement of confidence in God; (5) confession of sin;

---

1. In this discussion of psalm types, I am following the structure of Grant R. Osborne's presentation in *The Hermeneutical Spiral: A Comprehensive Introduction to Biblical Interpretation*, rev. ed. (Downers Grove, IL: InterVarsity Press, 2006), 232–36.

(6) vow to do certain things when God answers; and (7) praise or restatement of request.[2] It is noteworthy that even when the psalmist is unrestrained in his complaint (Ps. 3:1–2), in nearly the same breath, he expresses confidence in God (Ps. 3:3–8). Lament and faith are complementary expressions. Even Jesus' cry from the cross, "Why have you forsaken me?" is accompanied by the words of trust, "My God, my God" (Matt. 27:46; cf. Ps. 22:1).

Praise Psalms

These psalms are characterized by the prominent motif of praising God (Pss. 106; 111–113; 146; 150). God is praised as Creator (Ps. 104), Savior of Israel (Ps. 149), and Sovereign over history (Ps. 103).[3] The basic structure of these psalms includes: (1) address to God; (2) call to oneself and/or others to join in worship; (3) enumeration of reason(s) to praise God; and (4) blessing(s) or a repetition of the initial call to worship.[4]

Thanksgiving Psalms

As indicated by the title, these songs thank God for answering the request of the worshipper(s). The psalms are written for individuals (Pss. 18; 32; 40; 92) or groups (Pss. 65; 75; 107; 136). The normal components of a thanksgiving psalm are: (1) invitation to others to thank or praise God; (2) recounting of the psalmist's need for divine intervention; (3) praise to God for his salvation; (4) "temple language" of sacrifice, festive processions, pilgrimage, music, dancing, or incense; (5) blessing pronounced over worshippers; and (6) final exhortation.[5]

Celebration Psalms

These psalms "celebrate God's covenant relationship with the king and the nation."[6] Two subsets of the group are (a) royal psalms and (b) songs of Zion. Royal psalms (Pss. 2; 24; 93; 101; 110) celebrate the king of Israel as God's representative ruler and, on the other hand, the representative of the nation before God. Bruce Waltke convincingly argues that all the psalms are,

---

2. John H. Hayes, *Understanding the Psalms* (Valley Forge, PA: Judson, 1976), 58–59. Osborne draws his lament structure from Hayes (*Hermeneutical Spiral*, 232–33). Artur Weiser writes, "In their *formal structure* both community and individual laments are mostly composed of the following constituent parts: invocation; lamentation; supplication; motivation; vow. The sequence of these several items is not everywhere the same nor is it everywhere complete" (*The Psalms*, trans. Herbert Hartwell, The Old Testament Library [Philadelphia: Westminster Press, 1962], 67).

3. Gordon D. Fee and Douglas Stuart, *How to Read the Bible for All Its Worth*, 3rd ed. (Grand Rapids: Zondervan, 2003), 213.

4. Osborne, *Hermeneutical Spiral*, 233. Weiser offers a similar explanation of the praise psalms, or as he calls them, hymns (*Psalms*, 53).

5. Osborne, *Hermeneutical Spiral*, 234.

6. Ibid.

in some sense, royal, for either superscriptions (explicitly) or details within the psalms (implicitly) present the speaker as the king of Israel.[7] Furthermore, the psalmists' consistent assumption of a royal speaker legitimizes the New Testament messianic use of the psalms, with Jesus as the promised Davidic ruler.[8] Songs of Zion (Pss. 46; 76; 87; 125) thunder with praise for God's choice of Jerusalem (also called "Zion") as the location of his temple, pilgrimage festivals, and chosen king.

Wisdom Psalms

A hybrid of song and wisdom literature (see question 28, "How do we interpret proverbs?"), wisdom psalms deal with topics such as the divine source and nature of true wisdom (Pss. 1; 19; 119) and questions about injustices experienced or witnessed in this life (Ps. 73). Wisdom psalms recast the themes of wisdom literature as songs of worship. As the church's hymnbook often serves as the theology text for the average layperson, it is instructive how much robust theology we find in the hymnbook of the ancient Israelites.

Penitential Psalms

Penitential psalms, whether individual or corporate, give voice to the psalmist's repentance. Probably the best-known penitential psalm is Psalm 51, which records David's repentance over his adultery with Bathsheba and his murder of her husband, Uriah the Hittite (also see Pss. 6; 32; 38; 102; 130; 143).

Imprecatory Psalms

These are the "cursing psalms," of which the best known is Psalm 137 (also see Pss. 35; 60; 70; 109; 140). In such psalms, the speaker calls on God to enact his divine justice against the psalmist's enemies. Often the plea is accompanied by a recounting of the psalmist's innocence. Christians sometimes have trouble squaring such psalms with the biblical injunctions to forgive one's enemies (Matt. 5:43–48; Rom. 12:14, 17). Nevertheless, in both the Old and New Testaments, the authors of Scripture point to God's ultimate intervention against evildoers as a source of comfort (Ps. 73:17–20; Rom. 12:19; 2 Thess. 1:6–8). In calling out for God's intervention, the worshipper releases his emotions and relies upon the only Judge who knows all hearts, words, and actions (Ps. 44:21; Acts 1:24).[9] The same David who pronounced sharp imprecatory

---

7. Bruce K. Waltke, "A Canonical Process Approach to the Psalms," in *Tradition and Testament: Essays in Honor of Charles Lee Feinberg*, ed. John S. Feinberg and Paul D. Feinberg (Chicago: Moody Press, 1981), 11–13.

8. Ibid., 16.

9. D. A. Carson writes, "Although Christians turn the other cheek, this does not mean they are slack regarding justice. We hold that God is perfectly just, and he is the One who says, 'It is mine to avenge; I will repay' (Deut. 32:35). That is why we are to 'leave room for God's

prayers against Saul (Pss. 18; 52) was able to exhibit amazing restraint and grace toward his enemy in daily life (1 Sam. 18:18; 24:3–15; 26:9–11; 2 Sam. 1:17).[10] In reading the imprecatory psalms, it is also important to remember that the psalmist often speaks as king or representative of Israel, *God's people*. A call for vindication is a call for God to show himself faithful to his people. Also, the psalmist's protestations of innocence are situational (Ps. 73:13). That is, the psalmist is not claiming to be ontologically sinless, but in the matter disputed he is claiming that he is in the right. Similarly, if you were wrongly charged in a modern court with robbery, you might passionately appeal, "Listen, I've done *nothing* wrong!"

In reading the imprecatory psalms, we are also reminded that we have acted with injustice and wickedness toward others.[11] Other persons could rightly pray these prayers against us! How thankful we must be, then, for the gospel. Dietrich Bonhoeffer writes on the imprecatory psalms:

> God's vengeance did not strike the sinners, but the one sinless man who stood in the sinners' place, namely God's own Son. Jesus Christ bore the wrath of God, for the execution of which the psalm prays. He stilled God's wrath toward sin and prayed in the hour of the execution of divine judgment: "Father, forgive them, for they do not know what they do!" No other than he, who himself bore the wrath of God, could pray in this way. That was the end of all phony thoughts about the love of God which do not take sin seriously. God hates and redirects his enemies to the only righteous one, and this one asks forgiveness for them. Only in the cross of Jesus Christ is the love of God to be found.[12]

In praying for our enemies, let us make sure that we prefer to have them look to Christ in repentance for their sin rather than personally experience God's unbridled wrath.

---

wrath' (Rom. 12:19). He is the only One who can finally settle the books accurately, and to think otherwise is to pretend that we can take the place of God" (*For the Love of God: A Daily Companion for Discovering the Riches of God's Word*, vol. 1 [Wheaton, IL: Crossway, 1998], reflection for April 24).

10. Osborne, *Hermeneutical Spiral*, 236.

11. C. S. Lewis writes, "I, who am exceptionally blessed in having been allowed a way of life in which, having little power, I have had little opportunity of oppressing and embittering others. Let all of us who have never been school prefects, N.C.O.s [i.e., noncommissioned officers], schoolmasters, matrons of hospitals, prison wardens, or even magistrates, give hearty thanks for it" (*Reflections on the Psalms* [New York: Harcourt Brace Jovanovich, 1958], 25).

12. Dietrich Bonhoeffer, *Psalms: The Prayer Book of the Bible* (Minneapolis: Augsburg, 1970), 58. This book is a translation of the eighth edition of *Das Gebetbuch der Bibel* (Verlag für Missions und Bibel-Kunde, 1966).

If one were to survey a number of commentaries on the psalms, one would find more than these seven types of psalms discussed. Also, one would find varying terminology and sometimes the same psalm classified differently.[13] Part of the reason for the variation in classification is the mixed forms of psalms. That is, what one person might classify as an impassioned lament, another would label as an imprecatory psalm. Is Psalm 19 a praise psalm, honoring God as Creator (vv. 1–6), or a wisdom psalm, pointing hearers to inscripturated wisdom (vv. 7–14)? It seems the psalm fits both categories. And many other psalms arguably could be classified in more than one category.[14] Also, it is important to note that a number of psalms or songs are found in the Bible outside the book of Psalms (e.g., Exod. 15:1–18; Judg. 5; 1 Sam. 2:1–10; Luke 1:46–55).

REFLECTION QUESTIONS

1. Prior to reading the material above, were you aware of different subgenres within the Psalter?

2. What is the interpretive benefit of correctly classifying a psalm in the appropriate subgenre?

3. Which type of psalm most expresses your current life situation to God (e.g., thanksgiving, lament, praise)?

4. As God's people no longer live in the land of Israel under a Jewish monarch, what is the continuing significance of the royal psalms or songs of Zion?

5. Using the seven psalm categories discussed above, label the following psalms: 1, 13, 21, 48, 51, 95, 137.

---

13. Bonhoeffer discusses the psalms according to their main theological subject. He writes, "We shall arrange the subjects dealt with in the Psalter prayers in the following manner: the creation; the law; holy history; the Messiah; the church; life; suffering; guilt; enemies; the end" (*Psalms*, 27). On the basis of 1 Chronicle 16:4, Peter Gentry claims that all psalms should be classified in the broad categories of lament (petition), thanksgiving, and praise (personal conversation, October 8, 2008). Furthermore, Gentry sees the entire Psalter organized according to this broad movement (lament➔thanksgiving➔praise).

14. Note McCartney and Clayton's skeptical approach to psalm types: "When interpreting a psalm, it is better to determine its character by looking at the psalm itself before looking at any commentaries to see what its classification is 'supposed' to be. Some psalms defy grouping with any others, and forcing them into a classification can obscure, rather than elucidate, their meaning" (Dan McCartney and Charles Clayton, *Let the Reader Understand: A Guide to Interpreting and Applying the Bible*, 2nd ed. [Phillipsburg, NJ: P&R, 2002], 231).

FOR FURTHER STUDY

Bonhoeffer, Dietrich. *Psalms: The Prayer Book of the Bible*. Minneapolis: Augsburg, 1970.

Lewis, C. S. *Reflections on the Psalms*. New York: Harcourt Brace Jovanovich, 1958.

VanGemeren, Willem A. "Psalms." In *Expositor's Bible Commentary*, edited by Frank E. Gaebelein, 5:1–880. Grand Rapids: Zondervan, 1991. This excellent commentary is also available in Zondervan's digital version of the *Expositor's Bible Commentary*.

QUESTION 31

How Do We Interpret the Psalms? (Principles of Interpretation)

The book of Psalms often is referred to as the hymnbook of ancient Judaism and the Christian church. Why, then, are the psalms absent in many modern churches? Repetitive praise choruses are substituted for the reading or singing of the psalms. When psalms are used, only short selections are read. Difficult verses and entire psalms are ignored. If we are to reclaim the psalms for personal and corporate worship, we must first read and understand them. What are some principles to help Christians interpret the psalms?

Note the Organization of the Book of Psalms

The Psalter is the longest book in the Bible. One hundred fifty songs, some of surprising length (Ps. 119), can be overwhelming to the beginning interpreter. In light of this challenge, it can be helpful to note the structural divisions within the book itself, which organizes the songs into more manageable groupings. The psalms are divided into five separate books:

- Book 1: Psalms 1–41
- Book 2: Psalms 42–72
- Book 3: Psalms 73–89
- Book 4: Psalms 90–106
- Book 5: Psalms 107–150

Possibly, the psalms were grouped this way in conscious imitation of the Pentateuch, the five books of Moses (Genesis, Exodus, Leviticus, Numbers, and Deuteronomy). Some scholars have detected a general movement within the book of Psalms from petition to thanksgiving to praise, as if the entire collection were organized like a large lament psalm. Others have proposed that the five distinct books facilitated a regular reading schedule in the synagogue.[1] More tantalizing is the suggestion that sees a developing Davidic theme as the key to understanding the organization of the Psalms. Christopher Seitz summarizes his study of this issue.

> The fivefold structure of the Psalms assumes a roughly linear movement. We begin with an emphasis on the earthly David. Then David as such begins to play a far less prominent role, and the fate of the nation more broadly considered comes into play—culminating in punishment and exile. Then the special role of David in God's plans is recalled and lamented, leading to God's assertion of his justice as sovereign over all creation. Hopes once associated with David and Zion are then once again brought to the fore as the Psalter concludes with David singing songs of ascent.[2]

Read the Psalms

One can spend hours or even days reading introductory information about the Psalms. Much more important is the reading of the Psalms themselves. There is a reason the Psalms have been preserved for millennia, while hundreds of writings about them already have been lost or forgotten. Current studies of the Psalms, now acclaimed, also will be forgotten. The book of Psalms, however, will remain: "The grass withers and the flowers fall, but the word of our God stands forever" (Isa. 40:8).

As noted above (in question 21) Kierkegaard once remarked, "Christian scholarship is the human race's prodigious invention to defend itself against the New Testament, to ensure that one can continue to be a Christian without letting the New Testament come too close."[3] One could say the same thing about scholarship on the Psalms. Tomes of research propose various cultic or festival backgrounds to the Psalms. Other scholars reconstruct the supposed "evolution" of ancient Israelite religion and its parallels with other ancient Near Eastern literature.[4] Vast castles of speculation are built on the sands of supposition. Meanwhile, the words of the Psalms themselves are forgotten. Read the Psalms.

---

1. Pius Drijvers, *The Psalms: Their Structure and Meaning* (Freiburg: Herder; London: Burns & Oates, 1965), 20.
2. Christopher Seitz, "Royal Promises in the Canonical Books of Isaiah and the Psalms," in *Word Without End: The Old Testament as Abiding Theological Witness* (Grand Rapids: Eerdmans, 1998), 165.
3. Søren Kierkegaard, *Søren Kierkegaard's Journals and Papers*, ed. and trans. Howard V. Hong and Edna H. Hong (Bloomington, IN: Indiana University Press, 1975), 3:270.
4. Note J. G. S. S. Thomson and F. D. Kidner's criticism: "The legacy of Gunkel and Mowinckel remains, in the preoccupation of most commentators with the task of assigning each psalm to its proper class, and in the viewing of almost all the material as ecclesiastical [i.e., cultic]" ("Psalms, Book of," in *The Illustrated Bible Dictionary,* ed. J. D. Douglas [Leicester: Inter-Varsity Press, 1980], 3:1297).

Label the Subgenre of the Psalm

There are several recognizable subgenres within the book of Psalms. Seven of the main psalm types were discussed in the previous question. There are several reasons that it is helpful to label the psalm type one is studying:

1. Knowing the normal elements of the psalm subgenre that one is reading enables the interpreter to note when expected portions are missing or expanded. One is able to see with greater clarity the emphases of the psalm.

2. Especially with more challenging subgenres (e.g., imprecatory psalms), it can be helpful to keep in mind caveats discussed under the psalm types in question 30. We have nearly two thousand years of Christian reflection on the Psalms. We would be foolish not to learn from those who have gone before us. Indeed, the only reason we can see so far and so clearly is that we stand on the shoulders of giants who have preceded us.

3. Once one has identified the subgenre of the psalm in question, it can be helpful to look at other psalms of the same type. Also, it can be helpful to compare the psalm with psalms in other subgenres. Like proverbs, psalms often discuss particular situations without giving all exceptions or conditions. As we look at the whole Psalter, however, we begin to gain a more holistic view of God and a life lived as his followers.

Note Any Contextual Information Given in the Psalm Headings

Many psalms have superscriptions, which give the author and sometimes the occasion of the psalm in question (see figure 11). For example, the superscription in Psalm 51 reads, "For the director of music. A psalm of David. When the prophet Nathan came to him after David had committed adultery with Bathsheba." Scholars debate the antiquity and authenticity of these superscriptions, but the best and most ancient manuscripts of the Psalms include them. Moreover, New Testament usage of the Psalms seems to presuppose the truth of the information in the superscriptions.[5] It seems that the superscriptions should be accepted as authentic. Information in the

---

5. E.g., Matthew 22:43, 45; Mark 12:36, 37; Luke 20:42; Acts 1:16; 2:25; Romans 4:6; 11:9; Hebrews 4:7. Peter Gentry makes this point in an undated classroom handout titled "Psalm Titles: Psalms in the Life of David." Gentry also observes that other ancient Near Eastern hymns have similar superscriptions and subscriptions. That is, such material would have been expected in the psalm, or at least not unusual.

superscriptions sometimes adds concreteness to the anguish or joy expressed by the psalmist (e.g., Ps. 51).

FIGURE 11: ATTRIBUTION OF PSALMS	
PSALMS ATTRIBUTED TO . . .	**NUMBER OF PSALMS SO ATTRIBUTED**
David*	73
Asaph	12
The Sons of Korah	12
Solomon	2
Heman the Ezrahite	1
Ethan the Ezrahite	1
Moses	1
(no attribution given)	48
* The Greek translation of the Old Testament (the Septuagint, or LXX) ascribes 84 psalms to David (Bruce K. Waltke, "A Canonical Approach to the Psalms," in *Tradition and Testament: Essays in Honor of Charles Lee Feinberg*, ed. John S. Feinberg and Paul D. Feinberg [Chicago: Moody Press, 1981], 10).	

Pay Attention to the Segmentation of the Psalm

As Hebrew poetry, psalms are divided into various lines and strophes (or stanzas). Translators' decisions about how to format their English translations are based on syllabification, stress, and other markers in the original Hebrew text. Readers of English thus are dependent on translators to faithfully convey the poetic segmentation of the original text. Thankfully, we have many modern English translations that convey this information well. A quick glance at any page of the Psalms reveals a lot of white space around the typed lines. This space is a result of parallel lines being grouped together and strophes being separated. A sermon or lesson on a particular psalm should attempt to follow the structure of the psalm. In other words, if the psalm has four stanzas, the sermon might best be organized around four applications or propositions.

Recognize the Poetic Language of the Psalm

Psalms are poems to be sung. As such, they are filled with poetic language—metaphor, simile, alliteration, hyperbole, parallelism, etc. While overlapping with poetry in the English language, Hebrew poetry also has some unique features. So as not to misunderstand or misinterpret it, the reader is advised to consult question 29 ("How do we interpret poetry?").

Authors employ poetry as an aesthetic expression, or a memory device, or to convey intense emotion. As we seek to understand the psalms ourselves and teach them to others, we must guard, not only against misunderstanding

Hebraic poetry but also against reducing such thundering compositions into prosaic propositions. We must seek God's help to convey the intensity of the original songs to our modern hearers. Sometimes a dynamically equivalent translation or paraphrase, such as Eugene Peterson's rendering of the Psalms in *The Message*, can help us hear afresh these powerful poems.

Explore the Messianic Significance of the Psalm

God promised David that one of his descendants would always reign on his throne (2 Sam. 7:12–13). The New Testament declares that Jesus is this promised Davidic Ruler. In reference to Psalm 16:8–11, Peter declares to a Jewish crowd,

> Brothers, I can tell you confidently that the patriarch David died and was buried, and his tomb is here to this day. But he was a prophet and knew that God had promised him on oath that he would place one of his descendants on his throne. Seeing what was ahead, he spoke of the resurrection of the Christ, that he was not abandoned to the grave, nor did his body see decay. (Acts 2:29–31)

Peter here seems to say that David was conscious that his words were pointing forward to a specific, preeminent descendent—a propositional prediction fulfilled in one person, the Messiah. There are other psalms, however, the New Testament authors apply to Jesus that read most naturally as having an initial reference in David's own life (Ps. 69:9; cf. John 2:17). These psalms include, for example, confessions of David's wrongdoings (Ps. 69:5). Such use of the psalms is best understood as typological—presenting David as the type and Jesus as the corresponding antitype. For example, if David endured the opposition of the godless around him, how much more will the preeminent Righteous One have to endure the opposition of the wicked (Ps. 69:4). For further information on typology and the Christological nature of Scripture, see questions 18 ("Is the Bible really all about Jesus?") and 24 ("How do we interpret prophecy? [Typology]"). Only context will indicate whether the New Testament authors are claiming a psalm as a propositional prediction or as a typological correspondence.

Because nearly half of the Psalms are attributed to David, some scholars have argued for reading all the Davidic psalms as, in some sense, messianic. At the least, we can say every Davidic psalm quoted in the New Testament as fulfilled in Jesus is messianic. Furthermore, Jesus taught his disciples that the Psalms pointed to him (Luke 24:44). With some tentativeness, it seems to me that additional typological correspondences may be proposed for the other Davidic psalms, if not the whole Psalter.[6] Bonhoeffer certainly takes this approach. He writes,

---

6. Waltke argues that most, if not all, of the psalms are to be understood as uttered by the king—ultimately by the messianic King. He writes, "In all fairness, it seems as though the

According to the witness of the Bible, David is, as the anointed king of the chosen people of God, a prototype of Jesus Christ. What happens to him happens to him for the sake of the one who is in him and who is said to proceed from him, namely Jesus Christ. And he is not unaware of this, but "being therefore a prophet, and knowing that God had sworn with an oath to him that he would set one of his descendants upon his throne, he foresaw and spoke of the resurrection of the Christ" (Acts 2:30f.). David was a witness to Christ in his office, in his life, and in his words. The New Testament says even more. In the Psalms of David the promised Christ himself already speaks (Hebrews 2:12; 10:5) or, as may also be indicated, the Holy Spirit (Hebrews 3:7). These same words which David spoke, therefore, the future Messiah spoke through him. The prayers of David were prayed also by Christ. Or better, Christ himself prayed them through his forerunner David.[7]

Pray the Psalms

The psalms are poems and songs, but they are also prayers. As a diverse collection of prayers, they cover the entire range of emotions and experiences that people face in this variegated life. Moreover, they are *inspired* prayers—teaching us to pray for things and in ways that God desires. Bonhoeffer notes the pedagogical value of praying the Psalms.

> And so we must learn to pray. The child learns to speak because his father speaks to him. He learns the speech of his father. So we learn to speak to God because God has spoken to us and speaks to us. By means of the speech of the Father in heaven his children learn to speak with him. Repeating God's own words after him, we begin to pray to him.[8]

The psalms not only can be prayed word for word, but also can be meditated upon, mentally digested, and prayed contextually based on the unique situations we all face.[9] Also, it is noteworthy that many of the psalms are corporate prayers. The body of Christ, the church, is to pray together (Acts 1:14,

---

writers of the New Testament are not attempting to identify and limit the psalms that prefigure Christ but rather are assuming that the Psalter as a whole has Jesus Christ in view and that this should be the normative way of interpreting the psalms" ("Canonical Process Approach to the Psalms," 7).

7. Dietrich Bonhoeffer, *Psalms: The Prayer Book of the Bible* (Minneapolis: Augsburg, 1970), 18–19.

8. Ibid., 11. He also writes, "The richness of the Word of God ought to determine our prayer, not the poverty of our heart" (15).

9. Osborne comments, "The value of such psalms for every believer is obvious. Whether one is ill, beset by enemies or aware of sin, the lament psalms offer not only encouragement but models of prayer. Many have claimed that one should pray them directly; I agree but prefer to meditate, contextualize and then pray these psalms as they reflect upon my situation"

24; 4:24, 31; 13:3). When Jesus gave his disciples a model prayer ("The Lord's Prayer"), it was a corporate one (Matt. 6:9–13, "*Our* Father . . . Give *us* . . ."").

Memorize the Psalms

One way to begin praying the psalms is to memorize them. Then, both in focused prayer time and in the mundane tasks of daily life, one will find the words of the psalms on one's lips. For the importance of meditating on the psalms—for devotion, instruction, and inspiration—see these verses from Psalm 19:

> The law of the LORD is perfect, reviving the soul. The statutes of the LORD are trustworthy, making wise the simple. The precepts of the LORD are right, giving joy to the heart. The commands of the LORD are radiant, giving light to the eyes. The fear of the LORD is pure, enduring forever. The ordinances of the LORD are sure and altogether righteous. They are more precious than gold, than much pure gold; they are sweeter than honey, than honey from the comb. By them is your servant warned; in keeping them there is great reward. (Ps. 19:7–11)

Sing the Psalms

While it is a Christian's delight to read and meditate on any of the psalms, this portion of Scripture possibly finds its fullest expression in song. Originally written as individual and corporate worship songs, any psalms sung by God's people today are a continued chorus that has now echoed for more than three thousand years.

REFLECTION QUESTIONS

1. When reading the psalms, have you interpreted them in light of the information in the superscriptions?

2. Is it valid to read Davidic psalms as "messianic" if they are not so quoted in the New Testament?

3. Looking at the five-part book of Psalms, do you see any internal theological or thematic elements that would explain their grouping into five books?

4. Challenge: Learn a worship song or hymn that is based directly on a biblical psalm. Sing it to the Lord in person or in corporate worship. For a number of modern worship songs based on the psalms, see "These Things I Remember" at www.sojournmusic.com.

(Grant R. Osborne, *The Hermeneutical Spiral: A Comprehensive Introduction to Biblical Interpretation*, rev. ed. [Downers Grove, IL: InterVarsity, 2006], 233).

5. Challenge: Memorize a psalm (e.g., Ps. 19) and meditate on it throughout the day—when waiting for the bus, mowing the grass, changing the baby's diaper, etc.

FOR FURTHER STUDY

Bonhoeffer, Dietrich. *Psalms: The Prayer Book of the Bible.* Minneapolis: Augsburg, 1970.

Lewis, C. S. *Reflections on the Psalms.* New York: Harcourt Brace Jovanovich, 1958.

VanGemeren, Willem A. "Psalms." In *Expositor's Bible Commentary,* edited by Frank E. Gaebelein, 5:1–880. Grand Rapids: Zondervan, 1991. This excellent commentary is also available in Zondervan's digital version of the *Expositor's Bible Commentary.*

Primarily New Testament Genres

How Do We Interpret Parables? (History of Interpretation)

About one-third of Jesus' teaching is in parables. So influential are these parables that even people who have never read the Bible use expressions drawn from them (e.g., "the good Samaritan," or "the prodigal son"). Though widely known, Jesus' parables are also notorious for their frequent misinterpretation. In this question, I will define *parable* and give a brief historical survey of how they have been interpreted. Then, in the following question, I will offer some principles for interpreting parables.

When asked the definition of a parable, most Christians might respond, "An earthly story with a heavenly meaning." The dictionary definition is "a short fictitious story that illustrates a moral attitude or a religious principle."[1] While these definitions are correct, the most fundamental component of a parable is that there must be a comparison.[2] For example, in the parable of the hidden treasure, the kingdom of heaven is compared to a treasure ("The kingdom of heaven is like treasure hidden in a field," Matt. 13:44). The Greek word *parabolē*, which underlies our English word *parable* has a broad range of meaning. It can refer to proverbs, similes, figurative sayings, stories, etc. For our purposes, however, we will limit our discussion primarily to the story parables that are found in the Bible.

For a broad survey of the history of biblical interpretation, see question 9 ("How has the Bible been interpreted throughout church history?"). At this point, however, we will overview specifically the interpretation of parables. This summary will be helpful in two regards: (1) In seeing the interpretive

---

1. *Merriam-Webster's Collegiate Dictionary*, 10th ed. (Springfield, MA: Merriam-Webster, 1997)
2. Stein defines a parable as "a figure of speech in which there is a brief or extended comparison" (Robert H. Stein, *An Introduction to the Parables of Jesus* [Philadelphia: Westminster Press, 1981], 22). My understanding of the history of interpretation of parables has been greatly influenced by Stein.

missteps commonly taken throughout history, the reader will be forewarned not to repeat them; and (2) it can be instructive to see how scholarly insights resulted in significant shifts in the understanding of parables. The interpretation of parables is surveyed in five historical periods.

Jesus' Original Setting and the Writing of the Gospels

At the least, we can say that Jesus and the inspired Gospel authors properly understood his parables. Thus, when Jesus gives an explanation of his own parables (Matt. 13:36–43; Mark 4:13–20) or the Gospel authors give contextual clues as to the meaning of the parables (e.g., Luke 10:29; 15:1–2), those interpretations are definitive. It is important to note that while Jesus used parables to illustrate truth (Mark 12:12; Luke 10:36–37), he also used parables to conceal truth and increase the culpability of his hard-hearted opponents (Mark 4:10–12, 33–34; cf. 2 Thess. 2:11–12).[3]

The Early Church to the Reformation

Very soon after the completion of the New Testament, early Christians began interpreting the text allegorically. That is, they proposed many allegorical meanings unintended by the biblical authors. For example, every early post-New Testament interpretation of the parable of the good Samaritan (Luke 10:25–37) explains the story as an allegorical message of salvation, with the Good Samaritan signifying Jesus (see, e.g., figure 12). In the text, however, Jesus clearly tells the story to answer a Jewish legal expert's question, "Who is my neighbor?" (Luke 10:29).

Early Christians interpreted parables in this way for several reasons. (1) Jesus himself explains at least a few details of his parables allegorically (Mark 4:13–20; Matt. 13:36–43). If Jesus can do this, why not his followers? (2) Allegory was a common approach to interpreting religious texts in the Greco-Roman world. Early Christians uncritically adopted the interpretive methods of their day. (3) Allegorical interpretation emphasizes the interpreter's access to the "secret" meaning of the parables. Such a method is inevitably attractive to humans who have a propensity toward the secretive and conspiratorial.

The Reformation

The Protestant Reformers of the sixteenth century decried the allegorical excesses of their forebearers. Martin Luther (1483–1546) said that Origen's allegorical interpretations were "silly," "amazing twaddle," "absurd,"

---

3. Stein remarks, "The fact that for centuries the meaning of the parables has been lost through allegorical interpretation and ignorance of the *Sitz im Leben* of Jesus also indicates that the parables are not self-evident illustrations" (Robert H. Stein, *The Method and Message of Jesus' Teachings*, rev. ed. [Louisville, KY: Westminster John Knox, 1994], 40).

and "altogether useless."[4] While isolated voices throughout pre-Reformation church history had criticized illegitimate allegory, the Reformation was the first time that such focused criticism descended systematically even to the parables. Unfortunately, out of habit, carelessness, or other reasons, many Reformers continued to provide allegorical reflections on the parables. John Calvin (1509–1564), the prince of Reformation biblical expositors, was most consistent in keeping to the authorial intent of the parables. In reference to allegorical interpretation, specifically as represented in the allegorization of the parable of the good Samaritan, Calvin wrote,

> I acknowledge that I have no liking for any of these interpretations; but we ought to have a deeper reverence for Scripture than to reckon ourselves at liberty to disguise its natural meaning. And, indeed, any one may see that the curiosity of certain men has led them to contrive these speculations, contrary to the intention of Christ.[5]

The Reformation to the Late Nineteenth Century

The Reformation broke the allegorical stranglehold on much of the Bible, but a majority of Christian writers continued to allegorize the parables. The many unexplained and striking details in Jesus' stories were irresistible fodder to these interpreters, who, due to historical influences, were predisposed to see allegorical significance that the biblical authors did not intend.

The Late Nineteenth to the Early Twenty-first Century

Several important developments in the interpretation of parables have occurred in the last century and a half. In 1888, the German New Testament scholar Adolf Jülicher published the first of his two-volume work, *Die Gleichnisreden Jesu* (*The Parable-talks of Jesus*).[6] Jülicher's study sounded the death knell for allegorical interpretation of the parables.[7] Instead of allegorizing the details of a parable, he focused on the main point of why Jesus gave the parable. Unfortunately, Jülicher interpreted parables according to his skeptical and liberal theological predilections and mislabeled many legitimate teachings of Jesus as later historical accretions.[8]

---

4. Martin Luther, *Lectures on Genesis, Chapters 1–5,* in *Luther's Works,* ed. J. Pelikan (St. Louis: Concordia, 1958), 1:91, 98, 233.
5. John Calvin, *Commentary on a Harmony of the Evangelists, Matthew, Mark, and Luke,* trans. William Pringle (Edinburgh: Calvin Translation Society, n.d.; reprint, Grand Rapids: Baker, 2003), 3:63 (vol. 17 in reprint series).
6. Adolf Jülicher, *Die Gleichnisreden Jesu* (Freiburg: Mohr, 1888). This work has never been translated into English.
7. The death knell in scholarly circles, at least (K. R. Snodgrass, "Parables," in *DJG,* 591). Allegorical interpretation in more popular literature has continued to the present day.
8. Ibid., 591.

FIGURE 12: THE PARABLE OF THE GOOD SAMARITAN, AS INTERPRETED BY ORIGEN (A.D. 185–254)*	
PARABLE DETAILS	**ALLEGORICAL EXPLANATIONS**
Man going down to Jericho	Adam
Jerusalem	Paradise
Jericho	The world
Robbers	Hostile powers (John 10:8)
Priest	The Law
Levite	The Prophets
Samaritan	Christ
Wounds	Disobedience, vices, and sin
Beast (Donkey)	The Lord's body, which bears our sins
Stable (Inn)	The church
Two Denarii	Knowledge of the Father and the Son
Manager of the Stable (Innkeeper)	Head of the church "to whom its care has been entrusted" (guardian angel)
Promised Return of the Samaritan	Savior's second coming

*Origen, *Homiliae in Lucam* 34.3–9. Interestingly, Origen draws upon an unnamed predecessor for this interpretation. He begins, "One of the elders wanted to interpret the parable as follows" (*Homiliae in Lucam* 34.3). For an English translation of Origen's extant sermons on Luke, see *Origen: Homilies on Luke, Fragments on Luke*, trans. Joseph T. Lienhard, The Fathers of the Church 94 (Washington, DC: The Catholic University of America Press, 1996).

In the early to mid-twentieth century, scholars such as C. H. Dodd and Joachim Jeremias called for interpreters to hear parables as they were heard by Jesus' original, first-century Jewish Palestinian audience.[9] Jesus announced an inbreaking of God's kingdom mediated through his messianic reign. Any interpretation of the parables that fails to consider this original historical context is doomed to failure.

Beginning in the mid-twentieth century, scholars known as redaction critics drew attention to the final editorial contributions of the Gospel authors. For parables, this emphasis was important because Gospel authors gave their readers editorial clues to the proper interpretation of Jesus' parables. Through grouping similar parables, providing important contextual information, or employing other literary devices, the authors of the Gospels provided guidance to the correct understanding of Jesus' parables.

---

9. C. H. Dodd, *The Parables of the Kingdom* (London: Nisbet & Co., 1935); and Joachim Jeremias, *The Parables of Jesus*, trans. S. H. Hooke, rev. ed. (New York: Charles Scribner's Sons, 1963).

In the late twentieth and early twenty-first century, there has been somewhat of a regress toward early allegorical tendencies. On one front, some reader-response and "aesthetic" critics insist on reading the parables apart from the original historical context.[10] The parables are taken as having a dynamic meaning-producing polyvalent life of their own. While this description may sound somewhat appealing in the abstract, in real life it means parables can mean whatever the reader wants them to mean. Jesus, however, clearly used parables to convey specific, definable truths. Admittedly, the affective power of story cannot be reproduced in propositional summary, but the basic meaning of Jesus' parables can and should be so summarized.

On other fronts, there has been an increasing *uncritical* interest in the history of the church's interpretation of biblical texts.[11] In other words, various interpretations of biblical passages are valued in their own right and given a level of authority and influence that sometimes equals or exceeds that of the inspired text. While a study of reception history (the way a text has been received throughout history) can be quite informative, the text itself must maintain a clear primacy over aberrant interpretations.

REFLECTION QUESTIONS

1. If Jesus provided allegorical explanations for some details in his parables, what is wrong with taking the next step and providing such explanations for *all* details?

2. Allegory was one of the dominant approaches to literature in the early Greco-Roman world. What would you say is the dominant approach to literature in our day?

3. Look again at Origen's explanation of the parable of the good Samaritan. How would your church respond to a sermon on the parable that interpreted it in this way?

4. Do you recall hearing or reading an invalid allegorical interpretation of a parable? At the time you encountered it, did you find the interpretation convincing? Why or why not?

---

10. E.g., D. O. Via, *The Parables* (Philadelphia: Fortress, 1967).
11. See, for example, Treier's description of the theological interpretation of Scripture (TIS) movement (Daniel J. Treier, *Introducing Theological Interpretation of Scripture* [Grand Rapids: Baker, 2008], 39–55).

5. What would you say to someone who claimed, "Origen's interpretation of the Good Samaritan convinced me to trust in Christ for my salvation, so that interpretation must be correct"?

FOR FURTHER STUDY

Blomberg, Craig L. *Interpreting the Parables*. Downers Grove, IL: InterVarsity Press, 1990.

_____. *Preaching the Parables: From Responsible Interpretation to Powerful Proclamation*. Grand Rapids: Baker, 2004.

How Do We Interpret Parables? (Principles of Interpretation)

If parables have been so infamously misinterpreted throughout church history (see the previous question), what are some hermeneutical guidelines that will aid us in staying on the proper course?

As a start, it is important to note that Jesus often employed parables to teach about the kingdom of God. Klyne Snodgrass claims that the meaning of almost all parables can be subsumed under the theme of kingdom, which was the main subject of Jesus' preaching (Mark 1:15). In fact, many parables begin with an explicit introductory phrase such as, "This is what the kingdom of God is like" (Mark 4:26). Snodgrass writes,

> The primary focus of the parables is the coming of the kingdom of God and the resulting discipleship that is required. When Jesus proclaimed the kingdom he meant that God was exercising his power and rule to bring forgiveness, defeat evil and establish righteousness in fulfillment of Old Testament promises.[1]

This kingdom theme, in turn, often is expressed through three main theological sub-motifs: "the graciousness of God, the demands of discipleship, and the dangers of disobedience."[2]

Below are several suggestions for determining the author's intended meaning of a parable.[3]

---

1. K. R. Snodgrass, "Parables," in *DJG*, 599.
2. Craig L. Blomberg, *Interpreting the Parables* (Downers Grove, IL: InterVarsity Press, 1990), 326.
3. While the Gospel authors (Matthew, Mark, Luke, and John) are technically the authors of the parables (in that they wrote them down), we assume that, as inspired authors, they faithfully conveyed Jesus' meaning.

Determine the Main Point(s) of the Parable

The most important principle in interpreting the parables is to determine the reason the parable was uttered and why it was included in the canon of Scripture. There is some debate among evangelicals as to whether each parable teaches only one main point (e.g., Robert Stein) or whether a parable may have several main points (e.g., Craig Blomberg). In reality, these two perspectives are not as varied as they initially may appear.

For example, Craig Blomberg insists that parables can have one, two, or three main points, *determined by the number of main characters/items in the parable.*[4] Thus, for example, in the parable of the prodigal son (Luke 15:11–32), there are three main characters—the father, the older brother, and the younger brother. The three main points, based on the activity of the three representative characters, would be:

1. *The father:* God the Father is gracious and forgiving.

2. *The older brother:* Followers of God should beware of a begrudging attitude toward his grace and forgiveness exercised toward others.

3. *The younger brother:* God welcomes rebels who confess their sin, turn from it, and embrace his mercy.[5]

By contrast, Stein maintains that it is more helpful to express the main point in one sentence. He might explain the meaning of the parable as follows: God (represented by the father) is gracious to sinners (the younger brother), and therefore we should not despise his love to others (as did the older brother). The focus of the parable, according to Stein, is on the response of the older brother and his unwillingness to rejoice in his brother's return and his father's complete acceptance. This analysis is confirmed by the context, as Luke clearly indicates that Jesus is responding to the Pharisees for their begrudging attitude toward God's mercy (Luke 15:1–2).

But just how do we determine the main point(s) of a parable? Stein recommends these additional questions.[6]

---

4. Blomberg, *Interpreting the Parables,* 166.
5. Blomberg summarizes the main points: "(1) Even as the prodigal always had the option of repenting and returning home, so also all sinners, however wicked, may confess their sins and turn to God in contrition. (2) Even as the father went to elaborate lengths to offer reconciliation to the prodigal, so also God offers all people, however undeserving, lavish forgiveness of sins if they are willing to accept it. (3) Even as the older brother should not have begrudged his brother's reinstatement but rather rejoiced in it, so those who claim to be God's people should be glad and not mad that he extends his grace even to the most undeserving" (ibid., 174).
6. Questions adapted from Robert H. Stein, *A Basic Guide to Interpreting the Bible: Playing by the Rules* (Grand Rapids: Baker, 1994), 146–49.

1. *Who are the main characters?* As we have already seen with the parable of the prodigal son, the main characters are the father, the younger brother, and the older brother. Stein suggests that of the three, the father and the older brother should be given the most attention.

2. *What occurs at the end?* As Jesus often stresses his most important point at the end of a parable, the fact that the parable of the prodigal son ends with a rebuke of the older brother (Luke 15:31–32) further supports that Jesus is focusing on correcting a wicked attitude toward God's gracious treatment of sinners.

3. *What occurs in direct discourse (in quotation marks)?* Direct quotations draw the readers' or listeners' attention to the parable's emphasized point. For example, in the parable of the prodigal son, note the emphatic placement of the older brother's quoted words toward the end of the parable (Luke 15:29–30).

4. *Who/What gets the most space?* (That is, to whom or what are the most verses devoted?) Simply by giving the most literary space to a certain person or item in the parable, Jesus showed us where his emphasis lay.

Recognize Stock Imagery in the Parables

In my classroom lecture on parables, I sometimes ask for an international student as a volunteer. Addressing the student, I say, "Imagine you pick up a newspaper and find a cartoon with a donkey and an elephant talking to each other. What is the cartoon about?" The suggestions are inevitably amusing—and completely wrong. The Americans in the class immediately recognize the donkey as a symbol of the Democratic political party and the elephant as a symbol of the Republicans. We do so because we are accustomed to such stock imagery from our cultural conditioning.

Jesus' first-century audience and the early readers of the Gospels also were accustomed to certain stock imagery. These images, paralleled in Old Testament and other early Jewish sources, are found throughout Jesus' parables as main characters or central actions (see figure 12). Sometimes a non-stock image plays a central role, and careful study must determine its significance. Additional details in the story generally are intended simply to make the story interesting and memorable.

Note Striking or Unexpected Details

My wife and I once gave an Arabic "Jesus video" (Gospel of Luke video) to some new Sudanese immigrants. As we sat in their cramped living room, watching the video with them, I was struck by how many times the immigrants laughed or glanced at each other with amusement. Jesus was an amazing and interesting teacher. Sadly, our minds have been dulled by familiarity. Jesus' parables are filled with striking details, unexpected twists, shocking statements, and surprise outcomes. When such attention-getting components occur, we need to pay attention because an important point is being made. For example, in the parable of the unforgiving servant (Matt. 18:23–35), we should note the nearly unfathomable difference between the debt that the servant owed the king ("ten thousand talents" [NIV] or "millions of dollars" [NLT]) and the debt owed to him by another servant ("a hundred denarii" [NIV] or "a few thousand dollars" [NLT]). Here Jesus emphasizes the immense grace of God in forgiving the depth of our sin, while also putting in proper perspective the sins we are asked to forgive others. Another example of an attention-getting detail is found in the parable of the widow and the unjust judge (Luke 18:1–8). The brash persistence of the widow would have been scandalous—especially in the traditional society of Jesus' day. With this vivid picture of determination, Jesus calls his followers to persistence in prayer. Similarly, an older man running to anything, much less a reunion with a renegade son (Luke 15:20), would have been an undignified sight in first-century Israel. How much more surprising, then, is the eager graciousness of God the Father toward repentant sinners.

Do Not Press All Details for Meaning

Not all details in a parable have significance. Rather, many details simply make the story interesting, memorable, or true to life for the hearers. For example, in the parable of the unforgiving servant (Matt. 18:23–35), the amount of money ("ten thousand talents") and the unit of money ("talents") have no special significance—other than to denote a large debt in a known currency. Likewise, in the parable of the prodigal son, when the father greets his repentant son with new clothes, new shoes, a ring, and a banquet (Luke 15:22–23), these gifts signify acceptance and celebration. They do not each carry some symbolic meaning that must be decoded. In fact, to attempt such decoding is to head down the misguided path of allegorical interpretation.[7]

Since each *central* parable figure generally conveys only *one main point of comparison*, it should not surprise us that some characters act in untoward ways. The judge in the parable of Luke 18:1–8, in some sense, represents God, to whom we bring our requests. Yet, while the human judge is only pestered into justice (Luke 18:4–5), God is eager to intervene for his people (Luke 18:7). The main point of comparison in the parable is the need for persistence in

---

7. Tertullian (ca. 160–225), in fact, did just this with the parable of the good Samaritan. He interpreted the following parable images accordingly: good Samaritan – neighbor – Christ; thieves – rulers of darkness; wounds – fears, lusts, wraths, pains, deceits, pleasures; wine – blood of David's vine; oil – compassion of the Father; binding – love, faith, hope (noted in Robert H. Stein, *An Introduction to the Parables of Jesus* [Philadelphia: Westminster Press, 1981], 44).

prayer (Luke 18:1). In the parable of the wise and foolish virgins (Matt. 25:1–13), the wise maidens are commended for preparing appropriately by bringing enough oil for their lamps (Matt. 25:4). Though the bridegroom delayed his coming, the wise virgins were still ready for his arrival. In the same way, Jesus' followers are called always to be ready (by living in faithful obedience), though his coming may be delayed (Matt. 25:13). The fact that five virgins were wise and five foolish does not mean that fifty percent of the world will be saved and fifty percent damned. Neither is Jesus teaching us that we should not share (the wise virgins refused to share their oil [Matt. 25:9]). Jesus was a master storyteller, and he included many details simply to make his stories interesting.

FIGURE 12: STOCK IMAGERY IN JESUS' PARABLES

STOCK IMAGE	SIGNIFICANCE	EXAMPLE
Father	God	Luke 15:11–32
Master	God	Mark 12:1–11
Judge	God	Luke 18:1–8
Shepherd	God	Matt. 18:12–14
King	God	Matt. 18:23–35
Son	Israel, a follower of God	Luke 15:11–32
Vineyard	Israel	Matt. 21:33–41
Vine	Israel or God's People	John 15:5
Fig Tree	Israel	Mark 11:13
Sheep	God's people	Matt. 25:31–46
Servant	Follower of God	Matt. 25:14–30
Enemy	The devil	Matt. 13:24–30
Harvest	Judgment	Matt. 13:24–30
Wedding Feast	Messianic banquet, the coming age	Matt. 25:1–13

A friend once told me about the sermon his pastor preached on Matthew 13:44–46 (the parables of the treasure in the field and the pearl of great price). His pastor asserted that the treasure and the pearl stood for the Christian believer or the church and that Jesus was the one buying the treasure or the pearl. The pastor claimed that this interpretation must be true because we do not buy the kingdom. Rather, Jesus buys us with his blood. This interpretation sounds very pious, but it is based on a misunderstanding of parabolic language. In both parables, Jesus sets before his hearers a crisis, where everything else is less important than the treasure or pearl. Jesus' preaching calls us to "seek first his kingdom and his righteousness" (Matt. 6:33). Yes, ultimately, we can seek the kingdom only because of the grace given us (Eph. 2:8–10). In these parables, however, Jesus is calling people to respond by valuing him and his messianic kingdom above anything else. Divine sovereignty does not negate human responsibility.

Pay Attention to the Literary and Historical Context of the Parable

The authors of the Gospels often clue us to the meaning of a parable by including information about why Jesus uttered that parable or by grouping together parables on similar topics. An obvious example occurs at the beginning of the parable of the widow and the unjust judge (Luke 18:1–8). In the opening lines of the account, Luke notes, "Then Jesus told his disciples a parable to show them that they should always pray and not give up" (Luke 18:1). Any interpretation that neglects this authoritative word of guidance is sure to go astray.

Luke provides similarly helpful contextual information prior to Jesus' series of three parables in Luke 15 (culminating in the parable of the prodigal son). Luke tells us,

> Now the tax collectors and "sinners" were all gathering around to hear him. But the Pharisees and the teachers of the law muttered, "This man welcomes sinners and eats with them." Then Jesus told them this parable. (Luke 15:1–3)

Luke did not have to tell us this information, but this introduction helps us to see that these parables are given as a response to religious hypocrisy that fails to understand the graciousness of God toward sinners (cf. Luke 15:31–32). Also, both before and after the parable of the good Samaritan, Luke clearly shows that this parable is Jesus' response to a self-righteous inquirer who wants to illegitimately limit the term *neighbor* (Luke 10:25–29, 36–37; cf. Luke 14:7; 19:11).

Whether Jesus originally pronounced the four parables of Matthew 24:45–25:46 (the faithful and unfaithful slave, the ten bridesmaids, the talents, and the sheep and the goats) together without intervening comment, we do not know. But it is no mistake that we find them together and that they follow immediately on the heels of his eschatological discourse of Matthew 24:1–44. The parables all call Jesus' disciples to faithful obedience as they wait for his return.

Sometimes a knowledge of history or cultural backgrounds aids in the interpretation of a parable. For example, to understand more fully the parable of the good Samaritan, the reader should know that the Jews of Jesus' day discriminated against Samaritans. By making the Samaritan the only "neighborly" person in the story (Luke 10:33, 36), Jesus condemned his hypocritical contemporaries, who delimited love to exclude certain races or persons.[8]

---

8. Thus, it is fitting that in his modern paraphrase of the Gospels set in the Southeastern United States of the 1950s, Clarence Jordan replaces the Samaritan with an African-American. The

While such background information is often available from a careful reading of the entire Bible itself (e.g., John 4:9; 8:48), persons with less familiarity with the Bible may want to consult a study Bible (see question 13, "What are some helpful books or tools for interpreting the Bible?"). Also, highly recommended is Craig Blomberg's *Interpreting the Parables*, which gives a brief, insightful discussion of every parable in the Gospels.

REFLECTION QUESTIONS

1. Which do you find more convincing—the one-point-only approach to parables or the understanding that parables can have as many points as main characters?

2. Why, in your opinion, do Christian speakers and writers so frequently stray into allegorical interpretation of the parables?

3. Besides a donkey and elephant, can you think of any other widely recognized stock imagery in modern American culture?

4. Challenge: Choose one parable from Matthew 13 and apply the guidelines suggested above.

5. Challenge: Choose a parable and ask Stein's four suggested questions (Who are the main characters? What occurs at the end? What occurs in direct discourse? Who/What gets the most space?). Did answering these questions help in determining the main point?

FOR FURTHER STUDY

Blomberg, Craig L. *Interpreting the Parables*. Downers Grove, IL: InterVarsity Press, 1990.
_____. *Preaching the Parables: From Responsible Interpretation to Powerful Proclamation*. Grand Rapids: Baker, 2004.
Stein, Robert H. *An Introduction to the Parables of Jesus*. Philadelphia: Westminster Press, 1981.

---

priest and Levite are represented by "a white preacher" and "a white Gospel song leader" (*The Cotton Patch Version of Luke and Acts* [New York: Association Press, 1969], 46–47).

How Do We Interpret Letters or Epistles? (Structure and Nature)

Of the twenty-seven books in the New Testament, twenty-one are letters. Some are letters to individuals, but most are written to congregations. As the early Christian church expanded rapidly into distant lands, the apostles and their successors sent encouragement and instruction through such letters (also called epistles).[1] What we initially encounter as overheard conversation in the letters is in actuality a word from God addressed to us. The letters in the New Testament are more than time-bound communication; they are works inspired by the Holy Spirit, offering authoritative instruction to the church in every age.

In this first question dealing with letters, we will cover their structure, literary forms used within letters, their occasional nature, and the issue of pseudonymity. In the next question, we will overview practical guidelines for interpreting a New Testament letter.

The Structure of Ancient Letters

In structure, ancient letters are quite similar to modern letters or e-mails. New Testament letters usually begin by identifying the sender and receiver ("Paul, an apostle . . . To the churches in Galatia" [Gal. 1:1–2]).

---

1. Some scholars have used the term *epistles* to refer to letters carefully fashioned for public consumption, in distinction from more informal correspondence (e.g., Adolf Deissmann, *Light from the Ancient East: The New Testament Illustrated by Recently Discovered Texts of the Graeco-Roman World*, trans. Lionel R. M. Strachan [New York: George H. Doran, 1927; reprint, Peabody, MA: Hendrickson, 1995], 228–41). I am using the two terms (*letters* and *epistles*) interchangeably, as most scholars do now. Paul wrote letters to particular situations, but he also maintained a consciousness of his apostleship and the broader church community (1 Cor. 1:1–2; Col. 4:16).

Such a greeting usually is followed by a word of thanksgiving and/or prayer (1 Cor. 1:3–9). One may be tempted to skim quickly through the beginning portions of a New Testament letter, but the careful interpreter will note that ideas introduced at the beginning of a letter often will reappear as significant themes later. For example, in Galatians 1:1, Paul emphatically identifies himself as "Paul, an apostle—sent not from men nor by man, but by Jesus Christ and God the Father, who raised him from the dead." One does not need to read much farther in the letter to discover that the legitimacy of Paul's apostleship (and thus the apostolic gospel) has been challenged (Gal. 1:10–11). Scholars recognize that the introductions and conclusions of most letters in the New Testament provide hermeneutical "framing brackets," which enable one to see more clearly the work's emphases and purposes.[2]

Following the prayer and/or thanksgiving section is the body of the letter. This core sometimes can be divided broadly into theological (Eph. 2:1–3:21) and ethical (Eph. 4:1–6:20) instruction. Other letters are much more difficult to outline or subdivide (e.g., James, 1 John). Letters frequently conclude with a benediction or formalized greetings (Eph. 6:21–24). Of course, this structure is the *general* form of a letter, from which there are many possible deviations. For example, the author might not explicitly identify himself in the greeting (Hebrews), or he may skip the thanksgiving section (Galatians). When an author does deviate from the standard structure, the reader should ask whether there is a reason for such aberrations. In the case of Paul's letter to the Galatians, it appears that the Galatians' abandonment of the gospel made an apostolic thanksgiving unthinkable (Gal. 1:6). Figure 13 is a sample outline of a New Testament letter.

It should be noted that study Bibles and commentaries will provide more extensive outlines of the New Testament letters (see question 13, "What are some helpful books or tools for interpreting the Bible?"). Although it is always better to discover information for yourself, an outline of this sort can provide a helpful bird's-eye view of the author's argument.

Literary Forms Used Within Letters

When reading a commentary or study Bible notes, it is not uncommon to encounter the assertion that a New Testament letter is quoting an early hymn or Christian confession (e.g., Phil. 2:6–11; 2 Tim. 2:11–13). Scholars hypothesize such literary ancestry on the basis of contextual clues (introductory phrases), unusual vocabulary, stylized expressions, etc. In the end,

---

2. L. Ann Jervis, *The Purpose of Romans: A Comparative Letter Structure Investigation*, JSNTSup 55 (Sheffield: JSOT, 1991); P. Schubert, *Form and Function of Pauline Thanksgivings* (Berlin: Töpelmann, 1939); and P. T. O'Brien, *Introductory Thanksgivings in the Letters of Paul* (Leiden: Brill, 1977).

while the origins of particular portions of Scripture are matters of undeniable curiosity, a passage's origin has no effect on our interpretation. Concerning Philippians 2:6–11 (the famous "Christ hymn"), for example, whether Paul is quoting a hymn or composing the text as he writes, he clearly agrees with it. Knowing the origin of specific verses (e.g., Paul's Spirit-inspired thoughts, or an authoritative church tradition he is quoting) does not change the meaning of the text.

FIGURE 13: SAMPLE OUTLINE OF NEW TESTAMENT LETTER: PHILIPPIANS

I.   Introduction (1:1–11)

   A. Greeting (1:1–2)

   B. Thanksgiving for participation in the gospel and prayer for even greater fruitfulness (1:3–11)

II. A call to unity for the sake of the gospel (1:12–2:30)

   A. Paul as a model of one who lives wholly for the sake of the gospel (1:12–26)

   B. Exhortations for the church (1:27–2:18)

      1. A call to unity in living for the gospel (1:27–2:4)

      2. A call to imitate Jesus (2:5–11)

      3. A call to joyful obedience as God's children (2:12–18)

   C. Exhortations to imitation (2:19–30)

      1. Imitate Timothy (2:19–24)

      2. Imitate Epaphroditus (2:25–30)

III. A call to imitate Paul and not the false teachers (3:1–4:1)

   A. The value of repetition (3:1)

   B. Beware of the circumcision and follow Paul (3:2–11)

   C. Not a call for perfection (3:12–16)

   D. Follow those who set the right pattern (3:17–4:1)

IV. A final call to unity and joy (4:2–9)

V. Thanksgiving for the Philippians' commitment to the gospel expressed in their generosity to Paul (4:10–20)

VI. Final greetings and benediction (4:21–23)

Adapted directly from Thomas R. Schreiner, "Introduction to New Testament, Part II Notebook: Acts, Epistolary Literature, and the Revelation" (class notes, Southern Baptist Theological Seminary, n.d.), 35–37.

Another literary form that is foreign to some modern interpreters is the diatribe. A diatribe is a debate with a fictitious partner who represents a view one is trying to correct. Thus, when Paul writes, "But who are you, O man, to talk back to God?" (Rom. 9:20), the apostle does not have in mind a particular opponent but in diatribe style is correcting a fictitious adversary who gives voice to the theological or moral error he is seeking to correct (cf. James 2:18–20).

The Occasional Nature of Letters

The letters in the New Testament are not abstract treatises of systematic theology. They are often passionate appeals, written to specific persons in particular situations in the first century A.D. In a word, they are occasional—addressing specific occasions.

At one level, the occasional nature of New Testament letters makes them challenging to apply. The writer of 1 Corinthians, Paul, is long dead, along with all the believers in Corinth whom he addressed in the letter. Furthermore, while we find analogous situations in modern times, none of the matters addressed in the letter are *exactly* the same as those today. Yet, even in these occasional letters, we see intimations that the original authors and recipients saw a timeless authoritativeness in their composition. Paul's letters are called "Scripture" by Peter (2 Peter 3:16). Paul insists that his letters be copied and read by churches to which they were originally not addressed (Col. 4:16). Paul addresses 1 Corinthians not just to believers in Corinth, but also to "all those everywhere who call on the name of our Lord Jesus Christ" (1 Cor. 1:2). Furthermore, the authors of New Testament letters write authoritatively (1 Cor. 5:4–5), presenting their teaching, not as ad hoc suggestions, but as passing on "the faith that was once for all entrusted to the saints" (Jude 3). Even letters to individuals, such as Paul's letters to Philemon and Timothy, give intimations that the broader church is intended to hear and heed the personal letters' instructions (Philem. 2; 1 Tim. 6:21; 2 Tim. 4:22).[3]

The Issue of Pseudonymity

It is not uncommon for non-Christian or liberal Christian scholars to claim that certain letters in the New Testament were not written by the persons so named in their salutations.[4] Recently, however, even a few well-known evangelical scholars have suggested that some New Testament letters might be pseudonymous (that is, falsely written under another name).[5] These evangelical scholars have claimed that pseudonymity, if employed, must have been a transparent literary device—that is, known to both writer and readers so as to prevent culpable deceit.

---

3. In the Greek text, the plural form of "you" is employed in 1 Timothy 6:21 and 2 Timothy 4:22 (also see Titus 3:15).
4. See, e.g., W. G. Kümmel's discussion of the Pastoral Epistles in *Introduction to the New Testament*, trans. Howard Clark Kee, rev. ed. (Nashville: Abingdon, 1975), 370–87.
5. E.g., I. Howard Marshall, *New Testament Theology: Many Witnesses, One Gospel* (Downers Grove, IL: InterVarsity Press, 2004), 398.

D. A. Carson and Douglas Moo present a cogent case against pseudonymity in the New Testament epistles. An elaborate restatement of their argument is beyond the scope of this book, but a few brief points can be mentioned.[6]

1. Statements within the New Testament imply that pseudonymity was not acceptable (2 Thess. 2:2; 3:17).

2. If pseudonymity were accepted and *expected*, why do a number of New Testament letters fail to name an author (Hebrews, 1 John, 2 John)? That is, why did early Christians not feel compelled to add the name of an illustrious author to these formally "anonymous" works?

3. When recognized in the early church, pseudonymous writings were consistently condemned and rejected.[7] There is no record of the early church knowingly accepting any pseudonymous work.

REFLECTION QUESTIONS

1. The letters of the New Testament are both occasional and timeless. In what ways is this both a challenge and a benefit to the modern Christian interpreter?

2. When studying passages from New Testament letters, do you read them in light of the entire letter's historical setting? Why or why not?

3. When reading personal letters in the New Testament (e.g., 1, 2 Timothy, Titus, Philemon, 3 John), have you thought of these works as written first to individuals? Does it make a difference?

4. Does accepting pseudonymous authorship of biblical books undermine the Bible's authority and/or inspiration?

5. Of the evidence presented above, what is the best argument against accepting pseudonymous authorship of New Testament letters?

---

6. D. A. Carson and Douglas J. Moo, *An Introduction to the New Testament*, 2nd ed. (Grand Rapids: Zondervan, 2005), 337–50.

7. Tertullian, *De baptismo* 17; Eusebius, *Historia Ecclesiastica* 6.12.3; *Muratorian Canon* 64–65; and Cyril of Jerusalem, *Catechesis* 4.36 (examples cited by Carson and Moo, *Introduction to the New Testament*, 341–43).

FOR FURTHER STUDY

Carson, D. A., and Douglas J. Moo. *An Introduction to the New Testament*. 2nd ed. Grand Rapids: Zondervan, 2005. (See pp. 337–50.)

Klauck, Hans-Josef. *Ancient Letters and the New Testament: A Guide to Context and Exegesis*. Waco, TX: Baylor University Press, 2006.

Schreiner, Thomas R. *Interpreting the Pauline Epistles*. Grand Rapids: Baker, 1990.

How Do We Interpret Letters or Epistles? (General Guidelines)

In the previous question, we discussed a number of introductory matters for understanding New Testament letters (structure, literary forms used within letters, the occasional nature of letters, and arguments concerning authorship). This previous discussion will be assumed as we move on to present some general guidelines for understanding and interpreting New Testament letters.

Use Mirror Reading with Caution

In a college religion course, my professor illustrated the process of interpreting New Testament letters by handing out photocopies of country song lyrics.[1] He proceeded to show how through the sometimes obscure verses, we could reconstruct the situation behind the song. For example, from certain statements, we might hypothesize that the singer had previously enjoyed a fulfilling relationship and job, of which he now laments the loss. This interpretive process is called "mirror reading."[2] We regularly do similar analyses when we overhear someone talking on the phone and imagine the other side of the conversation. Similarly, when we read the letters in the New Testament, we do not have independent historical knowledge of the recipients' situations or the congregations' letters (if any) to the New Testament authors. Hearing only half the conversation (that of the inspired writer to the recipients), we inevitably must synthesize a number of comments to reconstruct the situation that occasioned the letter. But we must do this with caution.

---

1. This exercise was done by E. P. Sanders at Duke University.
2. J. M. G. Barclay, "Mirror-Reading a Polemical Letter: Galatians as a Test Case," *JSNT* 31 (1987): 73–93.

An example of this mirror reading process can be given from 1 John. We can draw these conclusions about the situation John addresses.

1. Some persons have split away from the community that John addresses (1 John 2:19).

2. The persons who departed hold to a Christological heresy (1 John 2:20–26; 4:1–6; cf. 2 John 7).

3. The persons who departed seem to have exhibited loveless and immoral behavior (1 John 2:3–6; 3:10–12).

4. The root issues of who truly belongs to God and the assurance of God's salvation seem to be troubling the community to which John writes (1 John 5:13).

There is no substitute for carefully reading a letter multiple times so as to reconstruct the historical situation behind its writing. As Pascal wisely noted, "People are generally better persuaded by the reasons which they have themselves discovered than by those which have come into the mind of others."[3] At the same time, many people will be aided by consulting the introductory comments on a New Testament letter in a study Bible. Furthermore, any cultural or historical information unavailable to the average reader (such as an explanation of "idol meat" in 1 Cor. 8–10) will be explained in a good study Bible. Also, before studying a letter in the New Testament, it might be advisable to read an overview of it in a New Testament survey text, such as *An Introduction to the New Testament*, by D. A. Carson and Douglas J. Moo.

To familiarize one's self with the setting of any book in the Bible takes time-consuming study. Yet, in interpreting individual sections of a letter, there is no greater aid than a good understanding of the whole work. This fact alone is a good argument for preaching and teaching through entire books of the Bible, section by section. Few of us have the time to do new mirror reading and background study every week, much less every day. It is much easier to build on an established foundation of knowledge.

Divide the Text into Discourse Units

As one studies through a letter, it is helpful to break the text into more manageable units. In doing so, we should follow the literary and structural

---

3. Pascal, *Pensées*, fragment 10, in *Great Books of the Western World: Pascal*, ed. Mortimer J. Adler, 2nd ed. (Chicago: Encyclopedia Britannica, 1990), 30:173. Within the volume, *Pensées* was translated by W. F. Trotter.

clues the author has given us. Does he change topics? Does he shift from third to second person? Do conjunctions or exclamations signal the movement to a new subject?

The translation and editorial committees of almost every modern Bible version will have asked themselves these questions (and many others) as they divided the text into paragraphs and larger discourse units. Most modern Bibles insert helpful subheadings for unified sections of thought.

When doing detailed study on a particular text, it is advisable to compare several modern translations and note where they differ in segmenting the text. Also, any good commentary will discuss the organization of the text (see question 13, "What are some helpful books or tools for interpreting the Bible?"). Where translations and commentaries disagree, the interpreter will have to assess the data and make his or her own decisions.

Understand the Organization Within a Literary Unit

Once a section of unified thought (a discourse unit) has been chosen, the interpreter must pay careful attention to the development of the writer's argument within the smaller unit. Is the author appealing to his readers' experiences, to the Old Testament, or to his own authority? What is the relationship between the phrases and sentences—causal ("because"), concessive ("although"), instrumental ("by means of"), etc.? There are various ways for getting a handle on these tighter literary connections, but an elementary suggestion is: write it down! Visually representing the logical flow of the text on paper helps most people in mental and spiritual digestion. In *Interpreting the Pauline Epistles*, Tom Schreiner offers two suggested methods of such visual analysis.[4] The main thing, however, is to try *something*, even if it is simply indenting and labeling subordinate sections of the text.

Determine the Meaning of Individual Words

Important theological words worthy of focused study are found throughout the Bible. Yet, in the dense, logical argument of many New Testament epistles, there is an especially high frequency of such words. While there are interpretive dangers to superficial word studies, never before have better word-study tools existed for the curious and diligent interpreter. For tools and caveats related to word studies, see question 13 ("What are some helpful books or tools for interpreting the Bible?"). At the most basic level, if the interpreter is having difficulty honing in on the exact sense of a word or phrase, several modern English translations can be compared (see question 7, "Which is the best English Bible translation?").

---

4. Thomas R. Schreiner, *Interpreting the Pauline Epistles* (Grand Rapids: Baker, 1990), 77–126.

Apply the Message Today

We do not study the letters of the New Testament for the ultimate purpose of arriving at the most convincing and accurate historical reconstruction. Rather, we do such historical and exegetical study to understand the inspired author's original message so that we might faithfully apply that message in analogous situations today.

It is sometimes challenging to determine whether instructions in a letter are culturally bound, case-specific, apply directly without change, or embody an underlying principle that must be applied differently in a new setting. In question 19 ("Do all the commands of the Bible apply today?"), many guidelines are given to help determine in what way the instructions of Scripture are to be applied today. A brief example, however, can be given from 1 Corinthians 8–10. In these chapters, Paul instructs the Corinthians about eating idol meat. Paul says that if a Christian buys meat in the marketplace that has been offered to idols or eats such meat at a nonbeliever's home, that action is not sin. Buying or eating meat that someone else has sacrificed to an idol is not, in and of itself, participating in idolatry. However, if there are new believers in the congregation who, because of weak consciences, think of eating such meat as worshipping an idol, Christians with stronger consciences should refrain from eating idol meat. If a strong Christian were to eat the meat, a weaker brother might be inclined to partake as well and sin against his conscience. Consideration for the building up of others takes priority over personal freedom.

Few persons reading this book are facing pressing ministry problems with idol meat. Timeless principles from 1 Corinthians 8–10, however, apply to many issues today. For example, such principles might include the following.[5]

1. Ethical reflection must be rooted in theological truth. (Paul appeals to biblical monotheism to show that idols are nothing in and of themselves [1 Cor. 8:4–6.])

2. From a biblical perspective, there are three moral categories—right, wrong, and inconsequentials (or *adiaphora*).

3. Even if a behavior is not objectively morally wrong, if a person thinks it is wrong and then commits that behavior, he sins.

4. A Christian should show sacrificial love in protecting other Christians from temptation and sin—even when those other Christians are somehow "weak" or "immature" in their judgment.

---

5. These principles are drawn directly from my article, "Eating Idol Meat in Corinth: Enduring Principles from Paul's Instructions," *SBJT* 6, no. 3 (2002): 58–74. This article is available online under the "Resources" link at www.sbts.edu.

5. A Christian's behavior should not be governed simply by the ultimate categories of "right" and "wrong." In the realm of *adiaphora*, a Christian's behavior must be shaped by a dual concern—(a) for other Christians' spiritual health and (b) for the conversion of nonbelievers.

REFLECTION QUESTIONS

1. Do you or your church currently study, teach, and preach through entire books of the Bible? If not, what would be the benefit of switching to this method?

2. When studying the Bible, have you ever engaged in a word study? What resources did you use? What did you learn?

3. When you prepare Bible studies or sermons, how do you decide what section of text to deal with (that is, where to start the study and where to end)?

4. In seeking to understand the structure of an epistolary passage, have you ever tried a visual method (that is, writing it out with indentations or diagramming)?

5. Challenge: Choose a favorite passage from the New Testament letters and study it afresh this next week in light of the suggested methods above.

FOR FURTHER STUDY

Carson, D. A., and Douglas J. Moo. *An Introduction to the New Testament.* 2nd ed. Grand Rapids: Zondervan, 2005. (See chap. 8, "New Testament Letters," 31–53.)

Schreiner, Thomas R. *Interpreting the Pauline Epistles.* Grand Rapids: Baker, 1990.

PART 4

Issues in Recent Discussion

What Does the Bible Tell Us About the Future?

People who have never shown an interest in the Bible for any other reason sometimes are curious about eschatology (that is, what the Bible affirms about the end of the world and eternity). Whether out of curiosity about their own fate or a desire to make sense of complex and unpredictable times, people will often listen to a teacher who claims to elucidate the Bible's predictions of the future. Unfortunately, false teachers also capitalize on this widespread curiosity by spreading odd and unbiblical teaching, just as Jesus said they would (Mark 13:21–23).

What the Bible Clearly Teaches About the Future

The Bible does make numerous clear affirmations about the future, and it is best to start with these truths rather than more speculative doctrines. Below is a list of scriptural teachings about the future that Bible-believing Christians can agree on.

1. *Jesus will come again in visible, bodily form to consummate his eternal kingdom.* In Acts 1:11, to the disciples who had just seen Jesus ascend, two angels declare, "Men of Galilee . . . why do you stand here looking into the sky? This same Jesus, who has been taken from you into heaven, will come back in the same way you have seen him go into heaven."[1] Many other New Testament passages affirm the second

---

1. Note that as Jesus ascended, a cloud hid him from their sight (Acts 1:9). In my opinion, it is best to understand heaven as a coexistent dimension of reality, the entrance to which is best symbolized by a movement upward. Thus, as the Russian cosmonaut Yuri Gagarin supposedly noted, he did not see God in outer space. But, the biblical record (1 Kings 8:22–23, 27; 2 Kings 2:11; 2 Chron. 7:1; Isa. 6:1; 2 Cor. 12:2; 1 Tim. 2:8), as well as universal human temperament, testify that God's greatness and power draw us to look and

coming of Jesus (e.g., Matt. 24:27–44; 1 Thess. 4:13–18; 1 John 3:2). For this promised return, Christians are repeatedly told to be ready or to watch (e.g., Matt. 24:42; 25:13; Mark 13:34–37; Luke 12:37; 1 Thess. 5:1–11; Rev. 16:15). Watching does not mean staring at the sky or making elaborate charts that speculate as to the timing of Jesus' coming. In fact, Jesus said, "No one knows about that day or hour, not even the angels in heaven, nor the Son, but only the Father" (Mark 13:32). As is clear from Jesus' teaching on his return, watching entails faithful stewardship of the time, abilities, and resources the Lord has entrusted to his people (Matt. 24:45–25:46). Christians are to serve the Lord faithfully, so that they will not be ashamed before him at his return (1 John 2:28–3:3). The lazy or careless Christian will find his inferior work shown for what it really is.

2. *The return of Jesus will reveal true believers.* There will be many false professors, persons who claim to be Christians but to whom the Lord will ultimately say, "I never knew you. Away from me, you evildoers!" (Matt. 7:23; see also Matt. 13:24–30). The changed hearts of those who truly know the Lord will be made clear by the revelation of their Spirit-directed words and deeds (Matt. 7:15–20; 12:36–37; James 2:14–26; 1 John 2:3–6).

3. *Between the time of Jesus' first and second coming, there will be a period of political, spiritual, and environmental turmoil.* In Jesus' famous "eschatological discourse" (Matt. 24:4–44; Mark 13:5–37; Luke 21:8–36), he describes the events between his first and second coming. Scholars debate which of these signs were fulfilled in the lifetime of his apostles and which are outstanding, but, excluding the destruction of Jerusalem (which happened in A.D. 70), it seems best to understand the predicted signs as characterizing the entire interadvent period (that is, descriptive of the entire time between Jesus' first and second coming).[2] Those signs include political instability, religious deceivers, wars, famines, earthquakes, and persecution of Jesus' followers. A glance at a history book or the daily newspaper demonstrates that Jesus accurately predicted the future.

When will this turmoil increase, and will we be able to discern this increase as a sign of Jesus' imminent return? Scholars disagree on these issues, but the Bible does clearly teach that a major opponent of Christ, the Antichrist, or "Man of Lawlessness," will arise

---

reach upward—not because God is physically in outer space but because we have no other way of thinking about an exalted heavenly dimension that is far beyond our ability to comprehend.

2. See Craig Blomberg's exposition of this passage in *Matthew*, NAC 22 (Nashville: Broadman, 1992), 351–80.

prior to Jesus' second coming (1 John 2:18; 4:3; 2 Thess. 2:3). How long the deceit of the Antichrist will be allowed and to what degree Christians will be able to recognize him prior to his defeat by Christ is not clear. Christians of previous centuries have labeled various evil leaders in their days as the Antichrist, but the passage of time has repeatedly proven them wrong. The apostle John noted that already in his day "many antichrists have arisen" (1 John 2:18, my translation), even though a final arch-opponent of Christ was still expected (1 John 2:18–22; 1 John 4:3). Similarly, Paul says that the secret power of lawlessness is already at work in the world, even though the final "man of lawlessness" is still anticipated (2 Thess. 2:3–7). A quick glance at previous attempts to pinpoint the Antichrist or the timing of Christ's return should caution us against such conjecture.

4. *One day, all persons will be resurrected and judged and will enter into an eternal, unchangeable state of glory or damnation.* Some of the details as to what happens between death and judgment are debated, but the Scriptures seem to teach the following sequence: When someone dies, if that person has trusted in Christ for the forgiveness of his sins, his spirit/soul goes to be with the Lord (2 Cor. 5:6–9; Phil. 1:21–24). If a person has not received God's forgiveness in Christ, he goes immediately to a place of torment (Luke 16:19–31). When Christ returns, the bodies of all persons who have died will be resurrected/reconstituted (Dan. 12:2; John 5:28–29; 1 Thess. 4:16). All persons (those formerly deceased and those still living at the time of Christ's return) will stand before the eternal Judge, going either to eternal bliss in his presence or eternal torment in his absence (Matt. 16:27; 25:31–33; John 5:22, 27; Acts 10:42; 2 Cor. 5:10; Rev. 20:1–15). Those justified by Jesus Christ (declared righteous on the basis of Jesus' life and death) will be given glorified bodies and enter into eternal bliss in God's presence (1 John 2:2; Rev. 7:14). Those who have been justified by faith will have demonstrated the reality of the indwelling Spirit through their behavior—as will be made clear in the final judgment (Matt. 25:35–40). The Scriptures also speak of degrees of reward for the glorified and gradations of punishment for the damned (Matt. 11:21–24; Luke 12:47–48; 19:11–27; 1 Cor. 3:14–15).

Eschatological Issues About Which Bible-Believing Christians Disagree

One of the greatest needs in the discussion of eschatology is humility.[3] We should seek to keep a proper perspective on such matters—not elevating a

---

3. Regarding eschatological speculation, T. C. Hammond writes, "Much harm has been done by well-meaning but incautious zealots who have allowed their enthusiasm to run riot in

minor issue to a major one, or making a litmus test out of debatable doctrine. This does not mean that we cannot have convictions on debatable matters, but we must recognize our finitude and the lack of explicit clarity in the Bible on some eschatological issues. Below is a brief list of end-times matters on which Christians legitimately disagree.

1. *The Rapture.* In 1 Thessalonians 4:16–17, Paul says that believers who are alive at the time of Jesus' return, along with resurrected saints, will be caught up in the air to meet the Lord. Bible-believing Christians agree on that much. But then what happens? Do the Christians immediately descend with their Lord to rule and reign (the right view, in my opinion)? Or are Christians secretly raptured out of the world, followed by a period of intense tribulation (a view first espoused by J. N. Darby in the 1830s and that has become quite popular among some conservative Christians)? These are only some of the disagreements that sincere, Jesus-loving, Bible-believing Christians have with regard to the rapture.

2. *The Book of Revelation.* Does the book of Revelation give us a blueprint of coming world turmoil (the futurist position)? Or have some of the events in Revelation already taken place throughout church history, with some still to come (the historicist or historical approach)? Or does Revelation report events that were current at the time of writing but are now completed (the preterist view)? Or does Revelation speak in a timeless, symbolic way of the life of the church between the comings of Christ (the symbolic or idealist view)? Or is some combination of these approaches the correct way to view Revelation?

3. *The Millennium.* When Christ returns, will he set up a thousand–year (millennium) kingdom that fulfills the literal promises of land and monarchy given to the nation of Israel (the premillennial view)? Or will Christ judge the world and immediately usher in the new heaven and new earth without an intervening millennial reign (the amillennial position, in which the thousand-year reign in Revelation 20 is often taken as symbolic of the interadvent church age)? Or is Christ providentially working through history to bring about a millennial golden age, to be followed by his glorious return (the once popular postmillennial position, which now has few adherents)?

---

wild and dogmatic assertions upon points where dogmatism is impossible. Still more harm has been done by those who have seized upon certain isolated texts and woven around them doctrines which are inconsistent with the rest of Scripture" (*In Understanding Be Men: An Introductory Handbook of Christian Doctrine*, rev. and ed. David F. Wright, 6th ed. [Leicester: Inter-Varsity Press, 1968], 179).

4. *The Nation of Israel.* Has the church truly become the new Israel, such that God makes no ongoing differentiation between ethnic Jews and Gentiles? Or does God continue to save a remnant of Jews (and thus they are in some sense distinct), with such saved Jews incorporated into the one people of God, the true Israel, the inheritors of the promises to David and Abraham (the biblical view, I believe)? Or are God's dealings with the church only a parenthesis in the history of his saving work? Is God going to return to Israel in the future and fulfill in a literal way the promises given to the patriarchs (the dispensational view popularized by books such as the *Left Behind* series)?

REFLECTION QUESTIONS

1. Did you grow up with any definite beliefs or expectations about the end of the world and Christ's return? Where did you acquire these beliefs?

2. In your opinion, what eschatological doctrines are absolutely essential for all Christians to believe? Why do you think this?

3. Have you ever run across any odd teachings about the end times? What do the Scriptures say with regard to these issues?

4. Of the approaches mentioned above, what is the correct way to view Revelation? Can you defend your position from the Bible?

5. Of the approaches mentioned above, what is the correct way to view ethnic Jews in relation to God's ongoing saving purposes?

FOR FURTHER STUDY

Erickson, Millard J. *Christian Theology.* 2nd ed. Grand Rapids: Baker, 1998. (See pp. 1155–1248.)
Grudem, Wayne. *Systematic Theology: An Introduction to Biblical Doctrine.* Grand Rapids: Zondervan; Leicester: Inter-Varsity Press, 1994. (See pp. 1091–1167.)
Hoekema, Anthony A. *The Bible and the Future.* Grand Rapids: Eerdmans, 1994.
Metzger, Bruce M. *Breaking the Code: Understanding the Book of Revelation.* Nashville: Abingdon, 1993.

What Is Biblical Criticism?

When people hear the word *criticism,* most think of a disparaging remark. In reality, biblical criticism or various critical approaches to the Bible are not about attacking the Bible but rather relate to the careful, academic study of it. Unfortunately, due to the antisupernatural presuppositions of many prominent biblical scholars in the last 250 years, biblical criticism has gotten a bad name. The term is often associated with a disingenuous objectivity that in reality is anti-Christian in its assumptions and conclusions. There are diverse forms of biblical criticism, some of them quite ancient (e.g., text and source criticism) and others more recent. We will survey some of the most significant forms of biblical criticism under the headings below.

Text Criticism

Text criticism is the careful study of ancient texts in an effort to establish what the original manuscripts of the Bible said. We have historical records of extensive text criticism from at least as far back as Origen (A.D. 185–254), but the modern flowering of the discipline followed the introduction of the printing press in Europe (1454) and the revival of scholars' knowledge of Greek and Hebrew at the time of the Reformation. Text criticism has flourished especially in the last two hundred years, with the many discoveries of ancient manuscripts and a growing scholarly consensus on methods. See question 5 ("Were the ancient manuscripts of the Bible transmitted accurately?") for more information on the findings of text criticism.

Historical Criticism

Historical criticism is the careful historical study of the documents in the Bible and related writings, events, and persons. The historical-critical method seeks to establish what actually happened in history and what a text meant to the original author and reader(s).[1] In a related vein, biblical scholars often speak of doing historical-grammatical exegesis. That is, beginning with a proper understanding of what the text says in the original language (grammatical), scholars investigate the Bible's claims about what happened (historical). Historical-grammatical exegesis can be done with Christian presuppositions (i.e., that what the Bible says is true) or with skeptical and anti-Christian prejudices. Because of abuse by liberal scholars, some conservative Christians decry the use of historical criticism (and most of the other criticism below as well). It must be remembered, however, that it is the presuppositions that accompany the method that result in anti-Christian conclusions. Surely, the call to study carefully the grammar and history of the biblical text cannot, in and of itself, be bad. However, some recent critics in the theological interpretation of Scripture movement have argued that, by making the modern application of the text secondary, the historical-critical method implicitly truncates the very nature of Scripture as God's Word to God's people (see question 39, "What is the 'theological interpretation of Scripture'?").

Form Criticism

Form criticism is the study of how various portions of the text (e.g., individual stories, laws, proverbs, poems) circulated in oral form before being written down. Much form-critical writing is devoted to speculation as to the historical settings in which the oral units originally circulated. For example, Hermann Gunkel (1862–1932) proposed extensive and often unfounded cultic backgrounds for most of the Psalms.[2] Liberal New Testament form critics have hypothesized a great deal about how the stories of Jesus were embellished or even created in periods of oral circulation.[3] Conservative form critics recognize the value of isolating and classifying formerly oral units, but they do not take a skeptical approach to the material's historicity.[4]

Source Criticism

Source criticism seeks to establish the literary sources the biblical author/editor drew upon. For example, Julius Wellhausen (1844–1918), a liberal Old Testament scholar, argued that the Pentateuch was composed of

---

1. Arthur G. Patzia and Anthony J. Petrotta, "Historical Criticism," in *Pocket Dictionary of Biblical Studies* (Downers Grove, IL: InterVarsity Press, 2002), 58.
2. Hermann Gunkel, *The Psalms: A Form-Critical Introduction*, trans. Thomas M. Horner (Philadelphia: Fortress, 1967).
3. E.g., Rudolf Bultmann, *The History of the Synoptic Tradition*, trans. John Marsh (New York: Harper & Row, 1963).
4. E.g., Vincent Taylor, *The Formation of the Gospel Tradition*, 2nd ed. (London: Macmillan, 1935).

four literary strands: the Yahwist or Jehovist (J), Elohistic (E), Priestly (P), and Deuteronomistic (D) sources.[5] The evidence for this JEPD construction is actually quite tenuous. The data support traditional Mosaic authorship of the Pentateuch, while obviously allowing for some gathering and editing of the Mosaic material.[6]

In the New Testament, source criticism is especially applied to Matthew, Mark, and Luke (the Synoptic Gospels) because of their close similarity in wording and order. The majority of New Testament scholars believe that Luke and Matthew used two main sources in their composition—the written gospel of Mark and "Q." "Q" is an abbreviation for the German word *Quelle* (source) and stands for a collection of written and oral sources that Matthew and Luke had in common. Indeed, Luke explicitly indicates that he drew upon multiple sources in the composition of his Gospel (Luke 1:1–4). As many early church fathers comment on the literary sources behind the Gospels (i.e., which Gospel author(s) were dependent on others), source criticism is truly an ancient discipline.[7]

Redaction Criticism

Redaction criticism is the study of the role of the redactor (editor) in the final composition of the biblical text. In other words, while many biblical authors had both firsthand knowledge of events (e.g., the apostle John) and oral and written sources from which to draw (e.g., Luke 1:1–4), the redactor ultimately showed his theological interests and purposes through selecting, omitting, editing, and summarizing the material for his text. (Of course, Christians assume the Holy Spirit was working through the redactors in this process.) Roughly between 1950 and 1990, redaction criticism was an especially popular method for studying the Synoptic Gospels (Matthew, Mark, Luke). The leading evangelical redaction critic is Robert H. Stein.[8]

Tradition Criticism

Tradition criticism seeks to establish the history of a text before it reached its final written form. Thus, tradition criticism encompasses both the oral

---

5. The basics of the theory predated Wellhausen (especially in the work of K. H. Graf), but it "was given its classic expression" in Wellhausen's writings (R. K. Harrison, *Introduction to the Old Testament* [Grand Rapids: Eerdmans, 1969; reprint, Peabody, MA: Prince (Hendrickson), 1999], 21). The theory is known as the documentary hypothesis or the Graf-Wellhausen hypothesis.

6. See Gleason L. Archer, *A Survey of Old Testament Introduction,* rev ed. (Chicago: Moody, 1994), 113–26.

7. E.g., Augustine, *The Harmony of the Gospels* 1.1–2 (*NPNF1* 6:77–78).

8. Robert H. Stein, *Gospels and Tradition: Studies on Redaction Criticism of the Synoptic Gospels* (Grand Rapids: Baker, 1991).

and literary background of a text. It includes form, source, and redaction criticism (see above).

Literary Criticism

Beginning in the 1980s, various kinds of literary criticism became increasingly popular with biblical scholars. As most previous critical methods had sought to explain the reconstructed physical or literary history behind the text, here was an approach that now allowed for the text to be studied as a unity while sidestepping debated questions of historicity or authorship. Literary criticism seemed to promise a new middle way between polarized liberal and conservative biblical scholars.

At the most fundament level, a literary approach to the Bible recognizes the various literary genres within the canon and studies those works as unified pieces of literature. Evangelicals generally have used literary criticism to call attention to authorial intent and the message of the text. However, there are many different permutations of a literary approach to the Bible. Influenced by secular literary trends, a reader-response approach to the Bible celebrates the reader's creation of meaning with little or no concern for the authorial intent. Another approach, technical literary analysis, was especially popular among biblical scholars during the heyday of literary criticism (1985–1995). Many dissertations, articles, and monographs claimed to elucidate the biblical text through the use of countless obscure terms such as *implied reader, ideal reader, implied author, implicit commentary,* etc. The near disappearance of such technically laden publications testifies that a more commonsense approach to literary interpretation is the type that will endure. Narrative criticism, a subset of literary criticism, employs a literary approach to study the narratives (stories) in Scripture.

Rhetorical Criticism

When people speak of rhetorical criticism of the Bible, they generally mean one of two things. In reference to the New Testament, they are often speaking of the labeling of recognized Greco-Roman categories of speech in the New Testament. From 1970 to 1990, many New Testament scholars sought to offer new insights on the structure and purpose of New Testament texts through rhetorical analysis. Most scholars are now agreed that the overly technical labeling of New Testament texts with Latin and Greek rhetorical categories will not stand up to broader scholarly scrutiny.

"Rhetorical criticism" also can refer to the detection of beautiful and effective patterns of speech in the text. This is sometimes called "new rhetoric" to distinguish it from the method of illegitimately imposing Greco-Roman categories on the New Testament.[9]

---

9. G. W. Hansen, "Rhetorical Criticism," in *DPL*, 824–25.

REFLECTION QUESTIONS

1. Before reading the material above, had you heard of any of these forms of biblical criticism? Which ones?

2. How does recognizing literary sources for biblical books affect our understanding of the authors' inspiration by the Holy Spirit?

3. Have you ever read an article or book in which a liberal scholar used one of the above methods with anti-Christian presuppositions and/or conclusions?

4. In your opinion, is it advisable for a Christian scholar to employ any of the above methods in the study of the Scripture? If not, what alternative approaches would you recommend?

5. Which of the above methods seems to hold the most promise for understanding the author's meaning in a text?

FOR FURTHER STUDY

Carson, D. A., and Douglas J. Moo. *An Introduction to the New Testament.* 2nd ed. Grand Rapids: Zondervan, 2005. (See chap. 1, "Thinking About the Study of the New Testament," 23–76.)

Firth, David G., and Jamie A. Grant. *Words and the Word: Explorations in Biblical Interpretation and Literary Theory.* Downers Grove, IL: InterVarsity Press, 2009.

Patzia, Arthur G., and Anthony J. Petrotta. *Pocket Dictionary of Biblical Studies.* Downers Grove, IL: InterVarsity Press, 2002.

Vanhoozer, Kevin J., ed. *Dictionary for Theological Interpretation of the Bible.* Grand Rapids: Baker; London: SPCK, 2005.

What Is "Speech Act Theory"?

Evangelical scholarly publications of the last two decades frequently include some discussion of speech act theory.[1] Yet, for students uninitiated into this linguistic and philosophical approach, it is difficult to find a succinct, understandable introduction to the theory. A critical evaluation is more difficult to locate. Why, in fact, have evangelicals shown special interest in speech act theory, and can the theory really deliver what its practitioners promise?

Brief Explanation of Speech Act Theory

When my wife says, "It smells in the kitchen," she is not simply making a factual declaration. Rather, we can paraphrase her words: "I request that you take out the garbage." Her words are in actuality an action (requesting) that sets in motion another action (her husband taking out the garbage). In fact, most, if not all, utterances can be understood in relation to the actions they express or set in motion. In a nutshell, this is speech act theory—that is, the recognition that language at its root is action based. Or, as D. A. Carson and Doug Moo aptly summarize, "Words in contexts do not simply *mean* something, they may *do* something. . . . Words *do* things as well as *teach* things."[2]

History of Speech Act Theory

Speech act theory as a distinct linguistic, philosophical movement traces its origins to John L. Austin's lectures at Harvard University in 1955.[3] The

---

1. E.g., Kevin J. Vanhoozer, "The Semantics of Biblical Literature," in *Hermeneutics, Authority, and Canon*, ed. D. A. Carson and John Woodbridge (Grand Rapids: Zondervan, 1986), 49–104; Millard J. Erickson, *Christian Theology*, 2nd ed. (Grand Rapids: Baker, 1998), 153–57, 247–48; and D. A. Carson and Douglas J. Moo, *An Introduction to the New Testament*, 2nd ed. (Grand Rapids: Zondervan, 2005), 73.
2. Carson and Moo, *Introduction to the New Testament*, 73.
3. The William James endowed lecture series. Austin, at the time, was a professor at Oxford University. Admittedly, the roots of speech act theory could be traced back further to the linguistic work of Wittgenstein or the theology of Karl Barth.

subsequent posthumous publication of the lectures (*How to Do Things with Words*, 1962),[4] along with John R. Searle's supporting studies, established the vocabulary and ground rules on which later speech act theorists continue to build.[5] Speech act theory has been widely hailed among literary critics and linguistic philosophers as an advance in understanding the way language works.[6]

The Vocabulary of Speech Act Theory

While more recent writers have greatly expanded the technical vocabulary of speech act theory, in this brief survey we will stay with three basic distinctions.

1. *Locutionary act:* the meaning of the utterance with respect to the normal sense of vocabulary and grammar.

2. *Illocutionary act:* the statement, with respect to the action performed in its utterance (e.g., request, command, promise, warning, blessing, etc.).

3. *Perlocutionary act:* an action created or brought about as a result of the utterance.[7]

An example from Scripture can illustrate this vocabulary. In Matthew 13:45–46, we read:

Again, the kingdom of heaven is like a merchant looking for fine pearls. When he found one of great value, he went away and sold everything he had and bought it.

In this short passage, the "locutionary act" is the statement of Jesus with reference to the things described. Or more precisely, the locutionary dimension of this passage is limited to the Greek words written by Matthew with respect to their normal descriptive sense. The illocutionary dimension of this

4. J. L. Austin, *How to Do Things with Words*, 2nd ed. (Oxford: Oxford University Press, 1975).
5. John R. Searle, *Speech-Acts: An Essay in the Philosophy of Language* (Cambridge, MA: Harvard University Press, 1969); and idem, *Expression and Meaning: Studies in Theory of Speech Acts* (Cambridge: Cambridge University Press, 1979).
6. W. Randolph Tate, "Speech Act Theory," in *Interpreting the Bible: A Handbook of Terms and Methods* (Peabody, MA: Hendrickson, 2006), 349–50.
7. See Carson and Moo's similar summary in *Introduction to the New Testament*, 73. For a more extensive survey of speech act vocabulary, see Richard S. Briggs, *Words in Action: Speech Act Theory and Biblical Interpretation: Toward a Hermeneutic of Self-Involvement* (Edinburgh: T & T Clark, 2001).

passage can be paraphrased, "I, Matthew, as a follower of Jesus, urge and request you to accept the Lord's teaching (here faithfully translated and transmitted). I charge you—value his kingdom above all else!"[8] The perlocutionary force of the passage is seen when readers (both ancient and modern) respond to this text by turning away from idolatrous valuations, placing ultimate value on God's kingdom.

Evangelicals and Speech Act Theory

Evangelical scholars recently have demonstrated a fascination with speech act theory. This interest seems to be driven by several concerns. First, speech act theory offers a new philosophical basis for grounding a text's meaning in the intention of the author. Simply put, if actions are traceable to the intentions of their respective agents, must not "word-actions" likewise be so intrinsically connected with their authors? Jeannine K. Brown notes:

> Speech-act theory reaffirms the interpersonal nature of textual communication. Autonomous texts cut off from their authors do not warn, promise, or covenant. People warn, people promise, people covenant. This is the case even if we do not know who wrote a text. The author remains, in theory, connected to the text's communicative aims.[9]

Frankly, from my experience, most students who are exposed to speech act theory do not see the necessity of going down this philosophical road to defend authorial intent. In the murky depths of linguistic philosophy, however, evangelical proponents of speech act theory are performing a useful apologetic function—arguing for the objective grounding of biblical interpretation in a broader academy committed to relativism and subjectivity.[10]

---

8. Vern Poythress warns, "Speech-act theory, if used simplistically, tends to make people think that each sentence-level act makes a single, simple speech commitment, defined as its 'illocutionary force': it either asserts, promises, commands, wishes, or the like. But a sentence in the Bible may often have, in addition to one more obvious and direct commitment, multiple, interlocking purposes, related in multiple ways to its literary context and its addressees. Speech-act theory, seen by some of its advocates as a way for enhancing our appreciation of multiple kinds of speech in the Bible, may at the same time artificially flatten and restrict the implications of any one kind of speech. The challenges increase when we move from considering sentences to considering the canon as a whole. The canon constitutes an exceedingly rich and complex product. It is easy to oversimplify if we try to fit it into a theory initially developed to deal with simple sentence-length utterances" (Vern Sheridan Poythress, "Canon and Speech Act: Limitations in Speech-Act Theory, with Implications for a Putative Theory of Canonical Speech Acts," *WTJ* 70 [2008]: 344–45).
9. Jeannine K. Brown, *Scripture as Communication: Introducing Biblical Hermeneutics* (Grand Rapids: Baker, 2007), 35.
10. Scott A. Blue, "Meaning, Intention, and Application: Speech Act Theory in the Hermeneutics of Francis Watson and Kevin J. Vanhoozer," *TrinJ* 23, no. 2 (2002): 161–84.

A second motivation for evangelical interest in speech act theory is the intersection of the theory with foundational Christian truths and the nature of Scripture. Theologians have long recognized the action-based dimension of God's words ("And God said, 'Let there be light,' and there was light" [Gen. 1:3]).[11] The words of Scripture are not just propositions; they are "words on a mission," as Vanhoozer fittingly says.[12] In this sense, speech act theory simply recognizes the truth of God's testimony as to the nature of his words in passages such as this:

> As the rain and the snow come down from heaven, and do not return to it without watering the earth and making it bud and flourish, so that it yields seed for the sower and bread for the eater, so is my word that goes out from my mouth: It will not return to me empty, but will accomplish what I desire and achieve the purpose for which I sent it. (Isa. 55:10–11)

Finally, evangelicals are interested (at least theoretically) in obeying the Bible as the Word of God. Consequently, speech act theory offers fertile ground for explaining possible relations between divine intentionality, the human author's intent, modern implications, and believing obedience to those implications. Evangelicals are still debating the exact relation of these practical hermeneutical dimensions and their purported grounding in speech act theory. For example, is the *modern* perlocutionary dimension of a passage (that is, obedience of the Christian to the text) included within the conscious intention of the human author? If not, how is it validly rooted in authorial intent?

Caveats and Comparisons

The current state of speech act theory can be compared with the use of rhetorical criticism in biblical interpretation. Following James Muilenburg's seminal work on rhetorical criticism in his 1968 presidential address to the Society of Biblical Literature, there was a flowering of rhetorical studies, especially among New Testament scholars. Countless commentaries and articles, not to mention doctoral dissertations, promised new insights into the text

---

11. McKenzie writes, "The word of Yahweh may be called sacramental in the sense that it effects what it signifies. When Yahweh posits the word-thing, nothing can prevent its emergence" (John L. McKenzie, "The Word of God in the Old Testament," *TS* 21 [1960]: 196).

12. Kevin J. Vanhoozer, *First Theology: God, Scripture and Hermeneutics* (Leicester: Apollos; Downers Grove, IL: InterVarsity Press, 2002), 179. Vanhoozer sees all speech acts in Scripture as infallible because of the divine origin of the Bible ("The Semantics of Biblical Literature," 95). Gregg R. Allison argues that a speech act theory approach to divine communication grounds both Scripture's infallibility and inerrancy ("Speech Act Theory and Its Implications for the Doctrine of the Inerrancy/Infallibility of Scripture," *Philosophia Christi* 18 [1995]: 1–23).

through labeling and discussing the rhetorical categories supposedly used by the biblical authors (e.g., *exordium, narratio, propositio, probatio, exhortatio,* etc.).[13]

As the fortieth anniversary of Muilenburg's address has come and gone, I think we can say that rhetorical criticism has come up short for several reasons. First, scholars often do not agree on the rhetorical labeling of the text. Indeed, if so-called experts in the field cannot agree on basic labels and divisions of the text, what is the likelihood that the average reader will be convinced or helped by these categories?

Second, scholars not engaged in rhetorical criticism are in general agreement that the rhetorical approach has produced little, if any, new insights into the text.[14] That is not to say that rhetorical critics have not offered helpful observations on the text but rather that their rhetorical-critical method is not indispensable.

Third, where insights have come through rhetorical critics' careful attention to the biblical author's argumentation, those insights often have been obscured by the overly technical vocabulary of rhetorical criticism. The same observations could have been made without the use of a dozen Latin words ending in *-tio.* Indeed, at its best, rhetorical criticism draws our attention to the persuasive and beautiful features of the authors' writing without parading itself as a faddish method.

Biblical scholars who use speech act theory can learn an important lesson from the history of rhetorical criticism. At its best, speech act theory will remind the interpreter of an often ignored dimension to language, namely, its inherent action component. When it is hermeneutically significant to note the action-related dimensions of speech, interpreters should do so, but with as little recourse to technical vocabulary as possible. Intelligibility and relevance will determine whether speech act theory is a passing fad or of lasting use in the study of Scripture. In one hundred years, speech act theory will likely only be an entry in dictionaries of hermeneutics. But, if speech act theorists are successful in awakening a generation of biblical interpreters to the action-dimension of language, then the movement will have succeeded, even if most of its technical vocabulary dies a well-deserved death.

Similarly, speech act theorists can learn from the story of verbal aspect theory. Some variation of verbal aspect theory is arguably the best way to understand the Greek verbal system. Very succinctly, verbal aspect theory says that the writer's subjective description of an action (viewed as a whole, in process, or completed with results) is the primary dimension of a Greek

---

13. For a brief overview of rhetorical criticism, see G. W. Hansen, "Rhetorical Criticism," in *DPL*, 822–26.
14. I am basing this observation on comments made by colleagues in biblical studies.

verb, with time of secondary importance *only* in the indicative mood.[15] Verbal aspect theory has been accepted nearly universally in some form among New Testament scholars and continues to influence the best of Greek grammars, New Testament commentaries, and other academic studies. What are some of the features that led to the theory's quick adoption and use? First, the theory has obvious implications for the reading of almost every sentence in the New Testament. If speech act theorists are going to exercise similar influence, they will need to improve in demonstrating the relevance of their theories.[16] Second, verbal aspect theory, while using a "technical vocabulary" (e.g., perfective, imperfective, stative), does not introduce too many new terms. Additionally, the terms are clearly defined and amply illustrated. Indeed, one could conceivably use verbal aspect theory without having any knowledge of the technical vocabulary—as long as the key insights are understood.[17] If speech act theorists can make their key concepts readily accessible and well illustrated, it is likely that they will exercise broad influence.[18]

At this point, the future of speech act theory is a bit uncertain. Biblical scholars are at the stage where they know they must offer some obeisance to the theory in their academic writing. It is yet to be shown whether speech act theory can really take hold in biblical studies through demonstrated relevance, clear and limited terminology, and understandable concepts. It is important to remember that insofar as speech act theory is actually a true description of reality, it only classifies undeniable language functions.[19]

REFLECTION QUESTIONS

1. Does the description of all language as being fundamentally action based seem correct to you?

---

15. Stan Porter, one of the primary proponents of verbal aspect theory, thinks that even in the indicative mood, time is only contextually determined (Stanley E. Porter, *Idioms of the Greek New Testament* [Sheffield: JSOT, 1992], 20–49).
16. One pioneer in this field is Anthony Thiselton. See especially his commentary on 1 Corinthians (Anthony C. Thiselton, *The First Epistle to the Corinthians*, NIGTC [Grand Rapids: Eerdmans, 2000]).
17. See the simplified description of verbal aspect theory advocated by Robert E. Picirilli, "The Meaning of the Tenses in New Testament Greek: Where Are We?" *JETS* 48, no. 3 (2005): 533–55.
18. For *locution, illocution,* and *perlocution,* Jeannine Brown proposes the following synonymous expressions: *speaker's saying, speaker's verbal action, hearer's response* (*Scripture as Communication*, 33).
19. Vern Poythress offers this helpful caveat: "Speech act theory, or genre theory, or any other theory, is not comprehensive in its attentiveness. So the danger arises that it . . . may over-optimistically be used as if it were the key to understanding, rather than a reminder of one more dimension of communication" ("Canon and Speech Act," 343).

2. In two minutes, could you explain the basics of speech act theory to someone else? Is the theory understandable and relevant?

3. Challenge: Choose a short passage in the Bible and discuss these dimensions: locutionary, illocutionary, perlocutionary (see above).

4. In the discussion above, speech act theory was compared with rhetorical criticism and verbal aspect theory. Can you think of any other academic approaches or theories that offer lessons to speech act advocates?

5. Can you think of any more accessible terms to substitute for *locutionary, illocutionary,* and *perlocutionary?*

FOR FURTHER STUDY

Briggs, Richard S. "Speech-Act Theory." In *Dictionary for Theological Interpretation of the Bible,* edited by Kevin J. Vanhoozer, 763–66. Grand Rapids: Baker; London: SPCK, 2005.

_____. *Words in Action: Speech Act Theory and Biblical Interpretation: Toward a Hermeneutic of Self-Involvement.* Edinburgh: T & T Clark, 2001.

Vanhoozer, Kevin J. *First Theology: God, Scripture and Hermeneutics.* Leicester: Apollos; Downers Grove, IL: InterVarsity Press, 2002.

_____. *Is There a Meaning in This Text? The Bible, the Reader, and the Morality of Literary Knowledge.* Grand Rapids: Zondervan, 1998.

What Is the "Theological Interpretation of Scripture"?

Biblical scholars gather once a year at the annual professional meeting of the Society of Biblical Literature. At the November 2008 meeting in Boston, some of the liveliest sessions focused on the "theological interpretation of Scripture" (TIS). Indeed, the recent publication of many titles related to TIS demonstrates that the fascination with this hermeneutical approach is only beginning.[1] At the same time, TIS is so new that even many Christian scholars have no clear sense of what it is. In a sentence, TIS is an academic movement that seeks to return reflection on the biblical text to the purview of the confessing Christian church. Below, we will survey the terminology, history, and characteristics of the theological interpretation of Scripture movement.

Terminology
At present, a number of interchangeable terms are used to identify a TIS approach to the Bible.

1. Theological interpretation of Scripture
2. Theological interpretation of the Bible
3. Theological interpretation
4. Theological hermeneutics
5. Theological commentary on the Bible
6. Theological exegesis

---

1. The Baker Academic Web site lists twenty-one books under the category of "theological interpretation." Included are a number of commentaries in the new Brazos Theological Commentary on the Bible series (www.bakeracademic.com [accessed December 13, 2008]). Baker appears to be the leading evangelical publisher in the area of theological interpretation.

Additionally, some recent works fit within the TIS framework but do not identify themselves explicitly with the terms listed above.[2]

History of the Theological Interpretation of Scripture Movement

As is clear from recent TIS authors' struggles to describe their movement, the theological interpretation of Scripture is still emerging as a defined approach to the Bible.[3] It is difficult to find a monograph before 2005 that uses the identifier "theological interpretation" in the technical sense that it has quickly acquired.[4] At the same time, advocates of theological interpretation do not see themselves as proposing something new but as returning to the church-based, transformative study of the Bible that characterized generations of Christians before the Enlightenment.[5]

Daniel J. Treier traces the interests of TIS authors to precursors in Karl Barth and the Yale School (a movement in literary criticism birthed at Yale).[6] Other more recent pioneers (from the 1990s) include Francis Watson, Stephen Fowl, and Kevin Vanhoozer.[7]

Indeed, as the movement has coalesced so recently, it is difficult to gain a balanced historical perspective on its origins. It seems, however, that a number of scholarly trends have intersected and combined, resulting in a new movement that only recently has found enough unity to consistently describe itself with its own moniker (i.e., TIS). The trends leading to TIS include: disillusionment with the historical-critical method and far-fetched ideologically driven interpretations (e.g., homosexual readings of Scripture), a desire for theological continuity with the pre-Enlightenment church, a growing acceptance in the academy of interpretive movements that bracket out skepticism and critical questions (e.g., reader-response approach,[8] canonical criticism, canonical process approach, narrative or literary criticism,

---

2. E.g., N. T. Wright, *The New Testament and the People of God* (Minneapolis: Fortress, 1992).
3. See Daniel J. Treier, *Introducing Theological Interpretation of Scripture: Recovering a Christian Practice* (Grand Rapids: Baker, 2008); and Kevin J. Vanhoozer, ed., *Dictionary for Theological Interpretation of the Bible* (Grand Rapids: Baker; London: SPCK, 2005), 19–25.
4. But see Stephen E. Fowl, ed., *The Theological Interpretation of Scripture: Classic and Contemporary Readings* (Cambridge, MA: Blackwell, 1997).
5. Note the subtitle of Treier's book—*Recovering a Christian Practice*.
6. Treier, *Introducing Theological Interpretation of Scripture*, 17–19.
7. Ibid., 11.
8. Interestingly, Erik M. Heen describes TIS as a kind of reader-response approach. He writes, "The 'Theological Interpretation of Scripture' has emerged as a new discipline within biblical studies. In this approach to the Bible the 'social location' of the contemporary interpreter is taken seriously. 'Theological Interpretation' can, therefore, be understood as kind of 'Reader-Response' criticism. In Theological Interpretation the primary interpretive community of readers is not understood to be a subset of the academy, as is assumed in many varieties of Reader Response Criticism; rather, the interpretive body is made up of those who self-identify as members of church communities. Theological Interpretation seeks then to bring together newer methods of biblical studies with confessionally based

reception history, effective history, etc.). For further descriptions of these precursors to TIS, see question 40 ("What are some other recent trends in biblical interpretation?").

Characteristics of the Theological Interpretation of Scripture Movement

"Can you tell me in one sentence what the theological interpretation of Scripture is?" Thus queried a colleague of mine at a recent gathering. Indeed, as the TIS movement is still developing, it is difficult to briefly define without being reductionistic. Below, I shall list some dominant characteristics and accompanying assessments of the TIS movement.

1. Practitioners of TIS generally are disillusioned with the historical-critical method, biblical theology, principles of interpretation, and ideologically driven interpretation as ends in themselves. It is important to note that TIS is in many ways a rejection of the status quo. To recent scholarly work on the Bible, TIS advocates would give two assessments: "Not enough" (by leaving theology in the cerebral realm) and "not faithful to the nature of Scripture and our identity as Christians" (by not reading as followers of Jesus who encounter God in the words of the Bible). Those advocating TIS are not advocating the complete neglect of historical criticism or other interpretive methods. But these methods in themselves (and what they have produced) are not enough.

   TIS authors especially dislike the idea that hermeneutics is a process of learning interpretive methods, applying those methods, and arriving at a propositional statement of authorial meaning. Such a hermeneutical model, it is argued, eviscerates and objectifies the text. The interpreter approaches the text as master rather than as servant.[9] Scripture becomes an ancient word to others rather than God's living Word to us today. While I certainly am sympathetic to criticisms of any method that would reduce hermeneutics to a cold semantic equation, it is equally true that many of the church fathers (generally revered by TIS) enumerate interpretive methods similar to the ones used in standard hermeneutics textbooks today.[10]

---

theological reflection in ways that historical-criticism did not always encourage" ("The Theological Interpretation of the Bible," *Lutheran Quarterly* 21, no. 4 [2007]: 373).

9. Kevin J. Vanhoozer, "Imprisoned or Free? Text, Status, and Theological Interpretation in the Master/Slave Discourse of Philemon," in *Reading Scripture with the Church: Toward a Hermeneutic for Theological Interpretation*, ed. A. K. M. Adam, Stephen E. Fowl, Kevin J. Vanhoozer, and Francis Watson (Grand Rapids: Baker, 2006), 92.

10. See, for example, the interpretive rules of Augustine in Book 2 of *De Doctrina Christiana* (*NPNF1* 2:535–55). Of course, in addition to standard interpretive principles, Augustine

Practitioners of TIS emphasize confessing Christians as participants and the audience of interpretation. According to TIS, interpretation must take place in the church and for the church. Some TIS
authors are liberal Protestants, others are Roman Catholics, and others
are evangelicals. But all desire to remain self-consciously ecclesiastical
in confession and concerns.

At its best, this bold call for a believing interpreter and audience
demonstrates that TIS authors are "not ashamed of the gospel" (Rom.
1:16). At its worst, writing in and for the church can be a capitulation
to the secular world's demands that religious faith remain subjective.
That is, in embracing the church context as the *only* legitimate realm
for theological reflection, Christians become just another reading
community rather than those who believe the truth they hold is for
all people.

2. Practitioners of TIS respect external theological parameters as guides
for interpretation. If one writes in and for the church, it is legitimate to
be bound by ecclesiastical confessions, argue TIS authors. That is, one
can unashamedly appeal to the "rule of faith" (early Christian summary of fundamental beliefs), creeds, confessions, and the contours of
the Christian canon. TIS authors point to the early church's use of the
"rule of faith" as one of its main interpretive principles.[11]

Admittedly, most interpretations of Scripture are influenced by
prior theological commitments, whether formalized in a creed or not.
Yet, ultimately, Scripture demands an authority above any doctrinal
précis. We do not want to lose what our forefathers in the faith fought
for in the Reformation. As Luther courageously declared in his defense
at the Diet [Assembly] of Worms (1521),

---

endorses a reverent, church-based, confessionally informed approach—the very desire of
TIS practitioners.
11. Treier's description of the new Brazos Theological Commentary on the Bible series illustrates the TIS commitment to doctrinal parameters: "The series 'presupposes that the
doctrinal tradition of the church can serve as a living and reliable basis for exegesis.' This
tradition, more specifically, is that doctrine surrounding the Nicene Creed. The series
promotes 'intratextual analysis' as its key 'method,' along with drawing upon 'the liturgical practices and spiritual disciplines of the church as a secondary dimension of the
canonical context for exegesis of scriptural texts.' Such an approach can lead to various
senses of Scripture, including 'allegorical' readings, and requires that contributors engage the history of exegesis, not in order to provide readers with a summary of past
interpretation, but in order to shape exegetical judgments in conversation with the tradition'" (*Introducing Theological Interpretation of Scripture*, 40). The quotations within
Treier's remarks are from a Brazos document describing the purpose of the series to
contributors.

Unless I am convinced by the testimony of the Scriptures or by clear reason (for I do not trust either in the pope or in councils alone, since it is well known that they have often erred and contradicted themselves), I am bound by the Scriptures I have quoted and my conscience is captive to the Word of God. I cannot and I will not retract anything, since it is neither safe nor right to go against conscience. I cannot do otherwise, here I stand, may God help me, Amen.[12]

3. Practitioners of TIS appreciate the narrative story line of Scripture. Scripture is approached not primarily as a set of propositions but as the story of the living God and his saving revelation of himself to wayward humans.[13] The language of drama is seen as a powerful metaphor for God's story in Scripture and the ongoing participation of Christians today in God's work in the world.[14]

4. Practitioners of TIS respect the way the Bible has been interpreted by previous generations of Christians. In fact, another scholarly trend that led directly into the TIS movement is the recent scholarly fascination with ancient church beliefs, writings, and practices.[15] While we can learn much from the early church, some TIS authors are too uncritical in their praise and appropriation of ancient and medieval church interpreters.[16] Martin Luther, on the other hand, judged Origen's exegesis as

12. *W.A.* 7:838. English translation by Roger A. Hornsby, "Luther at the Diet of Worms," in *Career of the Reformer II*, ed. George W. Forell, in *Luther's Works*, ed. Helmut T. Lehmann (Philadelphia: Muhlenberg, 1958), 32:112–13.

13. Vanhoozer writes, "We [as practitioners of TIS] do affirm the ecumenical consensus of the church down through the ages and across confessional lines that the Bible should be read as a unity and as *narrative testimony* to the identities and actions of God and of Jesus Christ" (Kevin J. Vanhoozer, "Introduction: What Is the Theological Interpretation of the Bible," in *Dictionary for Theological Interpretation of the Bible* [Grand Rapids: Baker; London: SPCK, 2005], 19 [my emphasis]).

14. Kevin J. Vanhoozer, *The Drama of Doctrine: A Canonical-Linguistic Approach to Christian Theology* (Louisville: Westminster John Knox, 2005).

15. E.g., Brian D. McLaren, *Finding Our Way Again: The Return of the Ancient Practices* (Nashville: Thomas Nelson, 2008); The Ancient Christian Commentary on Scripture Series (IVP); and The Church's Bible (Eerdmans).

16. E.g., David C. Steinmetz, "The Superiority of Pre-Critical Exegesis," in *The Theological Interpretation of Scripture: Classic and Contemporary Readings*, ed. Stephen E. Fowl (Cambridge, MA: Blackwell, 1997), 26–38; Stephen E. Fowl, "The Importance of a Multivoiced Literal Sense of Scripture: The Example of Thomas Aquinas," in *Reading Scripture with the Church: Toward a Hermeneutic for Theological Interpretation*, ed. A. K. M. Adam, Stephen E. Fowl, Kevin J. Vanhoozer, and Francis Watson (Grand Rapids: Baker, 2006), 35–50; and R. R. Reno, "'You Who Were Far Off Have Been Brought Near': Reflections on Theological Exegesis," *Ex Auditu* 16 (2000): 169–82.

"altogether useless."[17] Luther could make such a statement because of his commitment to the Bible's authority and clarity (as distinguished from Origen's allegorical flights of fancy, which added meaning unintended by the biblical authors).

5. Practitioners of TIS show an interest in the way the Bible has affected culture, art, politics, science, and other fields of knowledge. Technically, this subset of TIS is termed the study of a text's "effective history." Obviously, this sort of cross-disciplinary approach makes for interesting reading and allows readers to intersect the message of Scripture in ways quite foreign to traditional biblical studies. As TIS calls for the return of the Bible to the church (and the church is composed of much more than professional scholars), it is appropriate to ask how the Bible affects all of God's people and their lives.

6. Practitioners of TIS desire that the study of the Bible be transformative of the individual and the individual's faith community. Tying in with a growing interest in biblical spirituality, TIS authors advocate spiritually transformative study. Scripture cannot simply be viewed as a historical puzzle to be solved but as a word from God to his people.[18]

Projections

A colleague of mine recently noted that many people are writing books *about* the theological interpretation of Scripture, but very few are actually engaging in theological interpretation.[19] Of course, this situation is beginning to change with the new Brazos Theological Commentary on the Bible series and other forthcoming books. Still, it is difficult to evaluate the TIS movement until more of its interpretive fruit is available for sampling.

It is perhaps foolhardy to offer projections about how the TIS movement will develop, but I will offer some tentative projections. Initial euphoria over this new middle ground in biblical scholarship will likely give way to splintering. The issue of ultimate authority (Scripture? tradition? human reason?) will cause liberal Protestants, evangelicals, and Roman Catholics to part ways. Evangelicals will likely face division among themselves—some

---

17. Martin Luther, *Lectures on Genesis, Chapters 1–5*, in *Luther's Works*, ed. J. Pelikan (Saint Louis: Concordia, 1958), 1:233. Luther writes, "It is the historical sense alone which supplies the true and sound doctrine" (ibid.).

18. Joel B. Green favors "interpretive practices oriented toward shaping and nurturing the faith and life of God's people" (*Seized by Truth: Reading the Bible as Scripture* [Nashville: Abingdon, 2007], 79).

19. A comment by Jonathan Pennington. He is currently working on a book that seeks to apply concretely the TIS approach to the Gospels.

enamored with the broader academy's praise of TIS at the expense of biblical faithfulness.

A generational divide also will likely characterize evangelicals. Some younger evangelicals who embrace TIS will denigrate the work of their exegetical forefathers. Older evangelicals will misunderstand and dismiss the new movement, uncritically lumping it together with other recent trends (the emergent church, postmodern theology, post-conservative theology).

In spite of some dour expectations, I genuinely hope that my fears are unfounded and that the better aspects of the movement (especially the call for reverent submission to Scripture) influence evangelical colleges, seminaries, and churches for years to come.

REFLECTION QUESTIONS

1. Before reading the material above, had you ever heard of the theological interpretation of Scripture (TIS) movement?

2. What aspects of the TIS movement do you find most promising?

3. Do any characteristics of the TIS movement concern you?

4. Have you noticed any characteristics of the TIS movement in recent books you have read or speakers you have heard?

5. A few projections for the future of the TIS movement were made above. Which of these projections seem most likely to you?

FOR FURTHER STUDY

Adam, A. K. A., Stephen E. Fowl, Kevin J. Vanhoozer, and Francis Watson, eds. *Reading Scripture with the Church: Toward a Hermeneutic for Theological Interpretation*. Grand Rapids: Baker, 2006.

Bockmuehl, Markus. *Seeing the Word: Refocusing New Testament Study*. Studies in Theological Interpretation. Grand Rapids: Baker, 2007.

Davis, Ellen F., and Richard B. Hays, eds. *The Art of Reading Scripture*. Grand Rapids: Eerdmans, 2003.

Fowl, Stephen E., ed. *The Theological Interpretation of Scripture: Classic and Contemporary Readings*. Blackwell Readings in Modern Theology. Cambridge, MA: Blackwell, 1997.

Green, Joel B. *Seized by Truth: Reading the Bible as Scripture*. Nashville: Abingdon, 2007.

Treier, Daniel J. *Introducing Theological Interpretation of Scripture: Recovering a Christian Practice*. Grand Rapids: Baker, 2008.

Vanhoozer, Kevin J., ed. *Dictionary for the Theological Interpretation of the Bible*. Grand Rapids: Baker; London: SPCK, 2005.

_____. *The Drama of Doctrine: A Canonical-Linguistic Approach to Christian Theology*. Louisville, KY: Westminster John Knox, 2005.

What Are Some Other Recent Trends in Biblical Interpretation?

As this book is limited to forty questions, it is necessary to combine into one section a brief survey of some other current issues in the field of hermeneutics. It is my desire that the discussion below would give a concise introduction to trends and terms that the readers of this book may encounter in the area of biblical interpretation.

Biblical Theology

When used in the more technical sense, *biblical theology* refers to an approach to the study of the Bible that seeks to hear the nuances of the diverse biblical texts. The discipline often is criticized for being atomistic and having little concern for confessional application.[1] Any synthesis in biblical theology usually is attempted by exploring a common theme through the biblical books—again, with primary attention to the distinctions among the texts.

Biblical theology as a discipline traces its origins to the seminal address by J. P. Gabler (1787), in which he called for biblical scholars to focus on the grammatical-historical meaning of texts. Gabler then suggested that the conclusions of biblical theologians would be taken up and articulated to the current situation by dogmatic or systematic theologians. Modern scholars often decry the separation and competition that exists between systematic and biblical theologians. The theological interpretation of Scripture movement hopes to remove this divide between historical meaning and current-day significance (see question 39, "What is the 'Theological Interpretation of Scripture'?").

---

1. D. A. Carson, "New Testament Theology," in *Dictionary of the Later New Testament and Its Developments*, ed. Ralph P. Martin and Peter H. Davids (Downers Grove, IL: InterVarsity Press, 1997), 796–97.

Canonical Criticism

Canonical criticism is a scholarly approach to the study of the Bible that traces its origins to the writings of Brevard Childs (1923–2007) and the Yale School (i.e., a movement of literary criticism birthed at Yale). In actuality, Childs eschewed the label "canonical criticism," as he was not trying to set up another sterile academic approach to be lumped together with other "criticisms."[2] Still, many people see Childs as the grandfather of canonical criticism, an approach that embraces the completed canon in the context of confessional Christianity as the appropriate boundary within which to study texts and biblical themes. In other words, according to canonical criticism, biblical scholarship should not focus on hypothetical literary precursors or supposed historical influences but on the actual completed biblical books as they appear in the canon of the Christian church. Critics of canonical criticism have noted that, despite the benefits of viewing texts in their final form in relation to other canonical documents, valid literary and historical questions often are neglected by this approach.

Canonical Process Approach

Similar to canonical criticism, a canonical process approach to the Bible takes the completed canon as a starting point for studying the biblical writings. A canonical process approach respects each biblical author's original meaning, while seeing a progressive revelation of God's purposes in later biblical writings. Such later revelations give further insight into the original biblical author's intentions. An advocate of the canonical process approach, Bruce Waltke, explains:

> By the canonical process approach I mean the recognition that the text's intention became deeper and clearer as the parameters of the canon were expanded. Just as redemption itself has a progressive history, so also older texts in the canon underwent a correlative progressive perception of meaning as they became part of a growing canonical literature.[3]

Reception History

Reception history focuses on the way a biblical text has been received or understood by Christians throughout church history. In recent years, some

---

2. Gerald T. Sheppard, "Canonical Criticism," *ABD* 1:863.
3. Bruce K. Waltke, "A Canonical Process Approach to the Psalms," in *Tradition and Testament: Essays in Honor of Charles Lee Feinberg*, ed. John S. Feinberg and Paul D. Feinberg (Chicago: Moody Press, 1981), 7. Waltke also writes, "In contrast to canonical criticism . . . according to which the ancient texts were reworked in the progressive development of the canon in such a way that they may have lost their original historical significance, the canonical process approach holds that the original authorial intention was not changed in the progressive development of the canon but deepened and clarified" (ibid., 8).

biblical scholars have called for a focus on reception history as one way out of the impasse and confusion in the discipline of biblical theology.[4] Scholars must admit that even most experts know little about the way biblical texts were read before the eighteenth century. Moreover, attention to a text's history of interpretation possibly provides a more objective basis for ongoing discussion and helps reignite scholarly recognition of practical and confessional concerns. Unfortunately, a celebration of the way a text has been received can be a subtle acceptance of polyvalence (i.e., receiving various incongruous understandings as equally valid). Avoidance of the thorny issue of a text's truthfulness can be an implicit denial of that claim.

Effective History

The effective history of a biblical text looks not only at the way the text has been understood throughout church history (i.e., reception history) but also at the way a text has influenced the lives and environments of those reading the texts. Thus, *effective history* is a broader term than *reception history*, encompassing a text's influence on Christian behavior, church practices, art, culture, etc. Like reception history, the study of effective history has been proposed as a way forward in the splintered field of biblical studies.[5]

Intertextuality

Recently, at a graduation commencement at my seminary, the dean read the title of a doctoral dissertation that included the word *intertextuality*. A colleague leaned over and whispered, "I've never heard that word before." I replied, "It's a hot topic in biblical studies." In brief, intertextuality gives attention to the way that one biblical text is alluded to or used by another biblical author. Depending on a scholar's interests, an intertextual study can lean more toward literary, theological, or historical issues. Looking at the Bible as a unified book, some intertextual critics study the development of motifs throughout the diverse perspectives of the biblical writers. Patzia and Petrotta note:

> Generally the study of biblical intertextuality focuses more on the *processes* by which biblical texts were reworked and the *differences* between the texts: texts were extended in meaning but also transposed or even refuted. The

---

4. E.g., Judith Kovacs and Christopher Rowland, *Revelation: The Apocalypse of Jesus Christ,* Blackwell Bible Commentaries (Oxford: Blackwell, 2004), 1–38.

5. Markus Bockmuehl, *Seeing the Word: Refocusing New Testament Study*, Studies in Theological Interpretation (Grand Rapids: Baker, 2006), 64–68; and Kovacs and Rowland, *Revelation*, 31–38.

emphasis tends toward exploring the *plurality* of possible readings rather than the *conformity* of readings.[6]

Redemptive-Movement Hermeneutic

A redemptive-movement hermeneutic (or redemptive-trajectory herme-neutic) approaches the Bible with the supposition that the Scriptures provide a certain ethical trajectory that points to conclusions beyond (and possibly in contradiction to) those issues explicitly addressed in the text.[7] William Webb, an advocate of the redemptive-movement hermeneutic, writes,

> The Christian seeking to apply Scripture today should examine the move-ment between the biblical text and its surrounding social context. Once that movement has been discovered there needs to be an assessment of whether the movement is preliminary or absolute. If it is preliminary and further movement in the direction set by the text would produce a more fully real-ized ethic, then that is the course of action one must pursue. The interpreter extrapolates the biblical movement towards a more just, more equitable and more loving form. If a better ethic than the one expressed in the isolated words of the text is possible, and the biblical and canonical spirit is headed that direction, then that is where one ultimately wants to end up.[8]

For example, though slavery is regulated and assumed in the Old and New Testament, according to a redemptive-movement hermeneutic, we see an increasing recognition throughout Scripture that slavery is objectionable to God. Though the biblical text does not explicitly state abolitionist conclu-sions, if one continues to trace the redemptive critique of culture beyond the text, one will be led to see the sinfulness of slavery. Thus the redemptive-movement hermeneutic is the recognition of progressive patterns that reach their climax beyond the actual written words of Scripture. Scholars also have used a redemptive-movement hermeneutic to argue for the full participa-tion of women in pastoral ministry. This interpretive method, especially in arguing for women pastors (in clear contradiction to 1 Tim. 2:12), has been cogently critiqued by Thomas Schreiner.[9]

---

6. Arthur G. Patzia and Anthony J. Petrotta, *Pocket Dictionary of Biblical Studies* (Downers Grove, IL: InterVarsity Press, 2002), 63. Emphasis in original.
7. See, e.g., I. Howard Marshall, *Beyond the Bible: Moving from Scripture to Theology* (Grand Rapids: Baker, 2004); and Scot McKnight, *The Blue Parakeet: Rethinking How You Read the Bible* (Grand Rapids: Zondervan, 2008).
8. William J. Webb, *Slaves, Women and Homosexuals: Exploring the Hermeneutics of Cultural Analysis* (Downers Grove, IL: InterVarsity Press, 2001), 36.
9. Thomas R. Schreiner, "William J. Webb's *Slaves, Women, and Homosexuals*: A Review Article," *SBJT* 6, no. 1 (2002): 46–64. This article is available online under the "Resources" link at www.sbts.edu. See also the forthcoming dissertation critiquing the

Missional Hermeneutic

Missional is a relatively new word that continues to face some ambiguity in definition. The word has been taken up by a number of churches and biblical scholars as helpful in identifying the perpetually "sent" nature of the church. In other words, a church that is "missional" considers all of its beliefs and practices in light of the reality that God has sent that church to proclaim and embody the gospel to outsiders, especially in its immediate context. Likewise, a "missional" reading of the Scriptures or a "missional" hermeneutic sees God as the ever-sending God. The Bible contains a missional story because it reports God revealing himself savingly to wayward humans and commissioning other humans to this task as well. Advocates of a missional hermeneutic argue that when the Bible is extracted from its missional context and read solely as a systematic theology text, a fundamental dimension of God and his revelation is ignored.[10]

Philosophical Hermeneutics

One of my mentors, the New Testament scholar Robert Stein, once told me, "I wrote my text on hermeneutics because I could not understand the other books on the subject." While partly spoken in jest, his comment is instructive.

Many academic hermeneutics texts are difficult for the average lay reader to understand. Why? For one reason, a number of these books focus on foundational, philosophical issues. For example, how do we know that we know anything at all (epistemology)? How does language transmit meaning (semantics)? These and many other philosophical conundrums are explored, usually with a high frequency of obtuse terms. While exploring such issues is a worthy intellectual task, the majority of Christians are not aided by these rarefied treatises. Readers with a philosophical bent are referred to Anthony C. Thiselton's *The Two Horizons* for an analysis of philosophical questions that intersect hermeneutics.[11]

REFLECTION QUESTIONS

1. Of the terms and trends outlined above, which were new to you?

2. Do you see any commonalities among the recent interpretive approaches outlined above? What might those commonalities reveal about our current cultural context?

---

redemptive-movement hermeneutic by Benjamin Reaoch, a doctoral student at The Southern Baptist Theological Seminary.

10. E.g., Christopher J. H. Wright, *The Mission of God: Unlocking the Bible's Grand Narrative* (Downers Grove, IL: InterVarsity Press, 2006).

11. Anthony C. Thiselton, *The Two Horizons: New Testament Hermeneutics and Philosophical Description* (Grand Rapids: Eerdmans, 1980).

3. Does being aware of the missional nature of Scripture really make a difference in our understanding and application of it?

4. Challenge: Choose one of the methods explained above and study a specific biblical text in light of the chosen approach.

5. Challenge: Read Thomas Schreiner's review essay available at the Web site cited in the footnote in this section. Do you agree with Schreiner's assessment of Webb's redemptive-movement hermeneutic?

FOR FURTHER STUDY

Bockmuehl, Markus. *Seeing the Word: Refocusing New Testament Study*. Studies in Theological Interpretation. Grand Rapids: Baker, 2006.

Carson, D. A. "New Testament Theology." In *Dictionary of the Later New Testament and Its Developments*, edited by Ralph P. Martin and Peter H. Davids, 796–814. Downers Grove, IL: InterVarsity Press, 1997.

Patzia, Arthur G., and Anthony J. Petrotta. *Pocket Dictionary of Biblical Studies*. Downers Grove, IL: InterVarsity Press, 2002.

Thiselton, Anthony C. *The Two Horizons: New Testament Hermeneutics and Philosophical Description*. Grand Rapids: Eerdmans, 1980.

Wright, Christopher J. H. *The Mission of God: Unlocking the Bible's Grand Narrative*. Downers Grove, IL: InterVarsity Press, 2006.

Postscript

Imagine that you and I are talking together on a warm summer day. I describe in detail the delicious flavor of a new ice cream treat. I then pull one from a box and offer it to you. As you sink your teeth into the snack, you are suddenly struck by a rubbery, bland sensation in your mouth. A nearly invisible cellophane wrapper around the ice cream has prevented you from enjoying it.

This book is like a cellophane wrapper. I have spent a lot of time talking about the Bible, but unless you, the reader, actually pick up God's Word and savor it for yourself, this bland wrapper of a book will soon be forgotten. If, however, I succeed in motivating you to read, pray, sing, and meditate on the Scriptures, then this book will have served its purpose. May the God and Father of our Lord Jesus Christ, by the power of his Holy Spirit, guide you on a lifetime journey of delight in his Word.

—Rob Plummer
March 2010

"The law from your mouth is more precious to me
than thousands of pieces of silver and gold." (Ps. 119:72)

"How sweet are your words to my taste,
sweeter than honey to my mouth!" (Ps. 119:103)

Select Bibliography

Archer, Gleason. *A Survey of Old Testament Introduction*. Rev. ed. Chicago: Moody Press, 1994.

Beale, G. K. *The Erosion of Inerrancy in Evangelicalism: Responding to New Challenges to Biblical Authority*. Wheaton, IL: Crossway, 2008.

Bruce, F. F. *The New Testament Documents: Are They Reliable?* 6th ed. Downers Grove, IL: InterVarsity Press; Grand Rapids: Eerdmans, 1981.

Carson, D. A. *For the Love of God: A Daily Companion for Discovering the Riches of God's Word*. Vols. 1 and 2. Wheaton, IL: Crossway, 1998, 1999.

_____. *New Testament Commentary Survey*. 6th ed. Grand Rapids: Baker, 2007.

Carson, D. A., and Douglas J. Moo. *An Introduction to the New Testament*. 2nd ed. Grand Rapids: Zondervan, 2005.

ESV Study Bible. Wheaton, IL: Crossway, 2008.

Evans, Craig A. *Fabricating Jesus: How Modern Scholars Distort the Gospels*. Downers Grove, IL: InterVarsity Press, 2008.

Fee, Gordon D., and Mark L. Strauss. *How to Choose a Translation for All Its Worth*. Grand Rapids: Zondervan, 2007.

Glynn, John. *Commentary and Reference Survey: A Comprehensive Guide to Biblical and Theological Resources*. 10th ed. Grand Rapids: Kregel, 2007.

Grudem, Wayne. *Systematic Theology: An Introduction to Biblical Doctrine*. Grand Rapids: Zondervan; Leicester: Inter-Varsity Press, 1994.

Longman, Tremper. *Old Testament Commentary Survey*. 4th ed. Grand Rapids: Baker, 2007.

Stein, Robert H. *A Basic Guide to Interpreting the Bible: Playing by the Rules*. Grand Rapids: Baker, 1994.

Wegner, Paul D. *The Journey from Texts to Translations: The Origin and Development of the Bible*. Grand Rapids: Baker, 1999.

Zondervan NIV Study Bible, Rev. ed. Edited by Kenneth L. Barker, et al. Grand Rapids: Zondervan, 2008.

List of Figures

Scripture Index

Ancient Sources Index